MW01620933

The Maritime Landscape of the Isthmus of Panamá

UNIVERSITY PRESS OF FLORIDA

Florida A&M University, Tallahassee
Florida Atlantic University, Boca Raton
Florida Gulf Coast University, Ft. Myers
Florida International University, Miami
Florida State University, Tallahassee
New College of Florida, Sarasota
University of Central Florida, Orlando
University of Florida, Gainesville
University of North Florida, Jacksonville
University of South Florida, Tampa
University of West Florida, Pensacola

The Maritime Landscape of the Isthmus of PANAMÁ

JAMES P. DELGADO, TOMÁS MENDIZÁBAL,
FREDERICK H. HANSELMANN,
AND DOMINIQUE RISSOLO

University Press of Florida
Gainesville · Tallahassee · Tampa · Boca Raton
Pensacola · Orlando · Miami · Jacksonville · Ft. Myers · Sarasota

Printed in the United States of America on acid-free paper

This book may be available in an electronic edition.

21 20 19 18 17 16 6 5 4 3 2 1

Library of Congress Cataloging-in-Publication Data
Names: Delgado, James P., author. | Hernandez Mendizábal, Tomás, 1940– author. | Hanselmann, Frederick H., author. | Rissolo, Dominique, author.
Title: The maritime landscape of the Isthmus of Panamá / James P. Delgado, Tomás Mendizábal, Frederick H. Hanselmann, and Dominique Rissolo.
Description: Gainesville : University Press of Florida, [2016] | Includes bibliographical references and index.
Identifiers: LCCN 2016015353 | ISBN 9780813062877 (cloth)
Subjects: LCSH: Panama—History. | Panama, Isthmus of (Panama)—History. | Excavations (Archaeology)—Panama. | Underwater archaeology—Panama. | Panama—Antiquities. | Panama, Isthmus of (Panama)—Antiquities.
Classification: LCC F1566.45 .D45 2016 | DDC 972.87—dc23
LC record available at https://lccn.loc.gov/2016015353

The University Press of Florida is the scholarly publishing agency for the State University System of Florida, comprising Florida A&M University, Florida Atlantic University, Florida Gulf Coast University, Florida International University, Florida State University, New College of Florida, University of Central Florida, University of Florida, University of North Florida, University of South Florida, and University of West Florida.

University Press of Florida
15 Northwest 15th Street
Gainesville, FL 32611-2079
http://www.upf.com

CONTENTS

ILLUSTRATIONS

Maps

Figures

PREFACE

Described as a narrow "land bridge" that divided the Pacific from the Caribbean until the early twentieth-century completion of the Panamá Canal, for over 500 years the Isthmus of Panamá has been a maritime link of empire and a land dominated by its relationship to the sea and the many rivers that feed it. For more than 10,000 years, prehistoric peoples inhabited its lands and coasts, navigated its waters, and harvested its resources. This changed drastically with the "discovery" of Panamá by Rodrigo de Bastidas, followed shortly thereafter by Christopher Columbus on his fourth and final voyage. Successive Spanish explorers and conquerors soon followed, such as Vasco Nuñez de Balboa, whose expedition famously resulted in his being the first European to cross the isthmus and see the "great southern sea" (la Mar del Sur), the Pacific Ocean. In light of Balboa's explorations, Spain colonized and fortified the isthmus as a transoceanic link that carried resources from its Pacific colonies over the transisthmian route from Panamá City to Portobelo via the Río Chagres and thence to the Caribbean and ultimately to Spain. The trade route and the immense amount of gold and silver that traversed it proved enticing for those that sought to gain wealth through violence and competition, culminating in the destruction of Panamá City in 1671. Relocated and rebuilt, Panamá City and the transisthmian route continued to flourish into the eighteenth century, only to meet its decline as Spain's overseas fortunes ebbed and the route's utility diminished.

In response to the Industrial Revolution, by the turn of the nineteenth century local trade was growing; and with the rise of steam navigation in South America, Panamá was soon caught up in the California Gold Rush from 1848–1856. Quickly seen as the fastest and safest passage to California, Panamá prospered and was transformed by gold fever. Hundreds of thousands of fortune seekers crossed the isthmus, initially by way of the Chagres and overland pack trains and soon thereafter through the creation of the first transcontinental railroad in the Americas, the Panamá Railroad, which was completed between 1850 and 1855. Regular steamship voyages and the shipment of gold and mail across the "land bridge" revived Panamá's fortunes and again transformed the socioeconomic climate of the isthmus. The heyday of the Gold Rush also revived a centuries-old dream: a transisthmian canal.

Despite the post–Gold Rush economic decline, the late nineteenth century introduced a French-led engineering effort to span the isthmus with a sea-level canal, which was itself a transformative event in Panamá's history. Although that venture ultimately failed, it was succeeded by an American-led effort to manage the construction of the Panamá Canal and usher in yet another era of metamorphosis for Panamá. Gaining independence from Colombia, Panamá became a de facto colony of the United States, with the autonomous Canal Zone uniting the seas but dividing more than the land. Its landscape dramatically changed as Panamá became a major global shipping hub and U.S. interests dominated its politics and economy. Within the zone, the canal's entrances were defended by extensive U.S.-built seacoast fortifications, and much of the interior was left undeveloped as a rainforest to ensure adequate freshwater supplies to operate the canal.

By the dawn of the twenty-first century, Panamá had become owner and manager of the canal in the aftermath of the United States' cession of the Canal Zone in 1979 (and the Canal itself in 1999). Currently Panamá is ushering in a new era of construction, which will again change the landscape and the socioeconomic and political structure of the country. The canal will be enlarged for a new generation of super ships to accommodate international shipping demand and the increasing global nature of the nation's economy.

The Isthmus of Panamá, especially the former Canal Zone, reflects its long history through a wide array of paleontological, historical, and archaeological resources. Late Miocene and Pliocene fossils and geological deposits speak of the emergence of the Isthmus more than 3 million years ago, uniting the northern and southern American landmasses and the ensuing biological exchange. Paleo-Indian and pre-Columbian sites dot the islands, coastal areas, and highlands. Visible and extant structures of the fortresses, warehouses, and ruined buildings of Portobelo, Panamá Viejo, and the Castillo de San Lorenzo (at the mouth of the Chagres) are the haunting physical remains of colonial Spain. Stone-paved roads, the late seventeenth-century walled city, the Casco Viejo, and the drowned beds and rails of the Panamá Railroad now submerged beneath the canal—along with dozens of settlements—embody the early efforts of industry. The U.S. Army's reinforced batteries and bunkers, the massive concrete locks and the riveted steel lock gates, the former American enclaves of the "CZ," concrete and earthen dams, and the flooded areas and dredged channels that define the Panamá Canal itself: all of these elements epitomize the drastic transformations, both physical and cultural, that the isthmus has undergone for over 500 years.

One could easily place the archaeology of the isthmus within the contexts of pre-Columbian, colonial, contact, historic, urban, and industrial archaeology. In archaeologically assessing Panamá, both as a link of empires and as a "land bridge" that connects the Americas (and divides the Caribbean from the Pacific), it is tempting to conclude that much of the archaeological work there might fit within the categorization of the isthmus as a portage—a point of interruption and yet a juncture in the maritime world. That characterization would be somewhat apt, especially with regard to the last 500 years of history; as Makarov (1994) has noted in regard to medieval portages, these were "the most difficult sections of the routes and sites where travelers met and traded, and fees and taxes were collected" (Makarov 1994:13). The Isthmus of Panamá was and remains such a portage, as it has been for half a millennium; however, its maritime nature goes beyond that singular aspect. The isthmus is inherently a maritime landscape, both in its geography and culture and from prehistoric times until the present. The isthmus has been connected to the maritime world through coastal migration and trade and the harvesting of the sea. Its coastal inhabitants have always grappled with the spiritual nature of the sea and their relationship to it.

Drawing on the material record and assessing Panamá through application of both world systems and maritime cultural landscape theory, we examine and explain Panamá within a broader context that ties this landscape to prehistoric patterns of settlement, trade, and sustenance. This is not a maritime history, nor is a comprehensive review of Panamanian archaeology. We examine both the physical and intangible landscape of the shift from the initial characterization of the isthmus as a barrier to Columbus's dream of a direct oceanic route to the Orient to the colonial acquisition of Panamá as a potential source of riches. This includes an archaeological look at indigenous use and exploitation of its maritime resources, which is crucial for appreciating the region's contribution to the sustenance, trade, and meaning in the lives of its first inhabitants. This book explores the evidence for the intensive and extensive trade networks that existed before any European set foot in Panamá and that connected the isthmus to the world beyond (both north and south). Also covered here is how the Spanish invasion incorporated the isthmus into new, wider oceanic patterns of trade. Those latter patterns ebbed and flowed, but ultimately the isthmus was reincorporated with the rise of the global economy in the aftermath of the fall of the Spanish Empire. The creation of the Panamá Canal, one of the greatest engineering feats of the twentieth century, was the means by which yet another colonial power, the United States, came to economically and strategically dominate the isthmus. We assess the various physical manifestations of this century-long process and the most recent and yet biggest change to the maritime landscape. Throughout this volume, we look at the archaeological remains of the isthmus' maritime culture as a reminder of how Panamá represents, above all else, the simple truth that humans shape their environment for their own profit but do so at their own peril.

ACKNOWLEDGMENTS

The authors wish to acknowledge and thank a wide range of friends and colleagues for their generous support. The authors are grateful for the sharing of research, collegial interactions, and for collaborations in the best spirit of historical and archaeological engagement and inquiry. Any book is part of an ongoing dialogue with our peers and the interested public, and we look forward to years of additional discussion and sharing of ideas as well as both agreement and inevitable disagreement on certain issues. We look forward to the refinement of current ideas and new insights in response to what we have written here.

Regarding the study of Panamá, I wish to acknowledge and thank two mentors. The late Theodore C. Hinckley was the first professor to instruct me in the nuances of Latin American history, and Professor Hinckley's lessons remain with me to this day. The genesis of chapter 6 was an earlier chapter written for a book that unfortunately was not completed before he died. Professor John Haskell Kemble should also be acknowledged here: Jack was the first American historian to focus on the history of the Panamá route. His seminal research in the 1940s inspired me and many other scholars. Jack Kemble and Alfredo Castillero are giants in the study of the history of the isthmus as a transit point; the authors of this book are still his students in many respects. Before he died, Jack Kemble generously shared, guided, and ensured my admission as a research scholar at the Henry E. Huntington Library and Archives as a bachelor's degree student. My thanks go out to Professor Kemble. I would like to also acknowledge and thank Dr. Richard G. Cooke of the Smithsonian Tropical Research Institute (STRI) for his assistance and guidance and for his amazing and extensive work in the prehistoric and historic period archaeology of Panamá. These acknowledgments would be incomplete if I did not also thank our collaborators on this volume: Tomás Mendizábal, Fritz Hanselmann, and Dominique Rissolo.

I have worked with these colleagues and friends for many years, and the bonds that unite us are more than the integration of thought and words in this volume. As always I would like to thank my wife, Ann Goodhart, who is my muse and inspiration: thank you for your good counsel, constant support, careful reading, and for encouraging me at every step.

I also thank Robert C. Chandler, PhD; the late Steven Potash, Pacific Mail Steamship Company historian and collector extraordinaire (and a fine friend, like Bob Chandler); Robert V. Schwemmer; James Dertien; John Cloud, PhD; the late Cedric Ridgely-Nevitt; Roberto Gallardo; Susan Peschel; Carlos Fitzgerald Bernal; Christian G. Fritz; Domingo Varela; Linette Montenegro; Donald Geddes III; Peter Way; Facundo Bacardí; Ted Waitt; Wayne Lusardi; Juan Mendez; Filipe V. Castro; Deborah Marx; the entire *Sub Marine Explorer* team, and all those acknowledged in *Misadventures of a Civil War Submarine* (Texas A&M University Press, 2012). I also thank both Juan Sisto for his gracious permission to use his photograph and Alberto Maiquez for his photographs. As always, I also thank Jack Scott for his magic with maps.

James Delgado

I would like to acknowledge Dr. Richard Cooke of STRI and Dr. Beatriz Rovira from Universidad de Panamá, who were my most important mentors in teaching me about the archaeology and early history of Panamá. I owe another debt of gratitude to Mr. Jacinto Almendra, the father of materials conservation in Panamá, who has always been there with sound and knowledgeable advice on all matters archaeological. I also want to acknowledge Dr. Juan Guillermo Martín Rincon, whose friendship and help have been invaluable in both my professional and personal life and in gathering the information in this book. I also would like to thank Dr. Alfredo Castillero, who through many lengthy and enjoyable conversations has always supported my research interests and has enthusiastically shared information and keen insights on how and where to look for "wonderful things." I also acknowledge the assistance and images of Fernando Bustamante, Tom Wake, Vicente Pascual, and Félix Durán Ardila.

Tomás Mendizábal

I wish to thank my best friend and lovely wife Lyndee first and foremost for introducing me to the culture of Panamá, especially that of the Guna. Family trips to San Blas turned into undergraduate anthropological research and later professional archaeological endeavors. Along those same lines, I thank my in-laws, Joel and Carmen Orton, as well as Ana "Tía Ana" Ramón for welcoming me as one of their family and providing me with an even more extended Panamanian family, both in the United States and in Panamá.

Words oftentimes do not do justice, and such is the case with my three very close friends and coauthors on this book. I cannot thank Jim Delgado enough for being a wonderful mentor, involving me in this research in Panamá and encouraging me to develop other projects and initiatives. I also thank Tomás Mendizábal for all sorts of assistance in addition to his friendship. From letting me sleep on his couch when funds were low, to finding an x-ray facility for artifacts, to delving into the politics of permitting and official bureaucracy with me, he is a stalwart friend and colleague. Dominique Rissolo deserves immense thanks for having enough faith in us to jumpstart the Río Chagres Maritime Landscape Study and for being perhaps the strongest voice of sanity throughout this process.

I would also like to thank Peter Way and the Way family for support, encouragement, and for joining us in the field.

Andrew Sansom and my colleagues at the Meadows Center for Water and the Environment at Texas State University worked very hard behind the scenes to facilitate all of my work, or "adventures," according to them. Thank you all for making this possible and for being some of my biggest cheerleaders!

I also need to thank the individuals who have been involved in this project on a number of different levels throughout the years. None of our success would have been possible without David Conlin, PhD, Christopher Horrell, PhD, Melanie Damour, Bert Ho, Charles Garrison, Donald Geddes III, Facundo Bacardí, James Dertien, and Julieta de Arango. I similarly thank the staff of Patronato Panamá Viejo: Jacinto Almendra, Marcelina Godoy, Jose Espinosa, Andres Diaz, Jason Nunn, Jason Sturgis, Jonathan Kingston, Christopher Morris, Joseph Lepore, Donnie Reid, Edgardo Ochoa, Raul De Leon, Aaron Wallendorf, Juan Guillermo Martín, PhD, Ben Ford, PhD, Sam Meacham, Vicente Cortez, Fernando Montejo, Jacob Hooge, Barry Bleichner, Glen Henson, Callista Holmes, as well as the crew of the *Plan B* and the staff of the Waitt Institute for Discovery; the Instituto Nacional de Cultura and the Dirección de Patrimonio Histórico for permits; the Smithsonian Tropical Research Institute; Captain Morgan Rum; Diageo; Taylor Strategy; and Ping Pong Productions.

Frederick "Fritz" Hanselmann

I join my coauthors in thanking those who have guided and supported our research in Panamá. I echo their acknowledgment of Joseph Lepore and the enthusiastic crew of the good ship *Plan B* under the command of Captain David Passmore. I also wish to thank the ever capable Michael Dessner as well as Lance Milbrand, Liz Smith, Jeffrey Morris, and Steve Bilicki. In the Pearl Islands, we were fortunate to work with Gregory Packard, Michael Purcell, and Erich Horgan from Woods Hole Oceanographic Institution. Back home, the staff of the Waitt Institute for Discovery kept our field efforts afloat. I am truly grateful for the esprit de corps enjoyed among my coauthors, and I stand ready to join them on future endeavors.

Dominique Rissolo

The following institutions and organizations were very helpful and graciously provided access and copies as we researched: Bancroft Library, University of California, Berkeley; Henry E. Huntington Library and Archives, San Marino, California; New York Historical Society, New York, New York; California Historical Society, San Francisco; J. Porter Shaw Library at San Francisco Maritime National Historical Park; NOAA Central Library, Silver Spring, Maryland; the National Archives, Washington, D.C.; Baker Library, Harvard University; California State Library, Sacramento; Columbia University Library, New York; Explorers' Club Library, New York; Royal Geographical Society Library, Kensington; Mystic Seaport Museum, Mystic, Connecticut; The Mariners' Museum, Newport News, Virginia; Morgan Library and Museum, New York; Peabody Museum of Salem, Salem, Massachusetts; Society of California Pioneers, San Francisco; United States District Court for the Northern District of California; American Geographical Society Library, Milwaukee, Wisconsin; Yale University Library; W. B. and M. H. Chung Library of the Vancouver Maritime Museum, Vancouver, British Columbia; The Paterson Museum, Paterson, New Jersey; Patronato Panamá Viejo; Autoridad del Canal de Panamá; and Instituto Nacional de Cultura de Panamá.

We are also grateful to the external reviewers of the manuscript, Roger Smith and Ben Ford, and for their careful and diligent review and comments: both of you helped make this a better book. Last, but certainly not least, we are grateful to director Meredith Morris-Babb and the exceptional staff at the University Press of Florida. Thanks also to copy editor Michael Sandlin, project editor Catherine Nevil Parker, and book designer Larry Leshan.

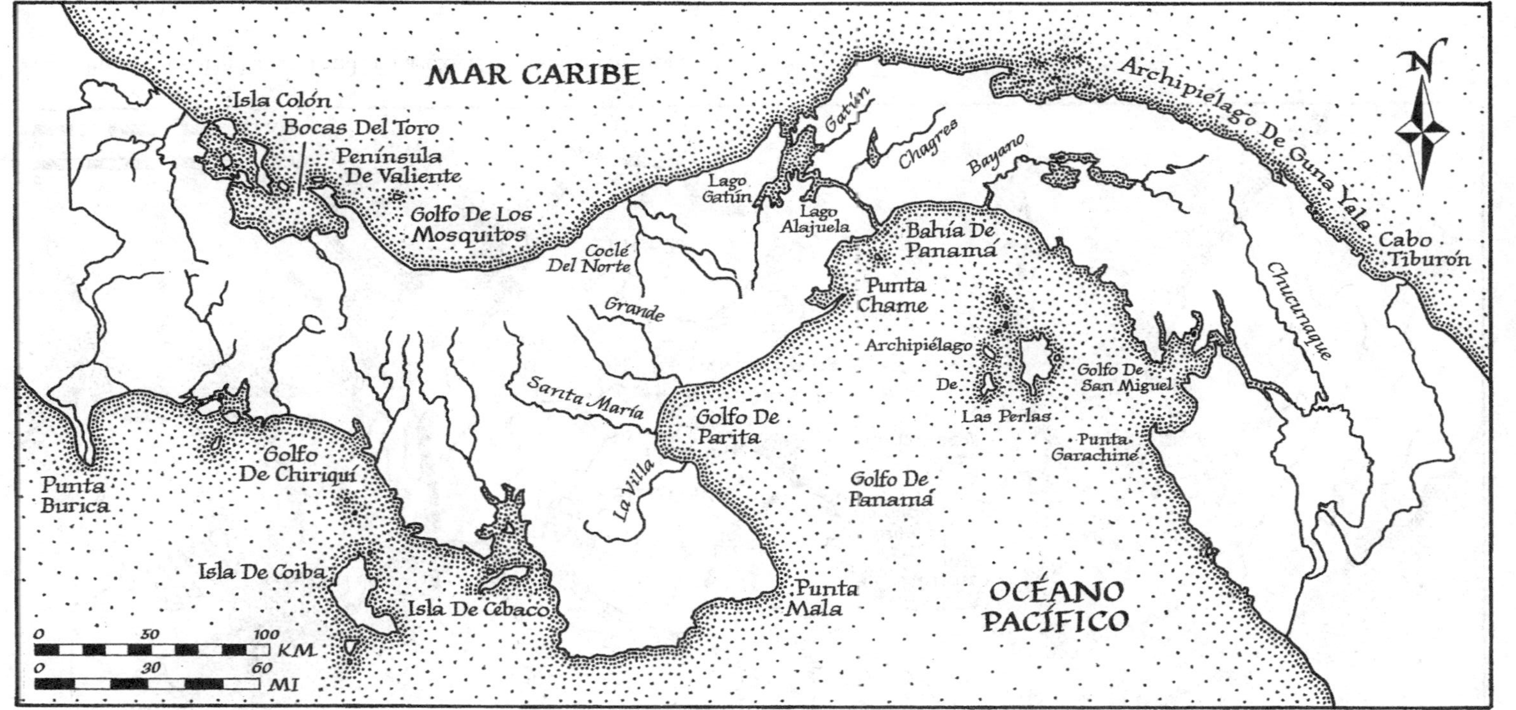

Map 1. Maritime Panamá, 2016. The maritime cultural landscape of Panamá has shaped the Central American isthmus as much as it has been shaped by it. Bordered by the Caribbean Sea and the Pacific Ocean (and spanned by rivers), for five centuries it has been both a settlement and a site marred by exploitation of its marine resources as well as a transportation link. The dominant element of the maritime cultural landscape is the Panamá Canal, delineated not only by its narrow cuts through the mountains but also by the massive confines of Lake Gatún. Map by Jack Scott.

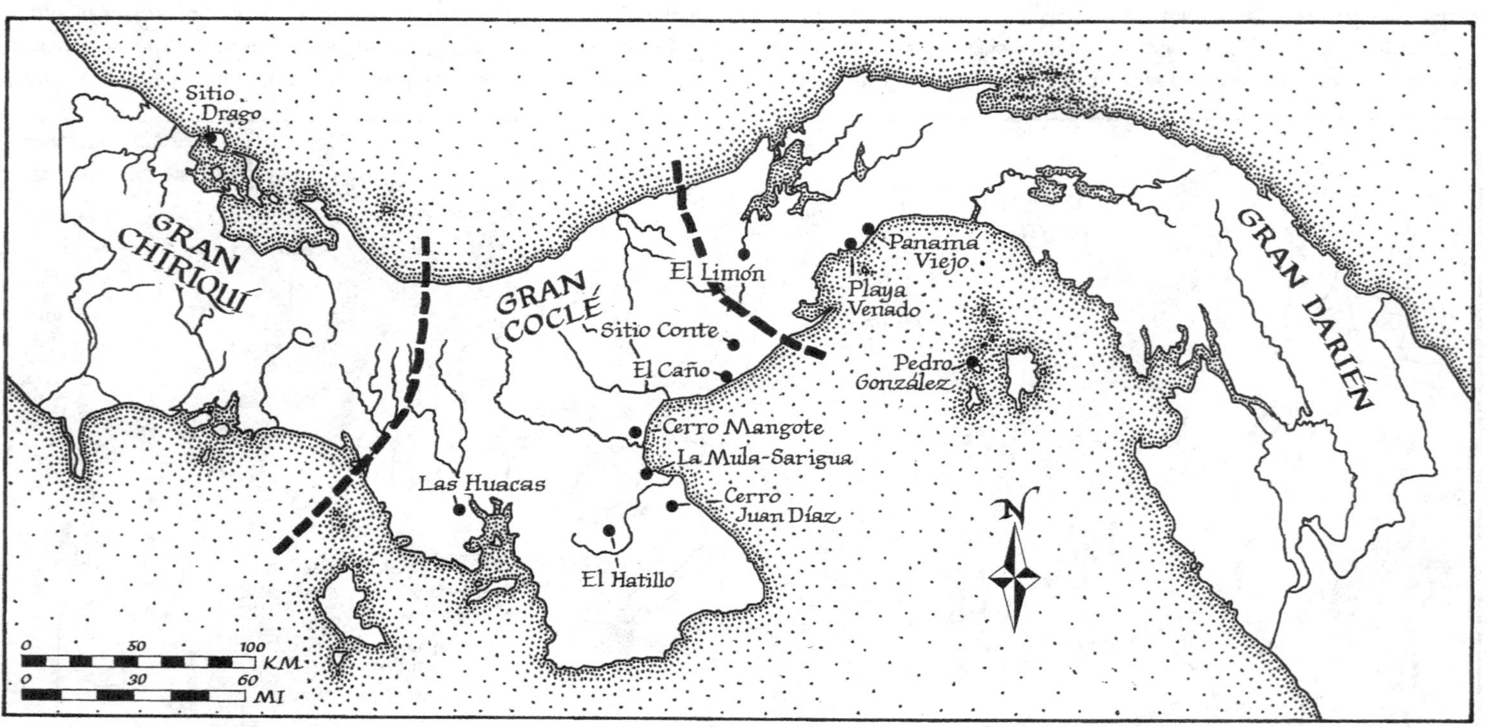

Map 2. Pre-Columbian Panamá and archaeological sites. Map by Jack Scott.

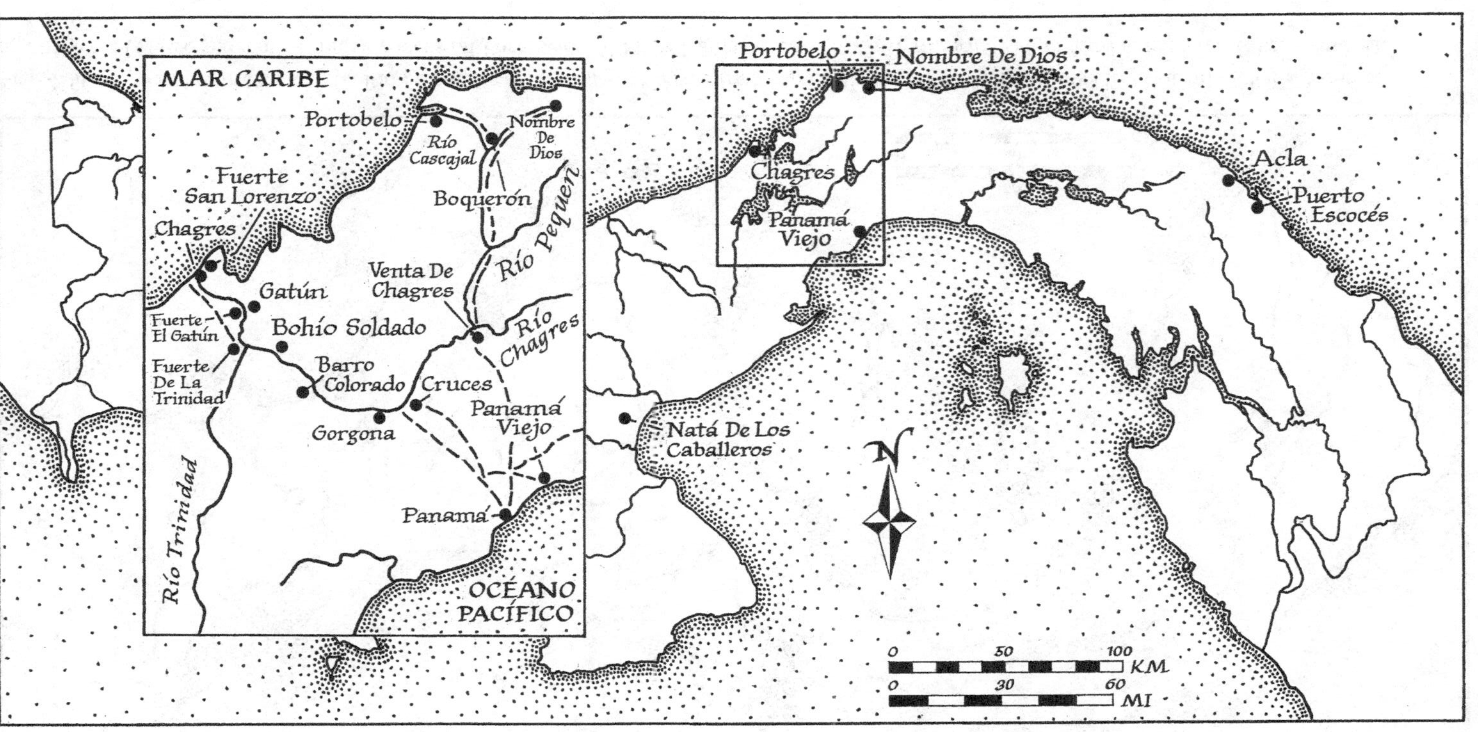

Map 3. Colonial Panamá archaeological sites. Map by Jack Scott.

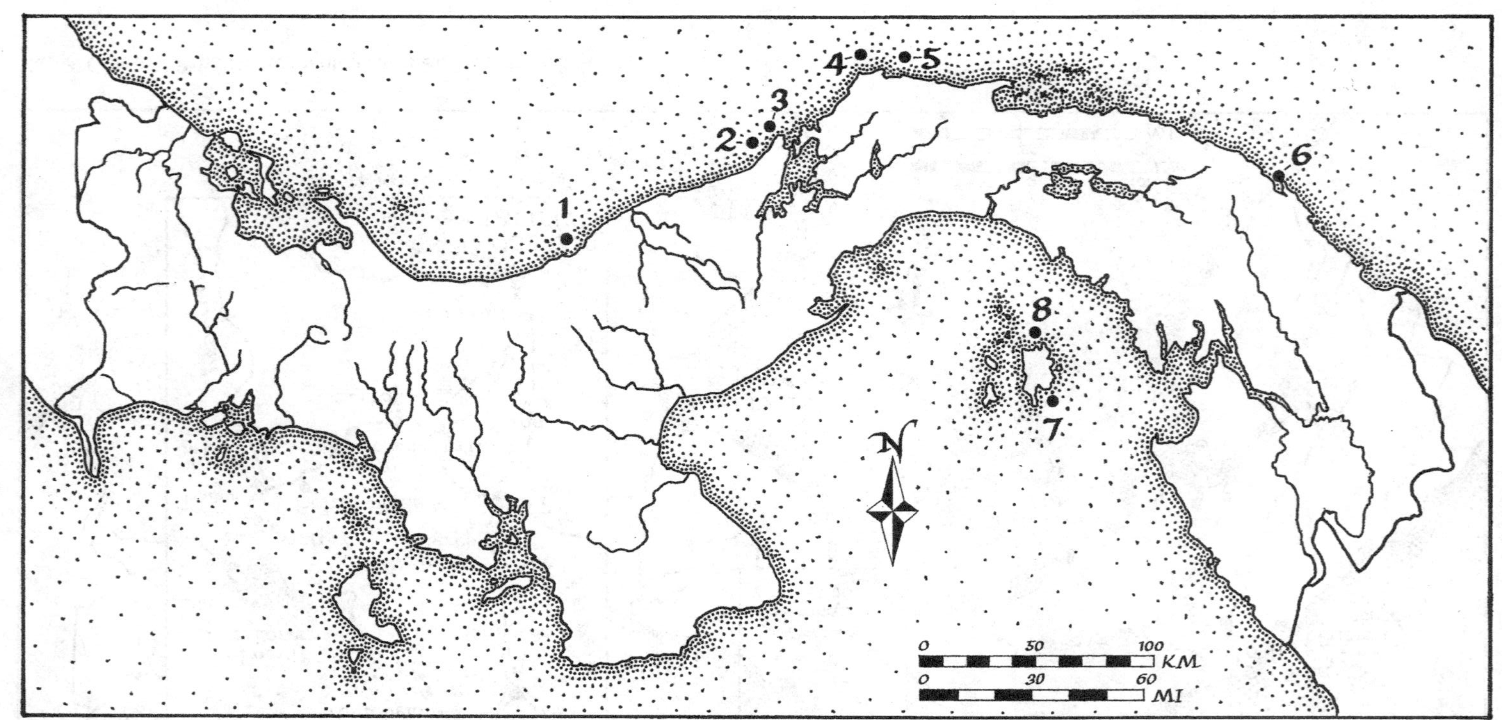

Map 4. Shipwreck sites in Panamá: (1) Río Belén, site of *La Gallega*; (2) *Nuestra Señora de la Encarnación*, Morgan's Fleet (including *Satisfaction*); (3) SS *Lafayette*; (4) two sixteenth-century wrecks off Portobelo; (5) Playa Damas wreck; (6) *Olive Branch*; (7) *Sub Marine Explorer*; (8) *San José*. Map by Jack Scott.

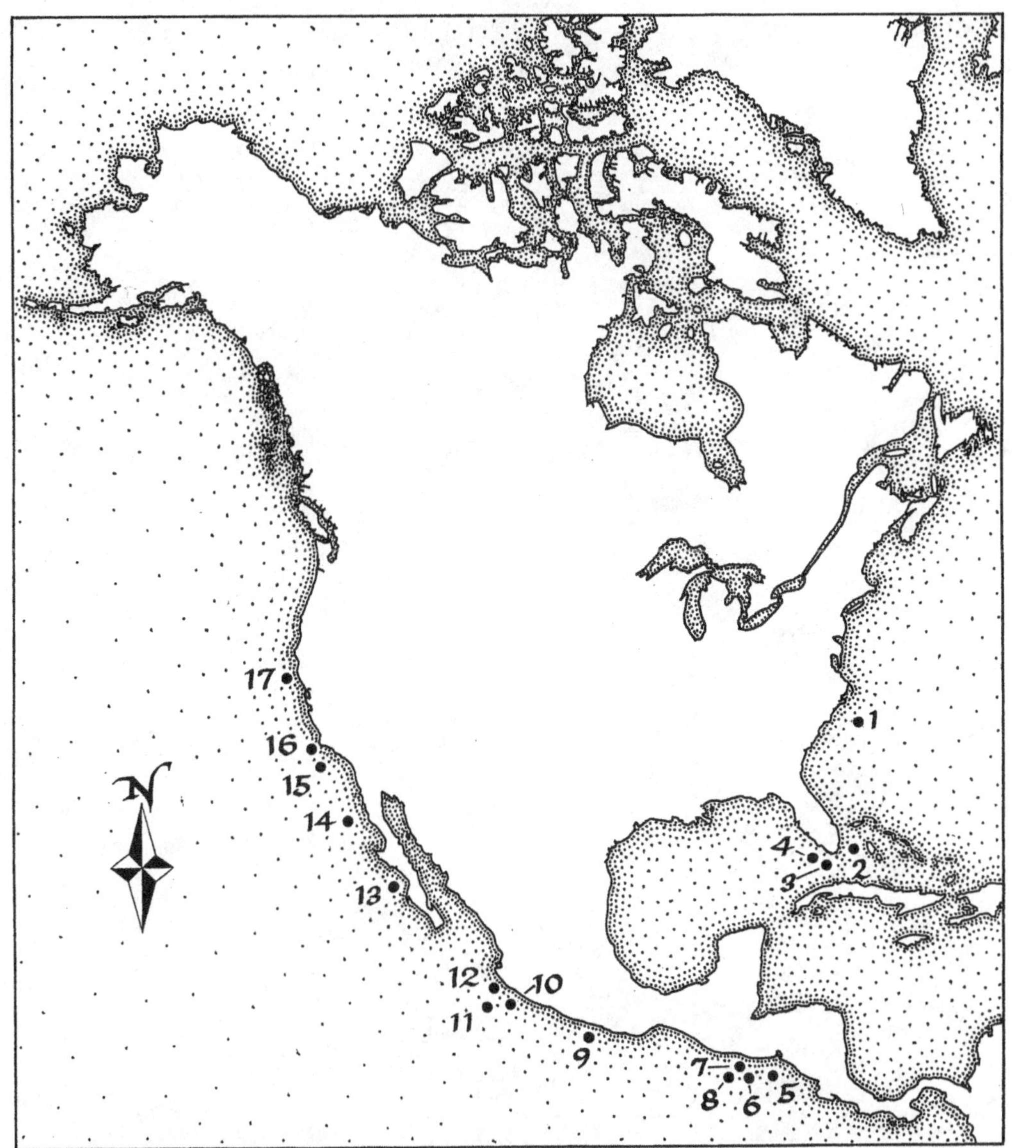

Map 5. Panamá route shipwreck sites beyond Panamá's borders: (1) SS *Central America*; (2) St. John's, Bahamas, wreck; (3) *Santa Margarita*; (4) *Nuestra Señora De Atocha*; (5) SS *Starbuck*; (6) SS *San Blas*; (7) SS *Colón*; (8) SS *Columbus*; (9) SS *North America*; (10) SS *Granada*; (11) SS *Colima*; (12) SS *Golden Gate*; (13) SS *Golden City*; (14) SS *Sacramento*; (15) SS *Winfield Scott*; (16) SS *Yankee Blade*; (17) SS *Tennessee*. Map by Jack Scott.

Introduction

Setting and Context

The Isthmus of Panamá occupies a unique place in the human geography of the world. It is, as geographer Eugene J. Palka has asserted, both the integral part of a narrow land bridge that spans two continents, and it is a one-time barrier, now a modern link, between the world's two largest oceans: "Panamá is the crossroads of the western hemisphere" (Palka 2005:3; Cooke 2005). It is a complex and diverse region forged by volcanic fire and shaped by geotectonic processes over a 150-million-year period. Yet it was in a "young landscape" that islands first appeared some 11 million years ago, followed a million years later by an archipelago that gradually emerged along with the Darién bridge of eastern Panamá (which emerged from the sea 10 million years ago). Then the mountains that form the western edge of Panamá were raised by shifting plates and volcanic eruptions (Coates 1999; Harmon 2005; Weil et al. 1972). This process created the reclined, S-shaped, generally east–west form of the isthmus known to the modern world (Harmon 2005:45).

This thin (60 km at its narrowest point) slice of earth includes, in the República de Panamá alone, some 3,000 km of coastline with approximately 1,450 km on the Pacific side and 815 km on the Caribbean shore. The Pacific coast is dotted with some one thousand islands of various sizes, including the Archipiélago de las Perlas, Isla Taboga, and Isla Coiba. For some 170 km the Caribbean is dotted by the approximately 380 islands of Guna Yala. The Caribbean is also defined by extensive coral reefs and a number of natural harbors that border a wide and gradual continental shelf, which forms the edge of a "semi-isolated sea" (Jackson and D'Croz 1999:39) known as the Laguna de Chiriquí. Fewer reefs and an even wider continental shelf with a rich, open-sea pelagic fishery are marine features that define the Pacific.

Figure 1. The shore near Portobelo as seen from the air reveals the typical maritime landscape of the isthmus: shallow, lined with mangroves and swamps, with numerous small channels. Rich in marine life, the coast was an ideal setting for pre-Columbian cultures to harvest its riches. In colonial and postcolonial times, the same landscape was part of a barrier to be conquered as the isthmus became a land-based transit point in global maritime trade. Alfredo Maiquez Photography, Panamá.

Other marked differences in the two coasts include distinct tidal regimes, with less than a 2 m rise and fall on the Caribbean coast as compared to a macro tidal range of 4 to 6 m on the Pacific coast (Palka 2005:6–7).

The climate is tropical, with a monthly mean temperature of 18 C and rainfall that varies from 2,970 mm annually on the Caribbean side to 1,650 mm on the Pacific coast. This humid, wet climate is one in which weathering and erosion formed an extensive network of river valleys, drainage basins, and the complex coastline (Palka 2005:7). Together with an intricate geomorphology, they have given rise to high environmental heterogeneity within this rather small territory, a marked differential seasonality between both ecologically dissimilar coastlines, and a considerable ecological diversity (see Cooke and Sánchez 2004:5; also Castro 2004). This is a "dynamic physical landscape that is continually reshaped by the forces of nature and one that is reflective of both the dominant geomorphic forces at work and the pervasive influence of climate and weather" (Palka 2005:6). Some five hundred rivers traverse the isthmian landscape, 350 of them discharging into the Pacific, and the others into the Caribbean, creating a multitude of valleys that facilitate perpendicular communication between the coastline and the mountains but impede them longitudinally. These include the most important of Panamá's rivers: the Río Chagres (Palka 2005:10).

The climate also created a series of natural vegetation zones ranging from forested mountains, hills, lowlands, savannas, coastal mangrove swamps, and tidal flats (Griggs 2005:18–38; Palka 2005:14). The geological and climatological forces, Palka notes, have left "an enduring imprint" not only on the landscape but also on its people (Palka 2005:5).

It is via this intersection of people and the environment that we can examine the maritime cultural landscape of the Isthmus of Panamá. As Jackson and D'Croz (1999) note, "Central America is a maritime land, every nation but Belize and El Salvador being bordered by both oceans, and the ratio of coastline to land is the highest in the continental Americas" (38). From the earliest known human presence on the isthmus some 11,000 years ago (Ranere and Cooke 2003) to modern times, the predominately maritime environment of the region has exerted a profound influence on human activity. And in time, human activity exerted an influence on the

Figure 2. The maritime cultural landscape of Panamá includes some 500 rivers and streams that originate in the highlands and flow to the coast. Many form coastal deltas. The most famous river, as well as one of the most navigable, is the Río Chagres on the Caribbean coast. It has been the setting for maritime activities from prehistoric times through the historic period. Today, contained by the Gatún Dam, the waters of the Chagres form much of the Panamá Canal. Photograph by James P. Delgado.

environment (Cooke and Sánchez 2001). Panamá is one of those places that exactly fits Westerdahl's (1995) original archaeological concept of combining sea and land to assess both as a larger maritime cultural landscape.

The 11,000-year human history of Panamá is one in which humans not only adapted to the isthmus' maritime environment but also increasingly adapted the isthmus for various maritime reasons, from harvesting resources to physically transforming the land to link two oceans. These millennia of maritime cultural activities, especially in the last five hundred years, have left a rich and diverse, tangible and intangible record, much of it archaeological but some of it ethnological and environmental—especially in the last century. To paraphrase Ford (2011:2), the Isthmus of Panamá existed before humans inhabited the area. It was a space that became a "place" because of human interaction: it was a place defined by an economic perspective that utilized its nature as a "maritime land." At first it was a place utilized by hunter-gatherers, then by settled agricultural societies, and later by colonial powers, which used it to direct and focus the flow of trade. In time, the expanding global economy (the so-called world-system) (Wallerstein 1974, 1980, and 1989) took control of this place to direct and focus world maritime trade to its advantage. Like the Suez's 100-mile stretch from the Mediterranean to the Red Sea, the Isthmus of Panamá "like no other corner of the globe offered humans the opportunity to connect two oceans with a short overland route" (Brady 1999:122).

The Isthmus of Panamá is particularly relevant with regard to Westerdahl's understanding of transport geography and transport zones, of which he asserts that "in a long perspective, it appears that heavy transport, *on land as well as on water* [original emphasis] primarily is concentrated to certain zones or corridors extended in a tangible direction" (Westerdahl 1998). In this regard, Panamá is not only a transport zone but also a transition zone in the maritime landscape—a place with obstacles that required the reloading of cargo (or people) and a switch to another means of transportation. This was certainly the case for the Isthmus of Panamá from the sixteenth through the twentieth centuries (Castillero 2010).

Indeed, Westerdahl's categorization of transport zones starts with "trans-isthmian (cross-ridge/cross watershed) land transport zones . . . with a combination of watersheds and waterways" (Westerdahl 1998). Westerdahl also notes how "the construction of ships and other vessels/vehicles and their techniques of propulsion are intimately adapted to the natural geography of the zone in question, the details of roads, coasts, routes, harbors (for example, the steepness and shallow banks) and the directions of prevailing currents and winds within the zone" (Westerdahl 1998). In this as well, Panamá's larger maritime cultural landscape reflects Westerdahl's maxim.

Another example that almost perfectly embodies Westerdahl's maxims is the modern practice of constructing ships to fit through the Panamá Canal as "Panamax" vessels. Anything larger has been known since 1914 as a "Post-Panamax" vessel. This basic split in vessel sizes began in 1914 with the opening of the canal and reflects the maximum size of a vessel that can fit into the canal's lock system (110 ft [33.53 m] wide, 1,000 ft [304.8 m] long, and 41.2 ft [12.56 m] deep for each chamber of the locks). With the construction of a new series of (larger) locks in the twenty-first century, there will soon be a "new Panamax" size, with the chambers being 180 ft (54.8 m) wide, 1,400 ft long (426.7 m) and 60 ft deep (18.3 m).

As Westerdahl notes, Panamax, post-Panamax, and new Panamax solidly demonstrate an

> *alternative view of the definition of a ship type.* The ship type is accordingly not just another archaeological type or implement. The functions of this floating combination of technological compounds could not be reduced to a simple archaeological type. It should rather be defined *in the process of explaining its use, of delimiting the vessel's function* from river to sea, from more or less closed transport zones to the open sea and then on to new zones that are gradually established along the way of change. The ship type concept thus would appear to be fruitfully bound up with the concept of the transport zones. (Westerdahl 1998 [original emphasis])

Westerdahl and others realize that assessing vessels and ship types with transport links and solely assessing ship types as a response to geography is not enough to inform a study, or the archaeology, of the maritime cultural landscape.

Westerdahl (1992) notes that a maritime cultural landscape "signifies human utilization (economy) of maritime space by boat, settlement, fishing, hunting, shipping, and its attendant subcultures, such as pilotage, lighthouse and seamark maintenance" (Westerdahl 1992:5–6). Westerdahl also includes cognitive, social, and cultural activities that are maritime in nature (1994:266). Other scholars, like O'Sullivan and Breen (2007), see this as "how people perceived and understood the sea and used this knowledge and understanding to order and constitute the landscape and societies that they live in" (15). In this way, maritime archaeology—first conceived in the 1960s as a ship-focused, "nautical archaeology"—was refined in the 1970s as a wider study of maritime culture. This study still focused on ships (Muckelroy 1978), but the emphasis on landscapes moved beyond the ship, and the shipwreck, to the broader environment ships are a part of.

This emphasis does not discard the shipwreck as a focal point, but it places it within a wider anthropological context. This context can simply be described as the archaeology of human interaction with maritime environment and space as well as the influence of this maritime world upon culture and maritime cultures' influence on environment and space. In Panamá, this is again strongly demonstrated by the canal and its attendant watershed rainforest, retained and managed to maintain an adequate supply of water to run the canal and keep a shipping lane vital to the global economy open for business.

Adding to Westerdahl's list, then, Ford (2011) notes that the maritime cultural landscape approach integrates maritime history and ethnography with the "physical residue of past maritime systems" that includes shipwrecks, ports, harbors, roadways, rail lines, modified rivers, villages, cottages, fortifications, shipyards, chandlers, warehouses, custom houses, commodities, insurance companies, lighthouses, and regulations (5) as well as the less tangible aspects of sound and smell and concepts of distance, perceived danger, and safety, which at times can be discerned through place names. In terms of the latter, utilizing a cultural landscape approach shows that different cultures, groups, and periods can have different perceptions, or at least different names for certain features in the physical world, and these can reflect behaviors tied to colonial or economic ambitions (i.e. "marketing") as well as spiritual belief. Indeed, a single place may have many names and reflect many beliefs, not only within the limits of its own space but also temporally as in a contiguous moment in time.

This volume will show how Panamá, as a space and as a place, reflects these theoretical perspectives within its relatively tight and limited boundaries, beginning with "prehistoric" times and continuing through to the present. The Isthmus of Panamá is examined from a maritime-cultural perspective so that the physical environment and the stamp of human endeavor upon it can be reconceptualized through a maritime-focused lens. In this way, we can assert that at its simplest, the archaeology of Panamá, beginning in prehistory, is dominated by its relationship to the marine environment. Maritime archaeology could be the study of a single shell mound, a ruined Spanish fortification, a stone-paved transisthmian road, the drowned rails of the original Panamá Railroad, the Gatún Dam, the use of the drowned bed of the flooded Chagres as part of the canal, a mid-nineteenth-century trash dump in the Casco, or the eroding graves of laborers on the banks of the canal. But maritime archaeology can just as easily encompass the study of a beached nineteenth-century pearl-diving submersible, a sunken canal dredge, or a colonial shipwreck.

With regard to shipwrecks, the global patterns of empire and capitalism that both influence (and have been influenced) by the Isthmus of Panamá have resulted in a number of shipwrecks that comprise an archaeological record not confined to the coastal waters of Panamá. These also include wrecks of ships bound from or for Panamá's Caribbean and Pacific shores in the precanal period, as well as all the vessels involved in Panamá-specific trades and activities: for example, the Gold Rush–era steamships of the United States Mail and Pacific Mail steamship companies of the nineteenth century, the wrecks of which lie in the Caribbean as well as along the Pacific and Atlantic coasts of the United States. These wrecks, as well as the remains of other ships built specifically for the Panamá route and lost in direct trade or association with the isthmian crossing—or which came to be lost, scuttled, or abandoned in isthmian waters—are part of the larger maritime cultural landscape of Panamá and will be included in this work. By necessity as well as a means of focus, this study excludes any ship, wrecked or otherwise, that ever transited the Panamá Canal.

In conclusion, the authors of this book agree with Flatman (2011) that in approaching the archaeology of Panamá as a maritime cultural landscape, we focus on what archaeology is all about: people. Through the model of "distinctive human societies in a distinctive environmental locale" (Flatman 2011:325), because "people make cultural landscapes," this study can focus on those who inhabited and changed both their culture and the landscape in response to the marine environment of Panamá as a space and not simply emphasize the typology of ships, bottles, or forts. By examining all tangible and intangible aspects of Panamá's past through a maritime focus, we can take a generalized theoretical approach, such as one emphasizing the maritime cultural landscape, and test what we have in Panamá against that model. As Flatman notes, this is part of a proactive, research-based process that is also good archaeology in that it is thoughtful, meaningful, and "allows a nuanced approach to a complex situation" (Flatman 2011:326).

We can now examine the 11,000-year flow of Panamá's history through a maritime lens, assessing sites, both submerged and on land, individually and collectively, as part of the maritime archaeological record of Panamá as a maritime cultural landscape. The chapters that follow are organized chronologically. However, there are aspects of the maritime cultural landscape that are consistent not only geographically but also culturally. Although the traditional histories suggest a near-total extinction of Panamá's native peoples, this is not the case, as will be seen with the Guna and the Emberá peoples, to name a few. Their persistence, politically and culturally, includes an ongoing interaction with the marine environment and represents an inherent and consistent indigenous thread in the overall fabric of the isthmian maritime cultural landscape.

Similarly, there is also a continuity of certain types of native maritime adaptations, including maritime craft. This continuity reflects not only adaptation to the marine environment but also the adaptation of certain aspects of pre-Columbian maritime culture by successive cultural and ethnic groups, including the successive African and European peoples of Panamá. There are other aspects as well. As will be shown in this book, archaeological evidence suggests that regular sustenance for the colonial-era inhabitants of Nombre de Dios (1519–1597) was essentially unchanged from indigenous food gathering of reef fish and crustaceans.

The chronological organization of this book begins with the pre-Columbian world of the isthmus some 11,000 years ago and continues to the 1501–1502 period of first contact. We then look at Christopher Ward's brilliant summary of isthmian commerce and trade, *Imperial Panamá* (1993), and his division of early isthmian history into four periods: the 1510–1519 period of conquest and the foundation of the first cities; the 1520–1532 period in which Spain consolidated the *encomienda* system on the isthmus and during which most of the native population was killed off or retreated beyond colonial reach; the 1532–1540 period of resource exploitation (primarily pearls and gold) and a time when Panamá served as a maritime base for the expeditions sent to conquer South America; and finally the period from 1540 to 1740 during which Panamá transformed into the Spanish Empire's economic maritime transisthmian link (Ward 1993:29).

We then divide the history and the development of the Panamanian maritime cultural landscape into the period 1740–1848, a time of relative stagnation that saw attempts to revive the old system. We examine the California Gold Rush–inspired revival of the isthmus as a maritime link through the American Civil War from 1849 to 1865. A second period of stagnation (1865–1904) followed, when France revived dreams of building a canal. This was also a period when colonial powers sought other means to incorporate Panamá into patterns of global commerce (such as reviving the pearling industry). Next our focus shifts to the American period of canal construction, operation, and modification from 1904 through 1979.

Finally, we look at the modern era, which began in 1980 and continues with the planned 2016 opening of new locks and an even larger Panamá Canal.

Each chapter will assess the maritime aspects of Panamanian history and culture, note the cultural adaptations and the formation of the maritime cultural landscape, and review the pertinent evidence, including archaeological work past and present. We conclude with an overview that revisits the 11,000-year record through the maritime cultural lens. As Flatman (2011) has also noted, a defining characteristic of landscape studies (including maritime cultural landscapes) is that they are about movement and change. Panamá's rich and diverse archaeological and cultural record reflects more than the movement of ships and people. It also reflects global change in patterns of empire and capitalism and the movement of capital while reflecting a massive change in the structure of the isthmus to better accommodate such movement. Through it all there is the persistence of certain peoples like the Guna and Emberá and the cross-cultural means of the ocean and the maritime world to connect all of humanity.

1

The Isthmus in the Pre-European World

The First Seafarers

Maritime culture is a response to the environment, and the first concept of maritime cultural landscape is evident in the first human settlement on the isthmus. Maritime culture may in fact be the first human culture to come to the isthmus, especially if the theory of coastal migration (that is, the rapid movement of the first humans in the Americas through the use of boats that followed the coasts and the sustenance provided by the marine environment) is to be believed (see Erlandson et al. 2007). Although no sites on the Isthmus of Panamá are known to have been in existence any earlier than 11,500 years ago, there is circumstantial evidence of people who passed through. And there may be evidence of some who stayed, especially on the now-submerged late glacial coastline. The discovery of a human skull in an underwater cave system at Hoyo Negro in Quintana Roo, Mexico, predates the inundation of the caves some 12,000 years ago (Chatters et al. 2014). The Hoyo Negro remains correspond to the earliest documented period of human settlement in the Mexico–Central America region. They may also point to other (as yet undiscovered) sites now underwater where early humans may have followed the coast as they headed into South America where sites such as Monte Verde, which dates to 14,800 years B.P. (Dillehay et al. 1982), indicate that people did pass through or near the isthmus, either on foot or by boat, in an earlier time. In fact, some researchers are skeptical that early peoples (pre-Clovis) entered South America without traversing Panamá and the Pacific route following the submerged coastline, which would offer a strong explanation for their current poor visibility (Cooke et al. 2013:3).

Panamá's location at the bottleneck of the Americas is logically situated to have witnessed some of the first human inhabitants in their settlement and their travels south. In spite of the dearth of Panamanian corroborative field data, the isthmian littoral (whose configuration has adjusted periodically to glacial cycles) should have played an important role in the continental dissemination of *Homo sapiens* (Cooke and Sánchez 2001:16). Evidence of very early coastal settlements elsewhere in the world and the colonization of remote islands such as Australia by necessarily maritime means set a perfectly acceptable precedent for the same happening in the Americas (see Piperno 2007:185–187).

Some of the most dramatic changes in the maritime landscape took place in the Gulf (or Bay) of Panamá, where the continental shelf is broad and presents a relatively slow gradient. At the height of the last glacial maximum that occurred around 20,000 years ago, with sea levels down almost 140 meters from their modern depth, the Gulf of Panamá was a vast dry and flat basin whose coastline could have stretched to nearly one hundred kilometers due south of Panamá City. This is a landscape covered in thorn woodland, low scrub, and wooded savanna vegetation, in which today's Pearl Islands would have stood as a low altitude hill chain. With the end of the Ice Age and the melting of the great ice sheets, sea levels started to steadily rise; however, by the time the first evidence of humans appears in mainland Panamá by 11,500 years ago, the future Gulf of Panamá was still a broad plain ready for colonization. Anyone taking the supposed Pacific route of entry into South America, following the shores in a route backed by archaeological, linguistic, and now genetic evidence, would have either settled in or traversed this area. That ancient early Holocene coastline, where people lived or, perhaps, walked or sailed heading south (with its habitation and catchment sites as yet undiscovered) is now submerged under more than a hundred meters of water. In any case, the spread of human groups from north to south, by water or land and by whatever social dynamic, left settlers all along the territories they crossed. These were people who stayed behind and made their permanent homes in the new lands, thus starting a millennia-long process of occupation and cultural development. These were people whose descendants received the Spanish well over 10,000 years later.

According to some models, the waters kept rising until they reached their current levels around 9,000 years ago (around 7000 BC; Cooke et al. 2015:4). It was during this time that the Pearls became islands, which were permanently separated although visible from the mainland. That separation, however, was of no consequence to maritime peoples, who used the water as a means of connection. Recent archaeological surveys and excavations in the archipelago by archaeologists from the Smithsonian Tropical Research Institute (STRI) and Patronato Panamá Viejo (PPV), led by Richard Cooke and Juan Guillermo Martín, have documented dozens of sites from the first millennium AD. Also documented is one early site that was first inhabited around 3700 BC and whose inhabitants reached the island by boat. It is located at the western edge of Isla Pedro González, where a large hotel development is currently taking place.

In a rare case of a real estate development company showing genuine interest in scientific research and conservation of cultural resources, the environmental impact assessment of Isla Pedro González has included a large investment in archaeological excavations, one that has focused principally on the excavation of preceramic site L19-L20, also known as Don Bernardo, on the namesake beach. Several test units have been dug at the site, revealing midden deposits at least 2.6 meters deep and laden with terrestrial and marine faunal remains and stone tools made mostly of agate. Carbonized vegetable remains are frequently found in the samples, which suggest these early inhabitants cleared forests with fire. Excavation stopped at the water table, but the archaeological deposits went deeper, suggesting earlier settlement on land covered by sea-level rise. Because of their systematic test-pit survey (but without excavating the entire area) Cooke and Martín estimate the site extends over an area of around 1,300 square meters (Martín et al. 2009, 2015). As of this writing, new open-area excavations on the site are about to commence in search of direct evidence of the ancient occupants in the form of post-holes or possibly burials.

The early inhabitants of the isthmus discovered that the chain of mountains separating the oceans was, like the water, no obstacle for cultural contact with their neighbors across the hills. The proximity of oceans with diverse and complementary coastal resources was well understood by the locals on each coast: they participated in a transisthmian exchange network that was archaeologically visible up to the sixteenth century AD and that also included lands beyond the isthmus. By at least 5000 BC, the peoples of the Pacific shores of Panamá, who already practiced fully developed agricultural methods, were utilizing the maritime littoral with a productivity that helped achieve a relative economic self-sufficiency and territorial stability (Cooke and Sánchez 2001:16).

Figure 3a–b. Excavations at Playa Don Bernardo, Isla Pedro Gonzalez, Archipiélago de las Perlas. Photographs by Fernando Bustamante.

The earliest evidence comes from sites on the shores of Parita Bay in central Panamá and dates from 5000 BC to AD 500. The coast here is steep, and during the dry season (December through April) it is subjected to upwelling, which supports a rich and diverse array of fish, mollusks, and crustaceans. Parita Bay is situated on mangrove-fringed waters and in a landscape that alternately floods and then experiences arid conditions during the dry season. With an erosion-formed coastline of mudflats, tidal channels, and high tidal flats, the marine environment was conducive to extensive maritime activity. Its maritime cultural landscape included weirs and traps built between the flats and in the channels; the use of boats to harvest fish, crustaceans, and mollusks; and the use of the flats as drying areas to harvest sea salt used to preserve the fish the people caught (Cooke et al. 2008:101).

The evidence comes mainly from two sites: Cerro Mangote, a preceramic village occupied between 5000 and 3600 BC and Sitio Sierra, a nucleated agricultural village inhabited between AD 1 and AD 400. At these sites, the inhabitants utilized "fences, harpoons, fishhooks and other primitive tools, many of them made from mangrove wood" to harvest "estuarine and coastal species such as the *Carangidae*, *Batrachoididae*, *Ariidae*, and *Aupeidae*" (Drude de Lacerda 2001:55). The result of thousands of years of harvesting and consumption of these species is found in shell mounds, which are also part of the pre-Columbian maritime cultural landscape. It is hardly surprising that the purveyors of marine foods at these two sites did not make forays into deep clear water to search out shoals of meat-eating fish and their prey; nor is it surprising that they did not fish around coral reefs or rocky substrates given the intrinsic taxonomic richness and productivity of the estuary. However, fish remains at Sitio Sierra do show that sometime after the abandonment of Cerro Mangote, the use of watercraft and gillnets grew in importance to be able to catch fish that do not take hooks.

Parita Bay fishers apparently stuck close to their very rich estuarine coastline, without the frequent need to head out farther. Even so, Cerro Mangote's age and Sitio Sierra's inland position (about 12 km) vis-à-vis the delta, confirm the longevity and geographical amplitude of pre-Columbian fishing in turbid littoral waters (Cooke and Ranere 1999:118).

The economy of Central Panamá during the late preceramic period and the early ceramic period (between 5000 and 1000 BC) was not entirely coastal or maritime but rather mixed. People lived in dispersed settlements near or on the shore, but they also practiced slash-and-burn agriculture, which forced them to constantly relocate. It seems likely that before and up to the first millennium BC the pre-Columbian populations of lower Central America and neighboring regions of South America were mostly self-sufficient and concentrated on the exchange of daily-use articles. They were at least somewhat aware of peoples beyond this region, and they certainly exchanged articles (such as manatee bones and seashells) from places that were several days' walk apart. But current data do not suggest a maritime route for trade. Most likely, up to this point in time, the relationship of these early peoples with the sea was limited to the harvesting of resources from coastal habitats where simple fishing and collecting technologies were enough. As shown below, this situation changed in later centuries.

Confident Navigators in the Pacific

Even if early pre-Columbian Parita Bay fishers stayed close to the shores in the procurement of aquatic resources, longer sea voyages became more commonplace, and these peoples developed into skilled maritime travelers who crossed the Gulf of Panamá on a regular basis (Martín and Sánchez 2007). There is plenty of archaeological evidence spanning the first millennium AD and up to the time of contact with the Europeans, which demonstrates that the native peoples of Panamá commonly plied the seas, resulting in cultural and commercial exchanges that made them aware of the existence of other lands and peoples. Crucial in the understanding of these interactions is the evidence available in island archaeology in the Pacific and Atlantic shores of the isthmus.

By the middle of the first millennium BC, archaeological, genetic, and linguistic evidence showed that there were enough people who had been living permanently in Panamá and for a long enough period of time that social and cultural differences began to appear. Broadly speaking, these differences began to appear mainly in three distinct regions of the isthmus: these were regions in which peoples shared cultural traits that were distinct from those of their neighbors in other regions. The differences in language, customs, and beliefs were noticeable to archaeologists first as changes in pottery manufacture and decoration. These cultural interaction spheres or regions with their discrete semiotic traditions occupied western, central, and eastern Panamá, extending to both the Atlantic and Pacific shores across the continental divide and are now called, respectively, Gran Chiriquí, Gran Coclé, and Gran Darién (Cooke et al. 2000:154) The frontiers between them were not static in time or space; they were not established formally but were rather fluid and porous, and archaeologists think there is proof of this in the Pearl Archipelago. The material evidence these three semiotic traditions left behind can be found in the archaeological record through to the Spanish invasion in 1501.

A "culture area" scheme with temporally and spatially immutable boundaries seems inappropriate. Cooke has proposed a revision of this, instead using the concept of three major "interaction spheres" in Panamá during the last 1,500 years of the pre-Columbian period, which are characterized as areas of "cooperation without domination" (Lange 1992:434). Within each one, relations between larger and smaller settlements, "cores" and "peripheries," and suppliers and recipients of goods, changed diachronically while reacting to inadequately understood demographic and economic parameters. The western and eastern spheres extended beyond Panamá's current frontiers into Costa Rica and Colombia, respectively.

The Pearl Archipelago of the Gulf of Panamá sits in a region between Gran Coclé and Gran Darién. There, the extensive surveys undertaken by STRI and PPV archaeologists have revealed the long-term and widespread inhabitations of the islands. Many refuse dumps, shell middens, and even human burials have been documented, all of which reveal much about the everyday lives of ancient islanders and their possible movements, as shown in the abundant ceramic, lithic, and faunal remains that have surfaced.

On the island of Pedro González for instance, after the preceramic occupations of Don Bernardo, the earliest ceramics found date to the beginning of the first millennium AD and consist of coarse earthenwares decorated principally by plastic means of incision (sgraffito), modeling, slip trailing, and low and high relief. These conforming pottery types archaeologists ascribe to eastern Panamanian peoples—that is, people from Gran Darién. However, by the mid-first millennium AD, painted pottery types from Gran Coclé had replaced the Gran Darién assemblage, which almost disappears from the record. One style of decoration in particular, known as the Cubitá style of Gran Coclé, dated between AD 550 and 700, spreads from the Azuero Peninsula all over the Gulf of Panamá and is found in coastal sites, well within Gran Darién and alongside local pots. But in the Pearl Islands, Cubitá pottery becomes the main assemblage for at least two centuries, before being replaced at the end of the first millennium, circa AD 800, by another ceramic group: this time, again, from Gran Darién. Pots with plastic decoration only, the trademark of Gran Darién, come back to the islands and dominate the archaeological record until the arrival of the Spanish (Martín and Sánchez 2007).

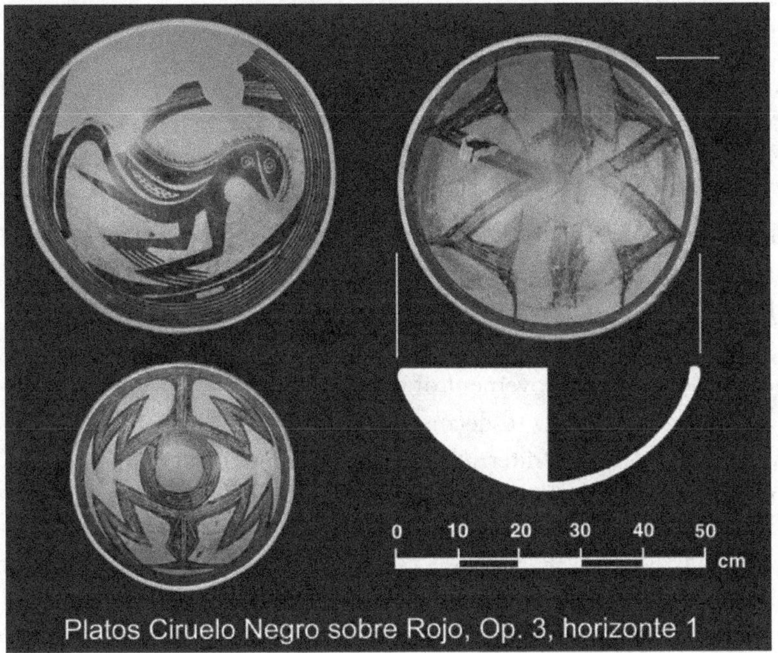

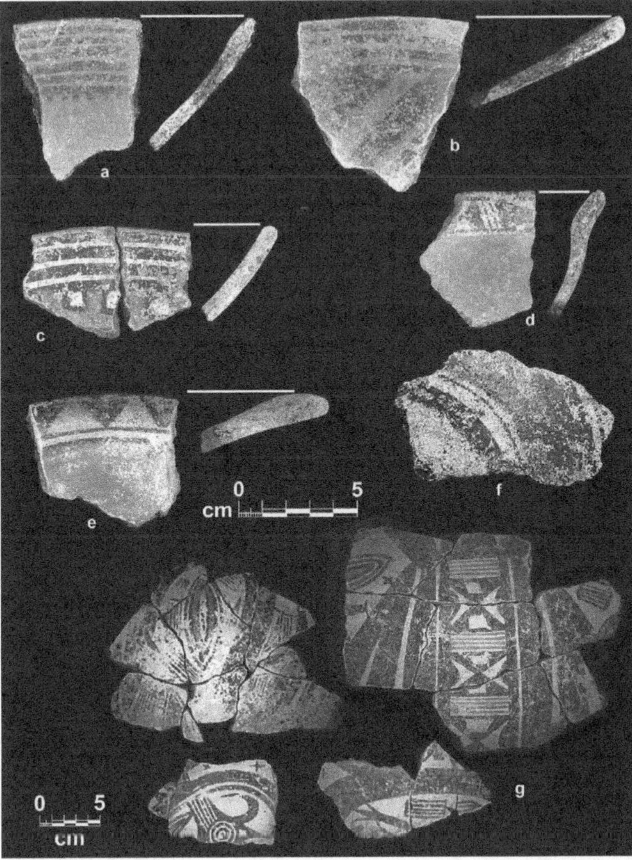

Figure 4a–b. Cubitá-style artifacts are evidence of the spread of the Gran Coclé culture throughout the Gulf of Panamá through maritime trade. Shown here are Cubitá-style plates of the Ciruelo black-on-red variety, excavated from Cerro Juan Díaz on the western shores of the Gulf, and Cubitá-style sherds recently excavated from sites on Isla Pedro Gonzalez in the Archipiélago de las Perlas. Photographs by Richard Cooke and Luis Sánchez, Smithsonian Tropical Research Institute.

Archaeologists hypothesize that the changes seen in the pottery assemblages could reflect actual movements of people migrating from one place to the other. More specifically, peoples from Gran Coclé on the western edge of the Bay of Panamá were encroaching on islands previously settled by Gran Darién peoples from the eastern edge who later retook them. But this is not necessarily the only plausible scenario. It could also be that Gran Darién Pearl islanders simply traded with Gran Coclé peoples on the western coastline of the gulf and adopted their fancy painted pottery styles: in other words, it was not a movement of people as much as an interchange of products or ideas on how to decorate pottery. In any case, the Gulf of Panamá became a sort of Mediterranean Sea for ancient Panamanians, who plied it with ease when making stopovers in the Pearl Islands. Gran Coclé pottery styles (not only Cubitá but some older and some more recent) are found in sites all along the Gulf of Panamá, from Azuero all the way down to Cupica in Colombia, which is more than 230 km southeast of the islands.

Ornaments from the Sea

Part of the explanation for the shifts in ceramic assemblages in the Pearls may be related to the commerce of seashell ornaments, which from the early to mid-first millennium AD became the main signifiers of status among the elites. Thorny oysters of species belonging to the *Spondylus* genus were particularly sought after for the manufacture of bodily adornments. These specimens live in subtidal waters of the Gulf of Panamá and the islands and attach themselves to rocks on the seabed. These oysters had to be pried off by divers, who represented just one group of the many professional specializations in pre-Columbian Panamá considering the sheer quantities of *Spondylus* shells being extracted and worked with. Pre-Columbian divers also harvested other species such as the pearl oyster (*Pinctada mazatlanica*) whose abundance amazed the Spanish and gave rise to the archipelago's current name. These elaborate ornaments have been documented at archaeological sites in Panamá as having had a wide distribution around the gulf during the first millennium AD. Cooke and Sánchez believe that the acquisition and exchange of these ornaments made of seashells from coral reefs and nonestuarine waters can be causally related to the expansion of the Gran Coclé ceramic tradition, particularly the Cubitá style of pottery around the Bay of Panamá and sites around it after AD 500 (2001:33).

Pinctada and *Spondylus* are the principal genera of seashells used in Cerro Juan Díaz, a large and long-lived habitation and burial site near the

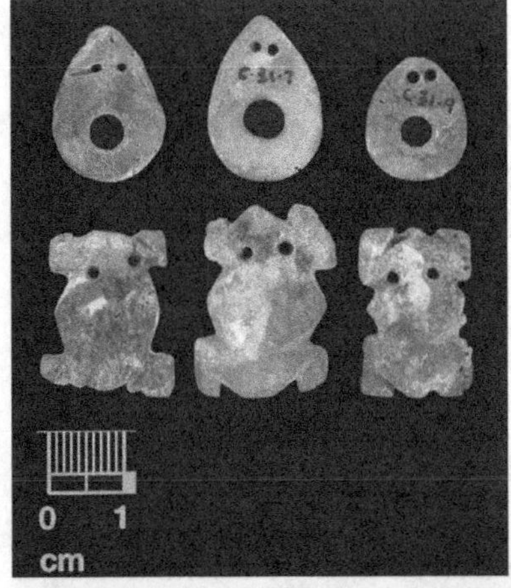

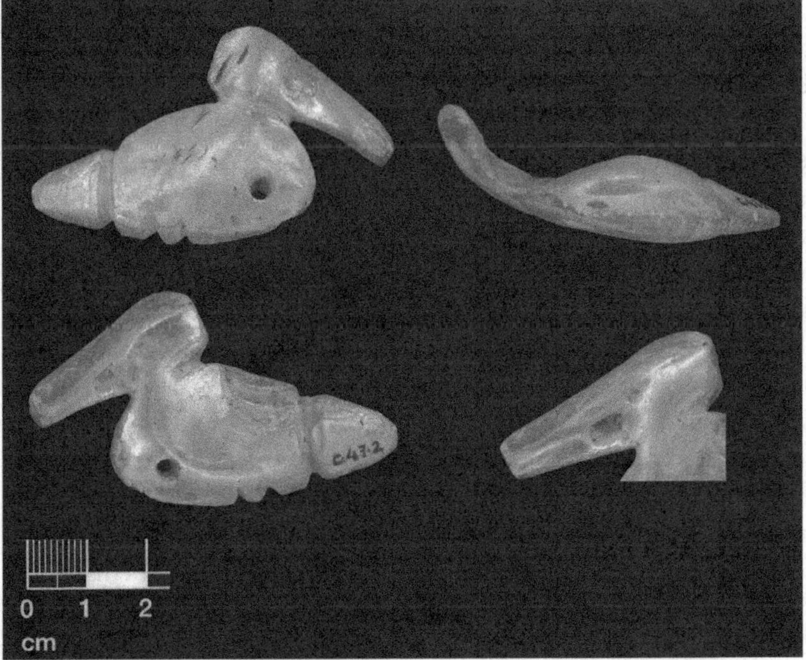

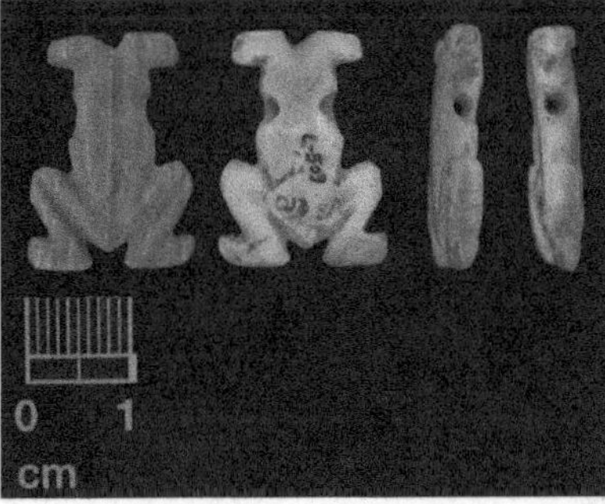

Figures 5a–c. Seashell artifacts from Cerro Juan Díaz, all dating from AD 200–AD 700. *Top to bottom*: group of *Spondylus princeps* decorations found in a multiple stage shaft tomb with bundle burials; hinge fragment from the valve of a pearl oyster (*Pinctada mazatlanica*) shaped into a pelican; *Spondylus princeps* decorations. Photographs by Elizabeth Morales, courtesy of Richard Cooke, Smithsonian Tropical Research Institute.

western coast of the Gulf of Panamá in Gran Coclé. These shells live in clear waters near rocky coral reefs and were fished in some locations such as Isla Iguana, at least 50 km from the shoreline. Some cut, perforated, and filed fragments have been observed in Cerro Juan Díaz, implying a local manufacture of which Julia Mayo documented a specialized workshop on site (Mayo and Cooke 2005).

The introduction and later apogee of seashell adornments, and what this implied from the point of view of their extraction, processing, and distribution, most likely had widespread social and cultural effects on the development of the agricultural communities of the central Pacific (Martín and Sánchez 2007:117) as it put them all in contact with each other. And perhaps the shared taste in shells led to a shared taste in Cubitá and later Conte pottery.

For now, the available archaeological evidence points to a specific geographic and chronological correlation between the Cubitá and Conte ceramic styles. The evidence also points to the apogee of the seashell artifact industry in sites in and around the Gulf of Panamá. Thus a grand maritime interaction zone between Gran Coclé and Gran Darién was established whose primary function was the exploitation and distribution of marine oysters and their derivative products—also stimulating the transfer of ideas, technologies, and materials. The geography of the gulf tends to favor this as it is full of islands and allows for long-distance sightlines, thus making long-distance canoe travel easier. Existing commercial relationships could have led to the exchange of polychrome pottery and raw or finished seashell artifacts. However, it is hard to trace the movements of a pot, for instance, from origin to destination. Additionally, Cubitá-style artifacts found in Gran Darién sites such as Playa Venado present technological particularities such as types of clays and surface finishes that could indicate local production instead of importation from Gran Coclé (Martín and Sánchez 2007:119–121). Then one would have to assume that either the idea of how to make and decorate a Cubitá pot traveled long distances or that the Cubitá peoples did.

Gold

The seashell's reign as the main symbol for wealth and rank in pre-Columbian societies would soon be over as the introduction of goldsmithing from Colombia and Ecuador, possibly by way of the sea, grabbed the attention of the elites. This does not mean that seashells disappear from the record. On the contrary, they would continue to be used. But gold increasingly became the preferred precious metal for the elites to be buried with, to wear and show off. Metalwork was unknown in Panamá. Whether it was the finished pieces or the technique to make them, whatever arrived first quickly caught on, and gold pieces were soon highly sought after by those in power.

Gold artifacts began appearing at burial sites and would almost completely displace seashell ornaments as the main elitist signifier for social ascendancy, as evidenced by the epitome of the craft in the Sitio Conte and El Caño chiefly burials, where the bodies of powerful men were interred with lavish gold offerings between AD 700 and 900. This custom continued right up to the Spanish invasion, as is famously narrated by Gaspar de Espinosa, who interrupted the burial ritual of Chief Antatara (also called "Paris" or "Parita") and ransacked his tomb and desiccated body, from which he obtained a rich cache of golden artifacts that he would later describe in detail in his report to the Governor of Panamá (cited in Torres de Araúz 1992: 134-144; see also Anderson 1911:212-3).

Technological and archaeological studies support the hypothesis that the manufacture of gold ornaments was in the hands of skilled artisans when metallurgy was introduced into lower Central America, but the available archaeological data cannot determine whether local people traveled to Colombia or Ecuador to learn the trade or if itinerant artisans or traders brought it to Panamá.

The fact that the very earliest gold artifacts found in Panamá share several icons with Gran Coclé pottery styles of the early to middle first millennium AD, with which they have been associated in burials, raises the question of whether one technology's ideology influenced the other's. Nevertheless, as archaeological knowledge of the La Mula painted pottery style from Gran Coclé (dated circa 200 BC–AD 200), which at that time was not a culture associated with metal, suggests that the motifs on pottery in this region were later incorporated on gold objects (Cooke et al. 2003:96).

Archaeologists surmise from this that all the activities associated with harvesting, transporting, elaborating, and distributing shell artifacts across the Gulf of Panamá would have suffered a collapse as the market for gold expanded and cultural tastes adapted to the new media for artistic and meaningful expression that gold represented. The seashell maritime trade network would have been gone or greatly reduced. It is possible then that the changes in pottery (or populations) seen in the Pearl Islands were connected or caused by the prevalence of the use of seashells and then by the shift to gold as one industry practically replaced the other. Although the connection between both phenomena has not been established or proved, at least the timing is right.

Still, the use of seashells did not disappear. There is documentary evidence from the early sixteenth century that the use and exchange of seashells still dominated maritime and land commerce in the isthmus. When Balboa reached the Pacific shore in 1513 he noticed the existence of commercial relationships between peoples on both coasts of Panamá as well as between the mainland and the Pearl Islands. Cooke and Sánchez (2001:35) state that a good example of how intensive pre-Columbian extraction of pearls was is the fact that the Spanish imposed a yearly tribute of 100 pearls on Dites, who was the chief of the largest island in the archipelago. These pearls came from the same species of oyster used to make ornaments recovered archaeologically. Chief Tumaco, who took Balboa to the island to meet Dites, had in one of his canoes objects adorned with mother of pearl. Balboa also tells of how Chief Comogre, in his town up the Chucunaque River, traded pearls for gold.

The Atlantic

While all these movements of goods, ideas, and peoples were happening in the Pacific, more evidence of natives developing a maritime culture has been recovered in the islands of the Bocas del Toro archipelago on the Caribbean coast. For more than ten years, archaeologist Tom Wake from the Cotsen Institute of Archaeology at UCLA has led an excavation at a place called Sitio Drago, a fifteen-hectare archaeological site sitting on a beautiful tropical Atlantic beach on the northern end of Isla Colón.

Based on the results of archaeological investigations undertaken between 2003 and 2012, Sitio Drago represents a nucleated chiefly settlement mainly used between the years AD 800 to 1200, although fifteen radiometric age determinations date the occupation of Sitio Drago to between AD 690 and 1410. Sitio Drago is like no other recorded site in Bocas del Toro as it consists of a dense cluster of at least fifteen artificial mounds on a stabilized beach ridge covering at least ten hectares (Wake 2006; Wake and Mendizábal [forthcoming]; Wake et al. 2004, 2012, 2013). This site configuration is markedly different from the diffuse scatter of one-hectare shell middens atop hills overlooking the water that previously characterized the region (see Gordon 1962, 1982; Linares and Ranere 1980). Surface investigation and test excavations all exhibit a high density of surface and buried artifacts including ceramics, lithics, human remains, and animal remains.

Sitio Drago has yielded a greater diversity of ceramic types and varieties, more carved stone, and more evidence of plant food processing than all other sites explored in the Bocas del Toro region, just from the limited test excavations conducted to date.

The ceramic artifacts collected from Sitio Drago exhibit a diversity of specimens that hint at external connections, including ceramic wares with an affinity for Chiriquí on the Pacific coast of Panamá, incised wares from Diquis in southwest Costa Rica, polychromes from the Valle Central of Costa Rica, Guanacaste, and possibly southwest Nicaragua, and polychromes from Veraguas and Coclé of Central Panamá. This diversity suggests that Sitio Drago may have functioned as a regional trading center. Carved stone "metate" fragments recovered from Sitio Drago are similar to complete examples found throughout Panamá and Costa Rica (Wake et al. 2004). The diverse array of artifacts recovered and the presence of a formal mortuary sector (especially in comparison to nearby archaeological sites) suggests that the prehistoric occupants of Sitio Drago achieved a higher level of sociopolitical complexity than was typical of most occupations in a tropical rainforest environment: and this indicated the presence of elite trade goods and the possibility of social ranking (Wake et al. 2013:1017).

Two major ceramic phases with clear stratigraphic boundaries have been identified at Sitio Drago. The first is characterized by pottery called "Biscuit Ware" because of its cream color and very thin, delicate, crackerlike appearance. It is present from 0 cm to 30 cm below the surface and dates to after AD 1200. With the exception of a few fragments, this ceramic ware has not been found at Sitio Drago below 40 cm. Below 30 cm the ceramic assemblage is dominated by Chiriquí ware. These Chiriquían ceramic types provide evidence of interaction with other parts of the Pacific coastal Mesoamerican region (Wake 2008:8).

Previous investigations have established the subsistence system as horticulture supplemented with hunting, foraging, and fishing. An imported raffia palm species was cultivated for its roots and seeds (Wake et al. 2004:3). Ongoing archaeological investigations at the site have determined so far that fishing and opportunistic hunting were important staples in the Sitio Drago subsistence system throughout all cultural phases.

The human burials, sealed in coffins made of coral stones, are in an area of the site where many remains of meaty animals have been found. This is an area that Wake associates with ritualized feasting and where social gatherings took place. In this same sector of the site can be found not only local ceramics but also fragments of pots that have been identified as imports

Figures 6a–b. Pre-Columbian site excavations at Sitio Drago, showing burials 1, 2, and 3 before and after excavation. Photographs by Tom Wake.

Figure 7. Pre-Columbian maritime ceramic motifs at Sitio Drago. Photograph by Tom Wake.

from Central America and central Panamá, with a range that covers over 200 km to the Azuero Peninsula in Gran Coclé, and more than 400 km to southern Nicaragua. It is possible that these fragile, foreign, and presumably valuable and special objects found their way to Sitio Drago by land. But at least the last leg of the trip, which would have been to Isla Colón and the site, was accomplished on a boat.

This suggests it is possible for some longer parts of those trips to have been by sea. Of course this would not be the case for items brought across the mountains from Coclé, which necessitated a land journey (although they could have been transported down the rivers), but it would seem easier and safer for such fragile items as ceramic pots to be brought over by sea in storage in a large canoe. There are several accounts of pre-Columbian ca-

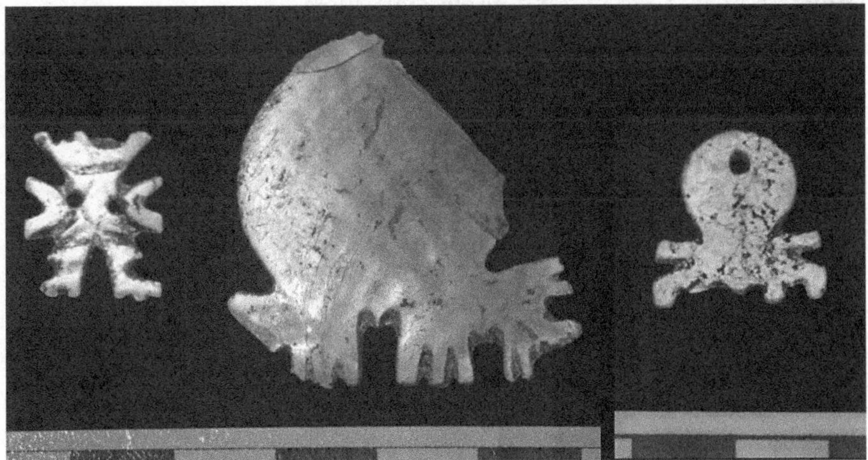

Figure 8. Mother-of-pearl artifacts from Sitio Drago. Photograph by Tom Wake.

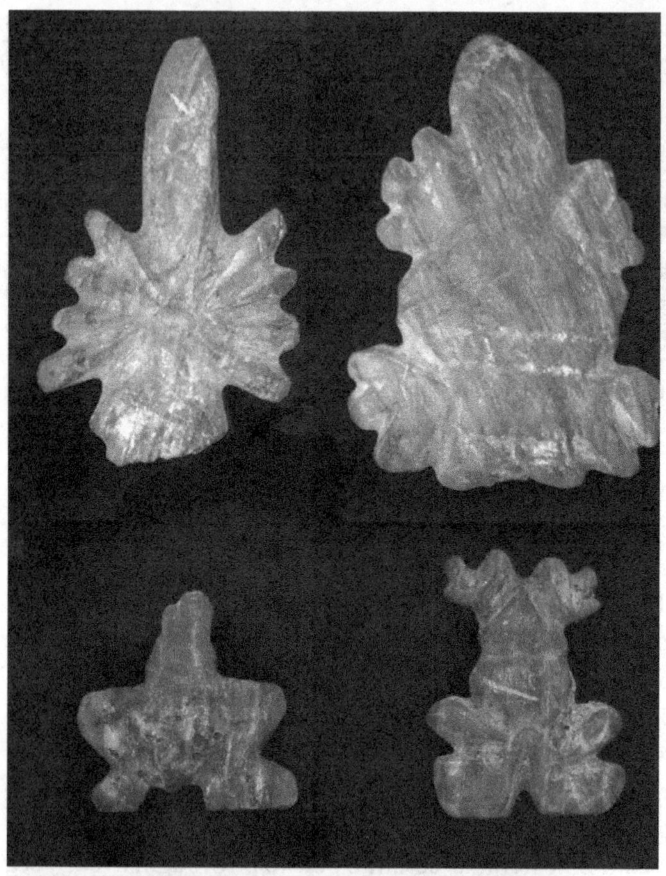

Figure 9a–b. *Spondylus* artifacts and trumpet shells from Sitio Drago. Photographs by Tom Wake.

noe voyages. This use of waterways was easier than by land, hand to hand, in a world with no draft or pack animals and carried on the backs of human porters all the way from Nicaragua. As was evident in the Pacific, and as will be seen in the next section, long distance maritime travels were common in the Caribbean Sea as well for the indigenous peoples living on its shores.

Maritime Trade and Contact

Cooke and Sánchez (2001:17) maintain that the Caribbean Sea was an open channel for extra isthmian barter during the European contact period, and although it is hard to gauge how far back this interaction goes between Panamanian and Mesoamerican groups, the recent data from Sitio Drago demonstrate that it dates to at least the end of the first millennium AD. As for the Pacific, both authors surmise that the extensive savannas, rivers, and estuaries would have allowed and fostered not only open mobilization on land but also, due to its coastal geography full of coves and natural ports, an agile access to the coast and islands by canoe. This was a transport system that according to early sixteenth-century documentation was used for commerce and war. Maritime culture was an important part of the daily lives of pre-Columbian peoples.

There are many accounts from early European voyagers in and around Panamá in which the extent of the indigenous peoples' skill at navigation is amply described. For instance, during the fourth and last voyage of Christopher Columbus (between 1502 and 1503), he traveled the Caribbean coast of Central America between Honduras and the Gulf of San Blas or Guna Yala archipelago in Panamá, where he was attracted by the incessant commercial activity and offered a perhaps somewhat exaggerated tally of "five large ports" in the coast of Veragua. Different accounts of people on this expedition also referred to large numbers of canoes that the locals not only plied the seas with but also used for trading purposes and to closely monitor the Spanish vessels.

For example, Ferdinand Columbus, son of the admiral, tells of how upon their arrival on an island in the "port" of Cerabaro (modern-day Almirante Bay or Isla Colón), they witnessed up to twenty canoes on land. Pedro de Ledesma, one of the pilots on this voyage, claimed that when the fleet arrived at Aburema, which would have been the next port somewhere in the Chiriquí Lagoon, they were approached by a still larger fleet of more than

Figure 10. This stylized image depicts an indigenous navigator in his small coastal dugout canoe. Carved from trees of various sizes, these craft worked the rivers and mangrove swamps and also navigated the Central American coast, the Caribbean, and the Bay of Panamá. From Gonzalo Fernández de Oviedo y Valdés, *Historia General y Natural de las Indias*, Madrid 1851.

eighty canoes filled with locals arriving to exchange all kinds of golden ornaments (Anderson 1911:93).

There are also other early accounts of foreigners in Panamá who could have arrived by sea. In another firsthand narrative, a man named Diego Mendez, who was also in Columbus's company, tells in his 1536 will of finding in the mouth of the Veragua River two canoes containing people whom he called "foreigners," presumably because they spoke a language that the local natives did not understand. These "foreigners" were so familiar with the locals that they knew of their intent to attack the Spaniards. They even ended up taking Mendez on their canoe upriver to the seat of the regional chief, the famous Quibián (Major 1870:212–216).

Along the Atlantic coast to the east, near the place where Nombre de Dios was founded, the chronicler Pascual de Andagoya talks of the place where the "chuchures" lived, who according to him were people who arrived from Honduras and spoke a different language than the locals (Jopling 1994:32), which in this case would have been the Cueva tongue that the Spanish so frequently refer to as being dominant in eastern Panamá and also very familiar to them. The most likely and easiest route from Honduras, as the later Mosquitos showed, was by boat.

Andagoya speaks of other encounters with Central American peoples on the Isthmus of Panamá. On one occasion, two years before the Spanish host arrived, an army of supposedly fierce cannibalistic warriors from Nicaragua was met by Chief Cutatura, ruler of the land of Paris (or Parita). Andagoya states that these Nicaraguans were feared by all the local chiefdoms, which consequently tried to appease the cannibals by bringing them young men to eat and other foodstuffs on the condition that these Nicaraguans set up in a savanna called Tauraba, which was near Parita. The warriors were soon struck by a disease that forced them to leave the site and "return to the coast of the sea." Andagoya got this information secondhand from the natives of Parita, and he never states whether they told him how these Nicaraguans got there. He implies, however, that the Nicaraguans arrived by boat and not on foot. The Nicaraguans allegedly met their end at the hands of Chief Cutatura, who took advantage of the foreigners' disease-ridden state to easily slaughter them in their sleep (Jopling 1994:35).

In 1522 Andagoya also speaks about the land of Chocama, in eastern Panamá or Gran Darién, situated on the Gulf of San Miguel on the eastern end of the Bay of Panamá, which was well populated with Cueva speakers. There he was told about how during every full moon people came by sea in canoes to wage war upon the locals and how they were so afraid of these attackers that they were too frightened to even go fishing. The attacking foreigners came from "a province called Birú, where corrupted the name it was called Pirú," and Andagoya states that having received a plea for help from Chocama to fight these invaders, he asked for people from Panamá City to mount an expedition that took six or seven days to arrive at that "province called Birú" (Jopling 1994:35).

There is also the well-known account of the "Sigua," a group most likely of Mexican origin which, in the first half of the sixteenth century, inhabited a region called Coaza, between the Sixaola and Changuinola rivers in what is now eastern Costa Rica and Bocas del Toro. The term "sigua" meant "foreigner" in the Chibchan languages of the region (Lothrop 1942; Cooke et al. 2003:112). It is odd that Columbus does not mention the Sigua in his narrative of forty years earlier, so it is possible they arrived after his journey. Several early documents point to their Mesoamerican origin because of some of the words they used to communicate with Spanish explorers. An example of this communication is found in the 1564 meeting of Juan Vásquez de Coronado with Sigua chief Yztolin in the village of Hara in the Coaza region. The chief was a man who called himself "a Mexican, cacique of the Chichimecs." After Yztolin submitted to the Spaniards, they embraced and then conversed in Yztolin's own tongue, which Coronado had learned in Mexico (Lothrop 1942:110).

The chronicler Juan de Estrada Ravago explains how the Sigua had told him they were sent by Emperor Moctezuma on a journey of more than six hundred leagues to the south to collect tribute consisting of many fine pieces of gold. Estrada narrates that he saw the "remnants of his soldiers and armies, who are called Nahuatatos." (Lothrop 1942:110). It is unknown whether this statement implies a formal relationship of vassalage between the inhabitants of the Atlantic coast of Panamá and the Aztec Empire or if they were sent to acquire gold pieces and also, as usual, spy on and reconnoiter the locals.

However, the possible status of tributary peoples to the Aztecs is further confirmed by information from Yñigo Aranza, governor of Veraguas in 1595, who states that "there are in the land called Duy more than six thousand Indian warriors, and it is reported that they have traffic with the Indians from Mexico who remained there when word reached them of the first entrance of the Spaniards, they having gone there for the tribute of gold which that province used to give to Montezuma" (qtd. in Lothrop 1942:111). Even if hearsay or secondhand misinterpreted information, this report points to a direct political link between the peoples of Atlantic Gran Chiriquí and the largest state polity in Mesoamerica, more than 2,000 km away. Surely if the peoples of Atlantic Panamá knew of Moctezuma, they must have known about other peoples in between them and Mexico.

Afterward the Sigua became hostile to Spanish incursions, and eventually, in league with other indigenous groups, they attacked the outpost of Santiago de Talamanca in 1610, which forced the European abandonment of the entire region. And despite repeated attempts at "pacification," the Spanish were unable to reestablish effective control. At some point after this, the Sigua abandoned the mainland and moved to the island of Tojar (Isla Colón, where Sitio Drago was excavated). They maintained trade with the continental peoples for hatchets, machetes, and foodstuffs. As Lothrop hypothesizes, it was to be expected that a group of warriors settling in a foreign land no doubt secured native women and that, with the passage of time, succeeding generations "although proud of their ancestry, took on the culture of the locality, including the language" (Lothrop 1942:112). They probably intermarried with Changuenas, Dorasques, and Terrabas, *ethniae* that spoke or still speak Chibchan-stock languages (Cooke et al. 2003:112).

They were still there in 1671 when Alexander Exquemelin described the inhabitants of Almirante Bay as "Indian tribes, whom the Spaniards have been unable to bring to submission. These tribes of Indios Bravos cannot understand each other's speech, and are constantly at war" (Exquemelin 1969:209). Apparently it was seaborne raids by Mosquito groups from Nicaragua that finally doomed the Sigua in the early 1700s. The last known account of this group was in 1763, when a Spanish priest described how the continuing Mosquito depredations forced the remnants of the Nicaraguans in Isla Colón to retreat to the hills and live in walled *palenques*.

In sum, the documentary data point to certain products of the Caribbean coast of Panamá being sufficiently abundant and accessible to attract groups of Mesoamericans to settle in the area. Even if gold was one of the primary catalysts for these commercial activities, it is hard to say which Panamanian pre-Columbian artifacts would have arrived in Mesoamerican localities (Cooke and Sánchez 2001:21). On the other hand, from the archaeological data obtained in Sitio Drago, it seems that at least exotic pottery was brought from Central America to exchange. We lack archaeological evidence of more signs of sustained trade, however, and so far Sitio Drago is the only site where there has been definite proof of exotic materials.

Even if the accounts listed here do not directly speak of Panamanian mariners but mainly of foreign sailors who arrived on the isthmus in pre-Columbian or precontact times, the possibility remains that the relationship was reciprocal and that Panamanian products, traders, and maybe even warriors also plied the seas to nearby regions beyond their local shores. The archaeological evidence points to Panamanian fishers staying mostly close to the coastlines, where aquatic resources were apparently abundant enough to preclude the necessity of risking of longer voyages. It is also likely that Panamanian fishers did not use a maritime technology more complex than the canoe (Cooke and Sánchez 2001:42).

Nevertheless it is known that isthmian peoples had good canoes, not only for coastal and island commerce but also for everyday transport and war. Gaspar de Espinosa tells of the chief of the island of Cébaco, to the west of Azuero Peninsula, taking 18 canoes with his men to attack an enemy's settlement on the mainland. No doubt many of the basalt stone axes found in archaeological sites after 1000 BC were specially made for crafting canoes, made out of a single tree according to early sixteenth-century documents. Speaking about the Cueva in Gran Darién, Oviedo remarks that "wherever there is the sea or rivers there are fish and fishermen"; he notes that fish provided their main sustenance and that the Cuevas were very fond of fishing as it was easier than hunting. The canoe was a most

Figures 11a–b. A lasting element in the maritime cultural landscape of Panamá—and one appropriated by Spanish conquerors—was the survival of dugout canoes. It is uncertain as to whether the forms predate colonial contact, but dugouts of all sizes were ideal craft for navigating, hunting, and fishing in shallow coastal waters and in the mangrove swamps. Gonzalo Fernández de Oviedo depicts the earliest Spanish modification to native craft by the addition of a mast and sails, although indigenous navigators most likely made alterations to their craft as well. Dugouts continue to be used by both surviving indigenous peoples and other Panamanians, but the introduction of fiberglass and metal boats has led to the abandonment of many of the traditional craft, like this canoe on the shores of Bahía Limón. Engraving from Gonzalo Fernández de Oviedo y Valdés, *Historia General y Natural de las Indias*, Madrid 1851. Photograph by James P. Delgado.

practical mode of transportation in a landscape full of estuaries, rivers, and swamps (Cooke and Sánchez 2001:38–39).

Even so, the maritime culture of Panamá's pre-Columbian peoples received a major shock and disruption as it collided with that of the European invaders. Although canoes were so effective that the Spanish happily and readily adopted them, even keeping small shipyards for their manufacture in several river mouths in the Azuero region (near Panamá and in the Pearl Islands), they were obviously outmatched by the large sailing vessels that fell upon them from the most distant of shores. It was a true clash of maritime cultures.

2

The Isthmus Encountered and Conquered, 1501–1540

At the beginning of the sixteenth century, the arrival of Europeans by sea in the service of Spain brought new concepts and gradual change to the isthmian maritime cultural landscape. At first (and at its simplest) the initial European contact by sea was part of a systematic search for an oceanic passage through this newly encountered maritime space to reach Asia, which was the original destination of these explorers. As various voyages defined and mapped the coastline, probing various rivers and inlets, it became obvious that what had been stumbled upon was, to the Europeans, a hitherto unknown landmass and that no oceanic passage to Asia existed. By 1513 they realized the narrowness of Central America and, in particular, that of the Isthmus of Panamá. The result was eventually a pragmatic decision to treat the ostensible barrier to maritime trade as a link, and Spain accordingly developed transisthmian routes to connect its Pacific and Atlantic trade by sea (Castillero 2004c, 2008; Brady 1999:122).

The gradual realization of the physical nature of the isthmus as a sea-focused economic link was part of the process of conceptualization in which this new space was rendered a maritime place. As Brady (1999) notes, this change came about through Spain's thorough, focused exploration of fluvial corridors in an effort to solve the "secreto del estrecho" or "strait secret": the understanding that many of these fluvial corridors maximized the ability of ships and boats to penetrate inland, thereby minimizing the slow, difficult, and expensive loading and offloading of cargo for land transportation. And finally there was the realization that even where land transportation was inevitable, the erosion caused by millennia of river flows had cut passes through the cordillera: the "spine" that bisected the isthmus (Brady 1999:126).

In this most sailorlike process, Spanish explorers redefined the Panamanian region as a maritime cultural landscape, and accordingly they not only sought the best ports for establishing the links in their globe-spanning maritime economic system but also sought "narrow spans of the land bridge that coincided with low, level gaps in its mountain spine," which allowed for inland penetration (Brady 1999:126). This process was aided by the use of previously established native trails and routes employed in pre-Columbian movement of people and goods.

In conceptualizing the isthmus and its neighborhood as part of Spain's expanding maritime trade, maps were drawn of the coast, and Spanish place names were bestowed on prominent land (that is, sea) marks. As a result, the isthmus began to evolve into a Spanish maritime cultural landscape. At the same time, charting and place names were not only a means for imposing a new rationale or thought processes on a physical space (Jacob 2006:205) but were also as much a part of the colonial process of dispossession and acquisition as the more formal ceremonies, including Spain's 1513 addition of the *requerimiento*, which was a legal document read aloud to the people about to be subjugated (Seed 1995:69). In discussing the act of explorers' putting names—toponyms—on the lands they "discovered," Seed (1995) notes that the toponym "is thus a signature, a claim of precedence and of symbolic ownership, analogous to the political and Colonial mastery suggested by the name of the sovereign" (205; see also Jaén Suárez 1998).

The initial European encounter with the isthmus came with the last of Christopher Columbus's four voyages to what he thought was the Orient. On his third voyage, undertaken in 1498, Columbus sailed south into new waters instead of heading back to Hispaniola (today's Haiti and the Dominican Republic). Seeking the elusive passage to the Orient, Columbus reconnoitered the northern coast of South America at the Gulf of Paria, encountering an island he named "Trinidad." After sailing farther along what is now the coast of Venezuela, Columbus's fleet also came into contact with the Orinoco's outflow before heading to Hispaniola. After he returned to Spain in chains for mismanagement and erratic behavior in 1500, Columbus's last voyage came as a crown-sponsored, tightly controlled expedition to continue coastal explorations along the edge of what would soon be defined as the eastern shores of the Caribbean (Cedeño Censi 1996; see also Varela and Gil 1997).

Departing from Spain in May 1502, Columbus's expeditionary force of four caravels pushed farther west, encountering and seizing a large Maya canoe full of traders and their goods. Before freeing them, Columbus's in

Figure 12. European explorers, and subsequently conquerors and colonizers, seized control of the maritime cultural landscape of Panamá through a variety of means. The process was violent, disruptive, and destructive despite later colonial depictions of the "discovery" and what followed as a welcomed and paternalistic set of actions. This nineteenth-century statue of Cristóbal Colón (Christopher Columbus) was a gift of French Empress Eugenie in 1870 as France commenced its own colonial intervention on the isthmus. Relocated four times in various acts of possession by French, U.S., and Panamanian officials, it now stands on Juan Demóstenes Arosemena Boulevard in Colón. Photograph by Daneistrada01, Wikimedia Commons.

terrogation through a Taíno interpreter encouraged him to continue west to seek the land of pearls, gold, and spices the Maya spoke of. After Columbus took the Maya canoe's captain, "Iumba," hostage (Columbus renamed him "Juan Pérez"), the expedition pushed on, carefully misled by "Pérez" so as to avoid the Maya heartland. Instead, the expedition proceeded west to the more remote non-Maya-controlled shores of today's Panamá.

Columbus arrived at Panamá's modern-day Almirante Bay in early October (Cedeño Censi 1996). His surveys of the Panamanian coast in the fall of 1502, along with findings from a 1501 voyage to the area by Rodrigo de Bastidas (who had successfully petitioned for a voyage of exploration on his own from 1499–1501), probed a coast they found to be full of people and rich in pearls and gold (Harris 1984). Columbus determined that he had finally reached the Orient. Among the ports he visited and named were Puerto Bello as well as the mouth of the Chagres River, a port known to the natives as *Huiva*. Columbus named the river Río de los Lagartos for its abundance of caimans and crocodiles. Toward the end of the year, the fleet anchored close by in a large bay that Columbus named Bahía Gordo, now known as Limón Bay. Columbus commented that the bay was so vast that the fleets of the world could moor in it (Castillero 2004a).

In January 1503, Columbus and his fleet sailed to the coast of Veragua and found a river that he named Santa María de Belén (Saint Mary of Bethlehem), as its "discovery" came on the day of the Feast of the Epiphany. Columbus and his ships stayed for a while, establishing a small settlement, Santa María de Belén, close to the river's mouth. They explored the region while trading with the natives for gold. Rising tensions soon led to open warfare. Columbus abandoned the Belén settlement along with one of his caravels, *La Gallega*, and in April he sailed for Hispaniola. Stopping at Puerto Bello, where rot forced Columbus to abandon another of his ships, *La Vizcaína*, he then pushed farther east, perhaps as far as Darién. The expedition left isthmian waters in May.

During his voyage and all along the isthmian shoreline, Columbus encountered large groups of organized indigenous peoples who navigated and worked along the coast. They also possessed much wealth and traded using these riches. Even if they were not subjects of the ruler of China, they had a land worth further exploration and exploitation, and soon others would follow in Columbus's wake.

Both Christopher Columbus and Rodrigo de Bastidas left what was ostensibly the initial Spanish imprint on the isthmian maritime cultural landscape: this imprint included place names (many of which have been

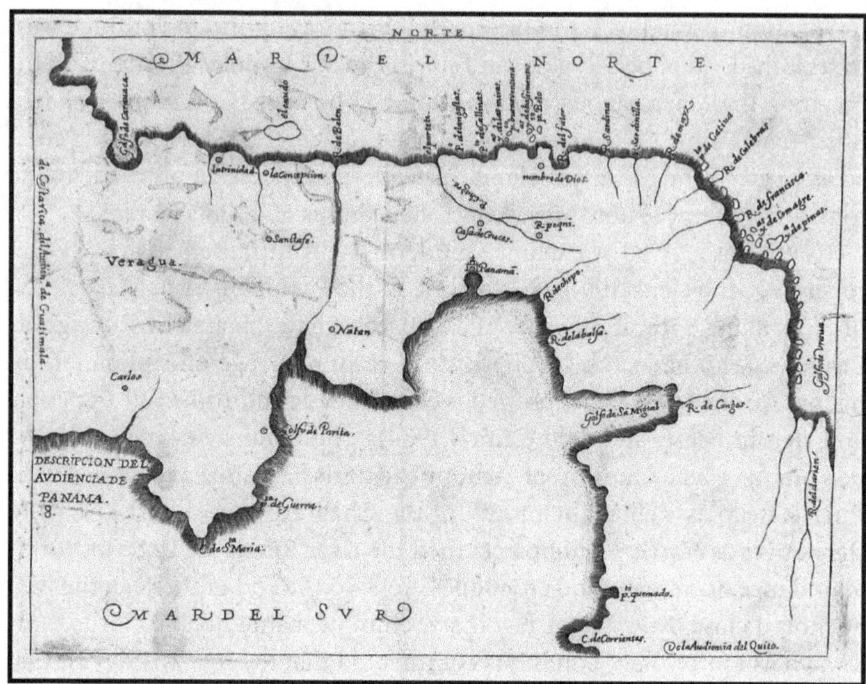

Figure 13. The emerging Spanish colonial maritime cultural landscape of the Isthmus of Panamá, as mapped in 1601. By this time, indigenous place names were disappearing in favor of new Spanish names. Some maritime features, including rivers, bays, and prominent coastal landmarks such as capes and islands are depicted, and the two principal settlements of Panamá and Nombre de Dios are also delineated. From Herrera y Tordesillas, *Historia General de los Hechos de los Castellanos en las Islas y Tierra Firme*, 1601.

retained over the years) and the archaeological remains of that first encounter, such as the site of Santa Maria de Belén and the abandoned hulks (or wrecks) of *La Gallega* and *La Vizcaína* (Griggs 1995). The first European map of the New World by Juan de la Cosa (c. 1500) clearly delineates these first onomastic markers of an evolving Spanish isthmian maritime cultural landscape.

Archaeological surveys have attempted to locate the remains of the settlement at Santa María de Belén as well as the wreck of *La Gallega*. As part of an ongoing initiative by the Institute of Nautical Archaeology (INA) and then taken up independently by Ships of Discovery, Inc., the quest to find these sunken vessels from Columbus's and other early voyages to the Americas focused on the Panamanian coast beginning in 1987. There, archaeologist Donald H. Keith and colleagues hoped to find the remains of the two ships Columbus had left behind on his fourth voyage. *La Gallega*, abandoned as a worm-eaten hulk on the banks of the Belén River on Easter Day in 1503, had been spotted by one of the men in Diego de Nicuesa's expedition in 1509, suggesting to Keith and his team that the vessel had neither been burned by the natives nor swept out to sea (Myers 1988:128). Detailed geomorphological studies, magnetometer surveys, and hydraulic probing undertaken from 1988 through 1990 did not locate the wreck, which may now no longer be in the river due to changes in the riverbanks over the last 500 years (Keith et al. 1990; see also Griggs 1995).

Following the abortive attempt at settling in Santa María de Belén, subsequent explorers probed the coast not only for a strait but also for habitable areas fit for new settlement.[1] With these voyages came the realization that unlike the islands they first encountered, this new region was solid land, or *tierra firme*. Thus began what historians describe as the first period in non-native Panamanian history, which was a brief time of conquest and the founding of cities that ran from 1510 to 1519 (Ward 1993:29). The maritime landscape of the isthmus is also rife with the as-yet-undiscovered wrecks of vessels lost or left by other explorers, including a caravel of the Guerra brothers lost in 1504 on the coast of Darién (they also lost another on the Colombian coast), four ships lost by Juan de la Cosa in 1505 in the Gulf of Darién, ships lost by Diego de Nicuesa near Nombre de Dios in 1510 and by Fernández de Enciso in 1510, and a *bergantín* lost by Francisco Hernández in 1513 (Ships of Discovery, 2014).

One of the more active explorers, Vasco Núñez de Balboa, had first come to the isthmus with Bastidas in 1500–1501, and in 1510 he finally selected a site for settlement after many misadventures near the western shores of the Gulf of Urabá on the isthmian coastline of present-day Colombia. After fighting the indigenous people for the site—a native village ruled by a cacique known to the Spaniards as Cémaco—and winning the battle, Balboa and his men renamed the village and built it into the settlement of Santa María la Antigua del Darién in 1510. It was the first successful Spanish settlement on Tierra Firme (Mena García 2011:111–216; Verlinden et al. 1958; Arcila Vélez 1986). From there, Balboa briefly governed the newly established Castilla del Oro (named for Columbus's claims of gold being found there) region and continued exploring through a clever policy of befriending the native peoples and forging such alliances as a "white chief" with a native wife (Aritio 2012:188–202).

In his quest for riches, Balboa and his men learned of a great "south sea" that existed beyond the mountains. After a long march, they stood atop a clear mountain summit and beheld the sea on September 25, 1513. It

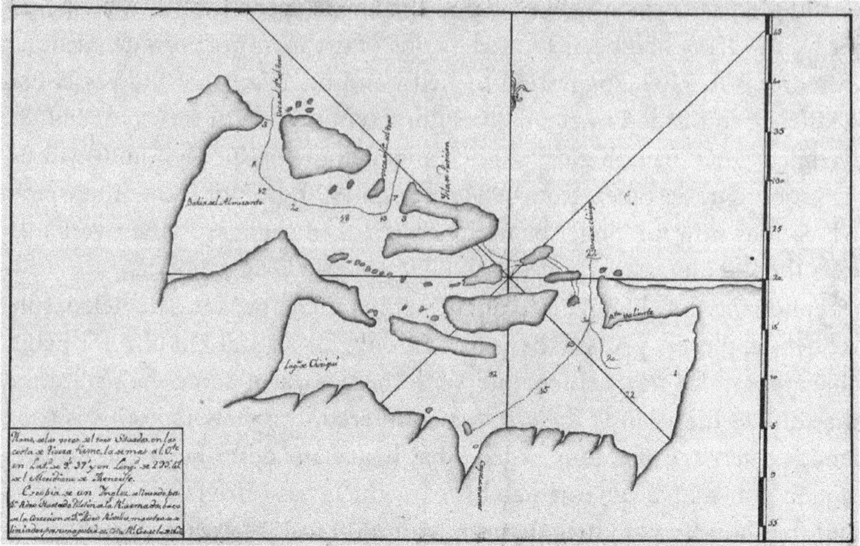

Figure 14. Bocas del Toro's islands and coast were settled in pre-Columbian times. The first recorded European visit was by Cristóbal Colón in 1502. This early Spanish map depicts the area. Library of Congress Geography and Map Division (LOC catalog no. 90680518).

was the Pacific, an ocean whose vastness would soon become apparent, as would the realization that beyond the Central American isthmus at last lay the oceanic highway to the riches of the Orient envisioned by Columbus. The narrowness of the Isthmus of Panamá and its possibilities as a land link and short cut for Spain's burgeoning Pacific trade would come in time. But when the port city of Panamá was founded by Pedro Arias Dávila in 1519, it was a center for Spain's control of the pearling beds that lay off the coast in an archipelago quickly dubbed the Islas de las Perlas as well as a base for further conquest and enslavement of the indigenous peoples of the immediate region and, later, for the invasion of Central and South America (Castillero 2013).

The site of the new settlement, known in the local language as *Panamá* (most likely meaning "fishing place") was a small native hamlet of fishing Indians (Castillero 2006:102–107). The Spanish Panamá was located approximately a mile away and in a swampy area that was not an ideal port. What it did have was an abundant forest that would supply the timber for ships needed to carry *conquistadores* farther in search of new conquests (Marley 2005:328).

Another Spanish settlement, Acla, was founded in 1516 northwest of Santa María La Antigua on the Caribbean side of the isthmus on the shores of San Blas (now Guna Yala). Panamá retained its primacy, even though Acla was the center for Balboa's activities. When Balboa was executed by his rival, Arias de Ávila, in 1519, Acla began to lose political importance, and disease kept the settlement from fully developing. It was abandoned after 1540, firmly establishing the supremacy of the transisthmian route between Panamá and Nombre de Dios. The site of Acla was found in the mid-twentieth century (Cruxent 1959) and has been archaeologically documented as well (Horton 1980; Higgins 1986).

With the Spanish settlement at Nombre de Dios, the Camino Real was created: what was, at first, a simple, rugged mule track therefore served as the initial portage for slaves, gold, and pearls that crossed the isthmus. In time, when Spanish ships finally crossed to the Pacific, it was hoped that the isthmus would also become part of the route through which spices would flow back to Spain. But that trade was ultimately captured farther north with the establishment of the Mexican port of Acapulco and the regular system of the Manila galleons (Castillero 2004c; Mena García 1992; Strassnig 2010). At the beginning of the Spanish-dominated isthmus, during what historians regard as the second period of non-native Panamanian history (1519–1532), Spanish activity focused on subjugating the area's peoples (by the end of the period, most of the native population had died) and annexing the isthmus into Spain's *encomienda* system (which dated from medieval times) to harvest whatever riches could be garnered through the tribute and labor of the conquered (Ward 1993:29). Thoughts of Panamá as a major link in a global maritime empire were decades away.

The bay that Nombre de Dios was founded on had been first surveyed by conquistador Diego de Nicuesa in 1509, although it is possible that Columbus also surveyed it in 1502 when he visited, describing a *Puerto de Bastimentos* in the area. Nicuesa established a small settlement and a fort but soon left for Santa María la Antigua del Darién upon hearing the news of Balboa's settlement there (Anderson 1911:146, 152). The site was reestablished as a settlement by Diego de Albítez in 1519 with Royal authorization to establish a town on the Caribbean shores of Tierra Firme.

The creation of this initial Spanish link through the "simultaneous establishment of Panamá City and Nombre de Dios immediately created a transoceanic trade system." Yet this trade system would take a few decades to evolve (Salamanca-Heyman 2009:4). Nombre de Dios and Panamá, joined by the road, served as the isthmian maritime conduit until 1597, when Nombre de Dios was abandoned in favor of Portobelo (Mena García 1992:229–282).

Olandus verſchafft/ das ein Carauel vnd etliche Hütten gebauwet worden. XIX.

VERAGVA PARS.

NIquesals deß Nachts ein groß Vngeſtümme entſtanden / wirdt mit ſeinem Schiff von ſeinen Geſellen hindan geriſſen vnnd verworffen. Welche als ſie auff die hundert Meylwegs gefahren/ vnnd jhn niergents antroffen/ auch gar nichts von jhm höreten/ haben ſie zum Oberſten erwöhlet/ biß der Niques widerkäme/ Olandum. Dieſer/ damit er ſeinen Geſellen alle hoffnung der Flucht entzöge/ ließ er die Schiff ſo vom Meer hin vnnd her getrieben worden/ freuentlicher weiß an das Land führen/ da ſie dann von den Felſen ſind zerſtoſſen vnd verſenckt worden/ da er aber baldt hernach ſeinen vnbedächtlichen Raht mit ſeinem ſchaden vermercket/ befalch er/ daß man auß den Brettern oder Dieln/ der zerbrochenen Schiffen ſolte ein Carauel zurichten/ das ſie daſſelbig in der Noth gebrauchen köndten. Darnach haben ſie angefangen Häuſer zu bauwen vnd Frucht zu ſäen. 21. Cap.

Die

Figure 15. The earliest Spanish voyages and adventures on the isthmus were recounted in the German-language edition of *America*, c. 1594, with illustrations by Theodor de Bry. This engraving, "Olandus verschafft das ein Caravel und eetliche Hütten gebauwet worden" depicts ship's carpenters building a new caravel after Diego de Nicuesa's ship was wrecked on the Veragua expedition. Library of Congress Prints and Photographs Division (LOC catalog no. 2006687182).

The archaeology of this early period has thus far yielded only the Playa Damas wreck, which is sometimes mistaken for Columbus's *La Vizcaína*. Within the range of the larger maritime cultural landscape, however, other sites have been searched for and studied, including Santa María la Antigua del Darién, Panamá Viejo, Nombre de Dios, and most recently the Camino Real and the site of Venta de Cruces.

Playa Damas Wreck

The Playa Damas wreck is named for its location just outside of Nombre de Dios Bay. Lying in 4.5 m (15 ft.) of water, the wreck was known to local fishermen for some time before being shown to American resident and treasure hunter Warren White in 1997 (Castro 2004:4; Brinkbäumer and Höges 2004).

Roughly defined as a 10 by 6 meter (60 m^2) exposed pile of ballast with three iron anchors and at least 12 iron cannon that line most of the surviving wooden hull, the wreck was visited and in part excavated by Investigaciones Marinas del Istmo S.A. (IMDI) in 2001. Archaeologists Roger Smith, Donald Keith, Cheryl Ward, Donny Hamilton, and Filipe Castro visited the site in 2002–2003: this visit was not part of IMDI's work but was rather to separately and independently assess the wreck in response to media reports that equated the site with Columbus's *La Vizcaína*. Those reports generated considerable excitement around the world, inspiring a documentary film and a magazine and book project from Germany's *Der Spiegel* media group, while also attracting not only offers of private sponsorship to scientifically excavate and recover the wreck and place it in a public museum but also the attention of treasure hunters who succeeded in maintaining control of the site. To date, no scientific work has been done on the site, and no reports exist other than the summaries of academic archaeologists who visited the wreck to assess it during the period of the ultimately unsuccessful negotiations to conduct a noncommercial, public archaeology project (Brinkbäumer and Höges 2004).

According to Castro, who examined the wreck without excavating it in September 2003 and then again in January 2004, it was a vessel that sank "during the first decades of the sixteenth century," which "was probably initially salvaged soon after its loss, and the only artifacts left were the heavy iron guns and anchors that were probably stored in the holds and were quickly buried by sand" (Castro and Fitzgerald 2006:38). Based on Castro's observations, the exposed hull components comprised the following measurements:

> Planking is 6 cm thick, frames are 17 to 18 cm square in section, and stringers are 27 by 7 cm in section. All these scantlings, the number of guns, and the size of the anchors indicate a ship larger than the 50 ton *Vizcaína*. (Castro 2004:4)

Figure 16. The Playa Damas shipwreck, off Nombre de Dios, is the earliest known shipwreck located in Panamanian waters. Originally suggested to be the wreck of Cristóbal Colón's *La Vizcaína*, the wreck dates to a few decades after Colón's voyage. It unfortunately has not been archaeologically excavated or studied and has been subjected to salvage. Photograph by Karl Vandenhole.

Dating from two wood samples placed the timbers at between 1530 and 1550, while a carbon-14 date derived from an olive jar sherd placed it at between 1450 and 1530 (Castro 2004:4).

Castro was able to observe a number of recovered artifacts being stored ashore in tanks of water in a warehouse but reported that IMDI denied him permission to photograph them. Working from wreck plans provided by Warren White, Smith, Keith, and Karl Vandenhole from *Der Spiegel*, Castro produced a brief summary of what he had observed, which summarized the recovery of a large number of artifacts prior to 2005 (Castro 2005). These included fifteen cannon and cannon parts, including *versos*, *bombardetas*, mortars, stone cannon balls, bottles and bottle fragments, 1,148 ceramic fragments, and a large number of concretions and unidentified artifacts (Castro 2005:2,4).

As noted, following the negotiations of *Der Spiegel* and the Institute of Nautical Archaeology at Texas A&M University with IMDI to conduct a complete excavation, analysis, conservation, and publication of the wreck, the discussions were unsuccessful. A treasure-hunting company from the United States, working with IMDI, reportedly conducted excavations and recoveries beginning in 2005 but with no reported results (Castro and

Figure 17. The exposed timbers of the Playa Damas Shipwreck. Photograph by Karl Vandenhole.

Fitzgerald 2006:40). The professional opinion of Castro and other archaeologists who study ships of this period is that the wreck dates from soon after Columbus's fourth voyage and could be a ship from the 1510 to 1530 period, making it the earliest known and located shipwreck in Panamá. The lack of scientific study and the likelihood that the artifacts have not been known to undergo conservation are exceptionally unfortunate given the significance of this site. Reports that the hull's remains were left exposed after excavation are a sad statement about the status of submerged cultural resource protection in Panamá: this is despite the fact that it was the first country in the world to ratify and pass as national law the 2001 UNESCO Convention on the Protection of the Underwater Cultural Heritage.

While the submerged record is scant and what has been found has been archaeologically compromised, maritime-related sites on land offer additional archaeological information and are elements of the early European maritime cultural landscape. These are the earliest isthmian settlements of Santa María la Antigua del Darién and Nombre de Dios.

Santa María la Antigua del Darién

As previously noted, Balboa founded Santa María la Antigua del Darién in 1510. It was the first successful Spanish settlement on Tierra Firme, a small and primitive base for further exploration for Balboa, who ruled his expanding territory from it. The town flourished as the capital of the Castilla del Oro region and became the first settlement to have the presence of a Catholic bishopric. Santa María proved to be initially successful but soon became entwined in the politics of colonial Spain. Balboa was replaced by Pedrarias Dávila, who brought with him approximately 2,000 more settlers, including soldiers, artists, doctors, and women in 1514. This sudden population influx taxed Santa María's agricultural resources and led to an eventual famine and epidemic. At the same time, Dávila sought other options, eventually founding Panamá City in 1519. The famous Spanish chronicler, Gonzalo Fernández de Oviedo, remained in charge of Santa María until Dávila ordered its abandonment in 1524 (Aram 2008; Aritio 2012; Altolaguirre y Duvale 1914; Fernández de Oviedo 1853; Romoli 1953).

Santa María la Antigua del Darién: The Site

The site of Santa María la Antigua del Darién was first discovered in 1950 by pioneering Colombian anthropologist Graciliano Arcila Vélez. It can be found in the Unguía municipality in the Department of El Chocó in Colombia, and it lies on a small elevation adjacent to the ancient bed of the Río Tanela, formerly known as Río Darién and near the Tilo and Cutí rivers almost 7.5 km from the Caribbean coastline (Mena García 2011:66–68; 2012:40). Limited test excavations sponsored by the former King of Belgium in 1956 probed the site (Verlinden et al. 1958), but further detailed excavations by Arcila for the University of Antioquia in the 1960s and 1970s yielded a range of artifacts as well as delineated some of the residential portions of the site (Arcila 1986). The predominant types of artifacts are ceramics (including bricks, pre-Columbian and European vessels) and crucibles (a key reminder of the quest for gold) as well as a range of metal artifacts, including ship spikes used in vessel construction, locks, knives, swords, horseshoes, badges, buckles, and scissors (Alzate Gallego 2011:9).

Since 2000, a reassessment of the collection at the University Museum of Antioquia has been undertaken (Alzate Gallego 2011). In 2006 a historico-archaeological project led by professors Virgilio Becerra and Paolo Vignolo of the Universidad Nacional de Colombia have explored the site (Mena García 2011:67), and beginning in 2013, a new excavation of the site commenced under the direction of the Colombian Institute of Anthropology and History (ICANH) led by Alberto Sarcina. Ernesto Montenegro of ICANH has been quoted as saying how the town was not "settled" but rather "installed," with its key components and settlers "loaded into a ship

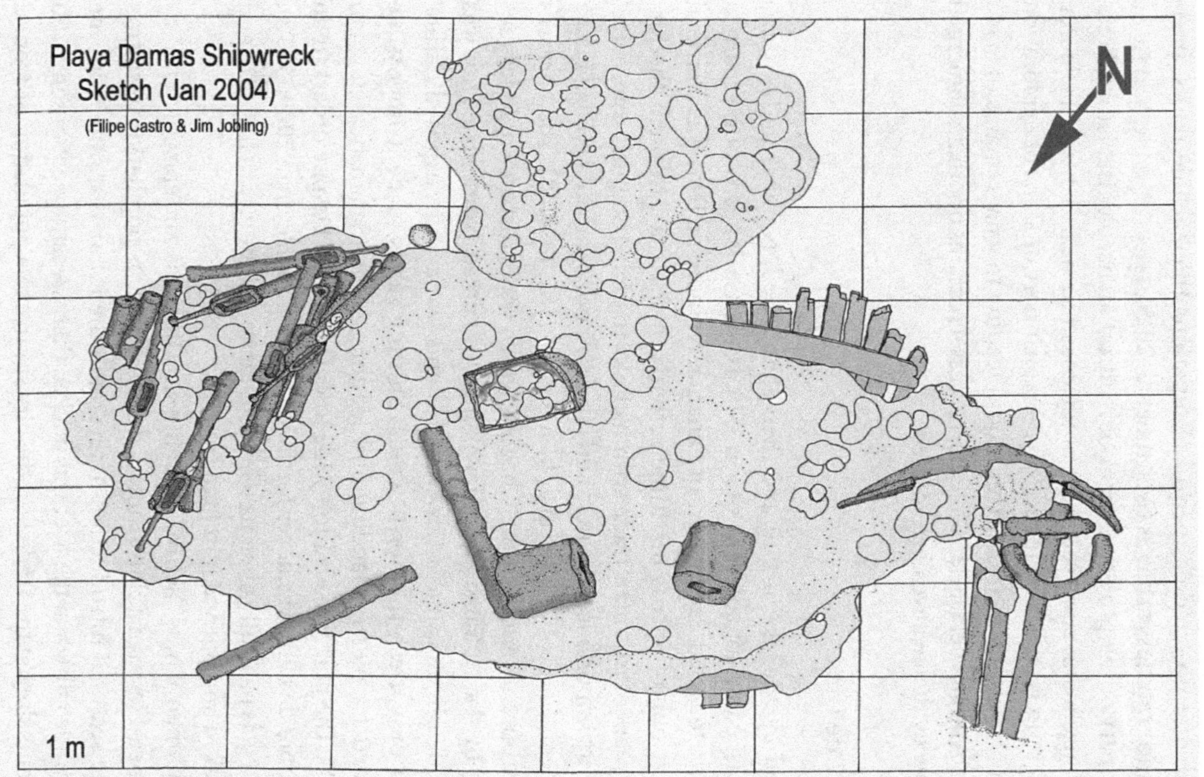

Figure 18. Playa Damas shipwreck site plan. Sketch by Filipe Castro and Jim Jobling after their reconnaissance dive, January 2004. Diagram created by Filipe Castro, Texas A&M University, Nautical Archaeology Program.

in Cadiz" and then unloaded at the site.[2] This aptly reflects how much this land site is part of the larger maritime cultural landscape. These most recent investigations have uncovered material remains from pre-Columbian, colonial, and postcolonial period occupations that include floors, postholes, and countless artifacts (Martín et al. 2015).

As a part of the project, a team of nautical archaeologists led by Frederick Hanselmann surveyed areas of the coastline near Bahía de la Gloria. They were in search of evidence of a Spanish port or ships of exploration that may have sunk near the river mouth leading to what remains of Santa María la Antigua del Darién. To date, no vessel remains or other submerged maritime evidence have been located.

Nombre de Dios

Founded by Nicuesa in 1510 and then abandoned, Nombre de Dios was reestablished on an adjacent site in 1519 as the Caribbean counterpart to the newly founded Pacific port of Panamá. Nombre de Dios was a critical transport hub of Spain's maritime activity on the coast through the formative years of isthmian trade with its links to global Spanish commerce. Despite its importance, the port and city were not compatible (Díaz Lopez 2001; Mena García 1992; see also Jaén Suárez 1985, 1998:40). The port was too far from the mouth of the Chagres, which was a distance of 18 leagues (50 nm) by sea. As Salamanca-Heyman (2009) notes, Nombre de Dios was surrounded by miasmatic low wetlands and was a wide, exposed harbor plagued by *nortes*—the north winds. Shifting sands made it impossible to construct a pier for landing and loading goods (Salamanca-Heyman 2009:79). The port was also too wide to defend (139). Despite orders to do so, Nombre de Dios was never fortified (Salamanca-Heyman 2009:77–78). That fact was painfully obvious when Drake raided the city in July 1572 and then sacked and burned it in January 1596.

Even when it was "active," Nombre de Dios was an "episodic city," as Salamanca-Heyman (2009) notes, due to shifts in population resulting from the seasonal introduction of fever and the influx that came with the annual trade fair when the fleet was docked there. A settlement of some 200 inhabitants during the trade fair, the city shrank to a population of around fifty between the fairs (Anderson 1911:276). Nombre de Dios was characterized by periods of intense commercial activity followed by longer periods of stagnation (Salamanca-Heyman 2009:6). As a "key oceanic port-of-call," Nombre de Dios nevertheless prospered due to its location within an of-

Figure 19. Nombre de Dios and its narrow, shallow port, as depicted in the illustrated sixteenth-century manuscript *Histoire Naturelle des Indies*, c. 1586. Pierpoint Morgan Library, New York, MA 3900, folio 97 recto, Bequest of Clara S. Peck, 1983.

ficial trade route controlled by the Spanish Crown (Salamanca-Heyman 2009:12,18,33). In addition to serving the needs of the annual fleet, Nombre de Dios also participated in regional maritime trade (153–154).

This explains how Nombre de Dios continued to exist despite the challenges of its location and thus its strategic vulnerability. It was only abandoned after an official decree to do so in 1584 made Portobelo the official port. The move took a decade to complete (Haring 1918:185). Despite the inadequacies of the site, this delay was largely due to the entrenched interests of the Panamanian merchants who seasonally occupied the city and did not want to see the status quo changed. Nonetheless, official interest in a new site did not wane. Work had just begun on the site at Portobelo when Drake's destruction of Nombre de Dios in January 1596 provided the final impetus for the shift (extensive discussion in Mena García 1992:229–264).

When Drake attacked Nombre de Dios, a church and close to a hundred buildings were there: approximately half of these were reportedly consumed by fire when Drake's men fired on the king's warehouse and the flames spread (Nichols 1653:57). Although some rebuilding may have taken place, Nombre de Dios was ultimately abandoned and cut off from the rest of the country as the Crown even ordered the part of the Camino Real that led to the city destroyed and rebuilt in the direction of Portobelo. The site was then reclaimed by nature. In 1682 William Dampier noted that although it was a "city once famous," Nombre de Dios was "now nothing but a name. I have lain ashore in the place where the City stood, but it is all overgrown with wood, so as to have no sign that any town hath been there" (Masefield 1906:88).

Nombre de Dios: The Site

In the five centuries since its founding, the landscape of the settlement and its harbor has changed in response to natural and human influences. The shoreline has been extended by several meters, and landside water sources have shifted and dried up.

Modern demolition and construction activities have all contributed to the disturbance of the archaeological site. A sixteenth-century fortification, the *morro*, was blown up; its stone was used to construct a landing quay; the road to Portobelo was graded; manganese mining operations involved in the quay project destroyed portions of the site (Salamanca-Heyman 2009:8); sand was dredged for the building of Gatún locks of the Panamá Canal between 1908 and 1912 (Isthmian Canal Commission [ICC] 1909:349–350); and pervasive looting occurred.

The earliest mention of archaeological remains at the site was during the construction of the Panamá Canal when the mouth of the Río Fató at Nombre de Dios was dredged for sand to be used in the concrete mixture for Gatún locks:

> The hull of an old vessel, which has every appearance of having been buried in the sand for several centuries was encountered during the latter part of September (of the year 1910). . . . The wreck was lying in the middle of the sand zone, about 300 feet distant from the beach line, and at from 18 to 20 feet below the surface of the ground. The dredge unearthed the old hulk for its entire length of about 60 feet. . . . The wood of which the ship was built resembles oak and was put together with wooden pins. (ICC 1911:54)

A second ship was unearthed in May 1911. It had

> an old hull at a point about 250 feet inside the shoreline and 20 feet below the surface of the ground. No effort has been made to take out the hull, because the dredge operates easily over it, but it appears to be about 100 feet long. The pumps have drawn up a small figurehead of brass, an iron pestle, and a large number of lead bullets from three-fourths to two inches in diameter. (ICC 1911:313)

The characteristics of the hull and its disposition are not known. It is possible the site "uncovered" was the Playa Damas wreck, but insufficient data exists to confirm that theory or the notion that there were one or more other shipwrecks associated with Nombre de Dios. The archival record of Nombre de Dios documents many accidents and losses in and around the harbor in the sixteenth century (such as Alonso Criado de Castilla's 1575 report, quoted in Salamanca-Heyman 2009:68–69).

Salamanca-Heyman (2009) notes that the first archaeological study of Nombre de Dios was undertaken by José María Cruxent in the 1970s. This work, which apparently did not involve excavation but rather the documentation of surface remains across the site (including scatters of roof tiles and approximately a hundred meters of extant stone-paved road), was not followed up (Salamanca-Heyman 2009:8). In 1993 archaeologist Beatriz Rovira called for renewed work and study, but that call was not heeded for some time. Historian John Thrower, with Michael Turner, who was a fellow member of the Drake Exploration Society, documented exposed features in 1993 and again in 1999 (Thrower 2001).

Thrower noted exposed remains of some three miles of the Camino Real south of the modern village, which is not on the site of the original town. According to Thrower, "The track is deeply indented into the hillside next to the highest prominence behind the bay . . . in 1999 all was changed. Two concrete wheel ways had been laid over the old trail to the top," all part of a series of intrusions, damage and looting that occurred at the site between 1993 and 1999. This included the destruction of much of the *morro* that fortified the harbor:

> In 1999 all was changed. The major part of the *morro* had been reduced to ground level. Its stone had been removed and used to convert the temporary pontoon jetty of the mining company into a permanent structure. It seemed a pity that a landmark that had survived so long should be sacrificed for a somewhat dubious purpose. Fortunately, the northern quarter remained complete with the face that had projected into the sea and enabled the fort to be recognized on the aerial photograph. (Thrower 2011:8)

As a result of an initial site visit in 2004, detailed work by Salamanca-Heyman began in 2007 (Salamanca-Heyman 2009:166). This included test excavation and documentation in a 19,800-square-meter area. The project also documented evidence of extensive looting and "cleaning" of exposed artifacts that had taken place between the 2004 and 2007 projects, highlighting the ongoing problem of site protection.

In documenting undisturbed features, the team achieved positive results using micro-resistivity to identify sediment-covered floors from now-vanished structures (Mojica et al. 2010) The buried floors, when test excavated, were found to be compacted pebbles similar to Colonial Spanish floors at Panamá Viejo (Mojica et al. 2010:129). Excavation followed, yielding stone foundations as well as the floors in depths ranging from 10 to 40 cm overlying sterile soil at 50 cm. (Salamanca-Heyman 2009:172).

The test excavations also yielded information about differing methods of construction of the town's buildings—as roof-tile remains, decorative elements, and ceramic-lined drainage canals were found—and further traced the Camino Real and other streets in the town. Among the architectural elements recovered were five decorative *azulejos* (or decorated tiles) as well as iron hardware including nails. The excavations yielded 40 ship's nails and 475 joiner's nails from buildings, along with 898 unidentifiable incomplete nails (Salamanca-Heyman 2009:194). The bulk of the identified nails was used for floors and braces as opposed to frames.

The work of Salamanca-Heyman and her colleagues ultimately resulted in an archaeologically based conjectural layout for the town. Their research also documented the survival of not only features but also artifacts and formed the basis of a doctoral dissertation by Salamanca-Heyman that provided a detailed archival as well as archaeological assessment of this first enduring, authentic Spanish maritime settlement on the isthmus (Salamanca-Heyman 2009). The nonstructural artifacts were a "diverse quantity" that reflected the town's use as a city-port including a ceramic assemblage of 3,172 fragments of which nearly 97 percent were imported (2009:203-4). Glass and metal artifacts reflected personal use, including locks and hinges for chests. Faunal remains showed that in addition to hunting and animal husbandry, the inhabitants harvested from the sea and rivers using canoes or boats. There have been findings of fish bones belonging to species with habitats that range from 50 to 600 meters as well as mollusks, which indicate reef harvesting. In addition to hooks, the excavations yielded lead net weights and a harpoon. Faunal remains also included birds, cattle, and pork (2009:208-12).

Salamanca-Heyman suggests that the lack of agricultural tools reported during excavation results from the dependence of the port on imported foodstuffs as well as from difficulties in cultivating the land. However, fields were cleared and certain products were eventually grown (2009:213). The ceramic assemblages included storage pots as well as *majolicas*, stoneware, and Kraak porcelain for the serving of food (217–236) and ornamental and consumption-related glassware from Catalonia and Venice (236–240). The variety of the ceramics and glass despite an "almost total lack of local manufactured products" indicates "the role played by Nombre de Dios in the Spanish commercial network" (Salamanca-Heyman 2009:240). Other evidence of the town's use as a port and its commercial networks were iron barrel hoops and fragments of *botijas* used in transport, which suggested an assemblage of approximately 72 vessels (259–262). Horse tack, horseshoes, hardware for extraction and weighing precious metals, and three coins were also recovered (265–270).

While additional excavation is needed, the work of Salamanca-Heyman and her colleagues allows for a more historically accurate sense of this key transport hub in the early colonial maritime cultural landscape. In particular, it takes a more focused look at the conjectural reconstruction of the cultural landscape of the town, which did not seem to conform to its environment but was laid out on a grid, with settlement patterning around a central plaza with socioeconomic distribution of lots (Salamanca-Heyman 2009:271–272). This pattern followed the typical medieval Spanish town distribution. Although not conforming to the curve of the bay, the town utilized the bay and surrounding waters not only as a port but also as a consistent and important dietary source. Salamanca-Heyman suggests that given the seasonal nature of the settlement, a smaller population base utilized the shallows during the winter months. In the summer, with a larger population due to the fleet's arrival, deep-water fishing provided additional food (272–273, 276).

In analyzing the town's failure to be a sustainable settlement, in addition to the geographical limitations, Salamanca-Heyman notes that the seasonal nature of the population in response to the annual arrival of the fleet did not inspire the development of community identity. The formation of identity came about as the result of the town's subordinate role to Panamá City and the fact that many of Nombre de Dios's upper class kept their permanent homes in Panamá City and not in Nombre de Dios (Mena García 1992:229). Changing regulations did not stir interest in the permanent development of infrastructure in the town, and its defenses were weak as a result (279–281).

However, Salamanca-Heyman demonstrates that this is a symptom of a larger problem: Nombre de Dios was located in a part of the maritime landscape that was ill-suited for development into a proper harbor with adequate defenses, given its open and shallow nature and problems with silting. Unlike other early ports that survived, such as Cartagena and Veracruz, Nombre de Dios was "abandoned due to geographical features that did not follow the Spanish urban plans for ports-of-call at the end of the sixteenth century" when a detailed inspection by the Crown highlighted its weaknesses (Salamanca-Heyman 2009:284).

3

The Isthmus Challenged and Fortified, 1540–1738

The maritime landscape of Panamá continued to change in the last half of the sixteenth century—and for 150 years after that—as the Spanish developed it as a major transoceanic hub. The creation of permanent transit nodes on both coasts, at Panamá City and Portobelo, was matched by the creation and ongoing evolution of transisthmian routes for the passage of goods and people both by land and via river. At the same time, maritime uses of the landscape included the ongoing harvest of its resources, both for sustenance and for wealth, the latter manifested by the development of a commercial pearl fishery on the Pacific coast.

The growing importance of the Isthmus of Panamá in the transit of wealth attracted colonial competition as well as piratical attacks, which were directed at shipping and coastal settlements. Scottish immigrants made a more peaceful (albeit failed) attempt to break the Spanish monopoly in the Darién Peninsula (Horton 2009; Prebble 2002). Dramatic capture of ports, robbery of treasure-laden mule trains crossing the isthmus, the capture, sack, and destruction of Panamá City in 1671, and British attacks in 1739–1740 led to the development of permanent fortifications that left prominent traces in the maritime cultural landscape.

These developments also encapsulate the most important period of the isthmus in terms of commercial activity as part of the Spanish Empire. Historians see the period from 1540 to 1739, (when the last Portobelo trade fair was held) as a time when the transisthmian economy consolidated its regular flow of goods and treasure (Ward 1993:29).

One of the factors that greatly influenced the growth of isthmian traffic was the successful conquest of Pacific Central and South America and the consequent absorption of the Inca Empire and its resources. The departure of Francisco Pizarro and his men from Panamá to the coast of South America and their conquest of the empire of the Inca in 1532–1533, gave

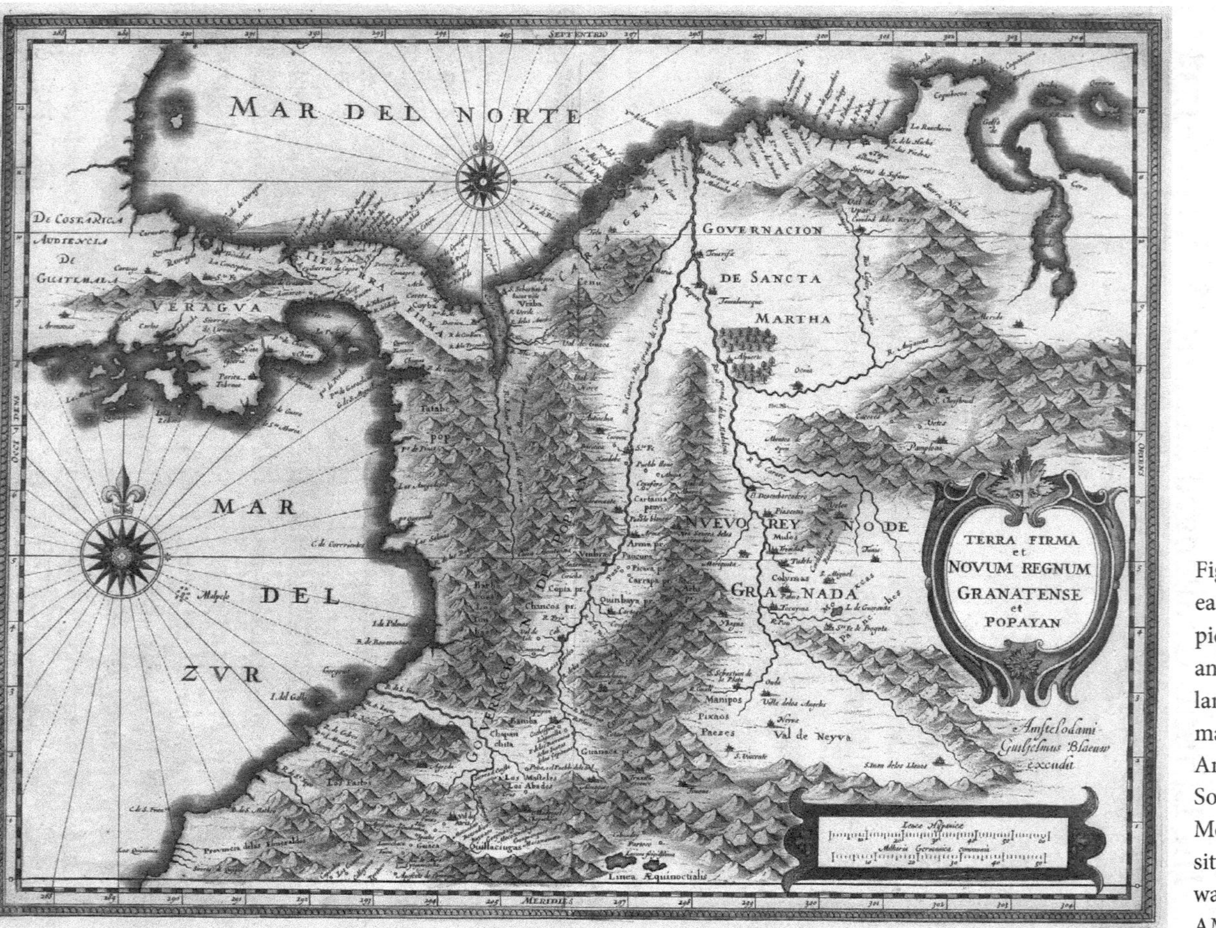

Figure 20. Among the earliest published depictions of the isthmus and its surrounding landscape is this c. 1642 map by Johannes Blaeu. American Geographic Society Collection, Meier Library, University of Wisconsin–Milwaukee (digital file no. AM010444).

Panamá a new role as the means by which the captured riches of the Inca flowed in ships up the coast. Panamá now became "the most vital link in the transportation system between Spain and Peru" (Haring 1918:181). Over time, approximately 60 percent of all silver shipped from the colonies to Spain passed through Panamá (Hamilton 1934:47,56; Castillero 2004c:356, 2008; Jaén Suárez 2014). What facilitated this flow of treasure was the creation of a more permanent system of crossing the isthmus with roads, way stations known as *ventas*, and the fortified port cities at the northern and southern ends of the Camino Real (see Hussey 1960; Bohn and Joly 1978; Castillero 2004c). The Camino Real de Panamá was and remains a dominant part of the isthmian maritime cultural landscape. The other major transisthmian route was the Camino de Cruces, which connected Panamá City and the fortress of San Lorenzo at the mouth of the Río Chagres. The Camino de Cruces consisted of a paved trail from the city to Venta de Cruces, a small town on the river, then connected to the Chagres, with the voyage continuing by boat down the river to the Caribbean Sea. These were the two essential links between both oceans in Panamá. The Camino Real, "in addition to its importance for the Spanish Colonial empire and global trade . . . had a lasting mark on Panamanian history and molded the formation of the Panamanian economy, population and culture. Its historical role is often compared to the current importance of the Panamá Canal" (Strassnig 2010:159; see also Mena García 1992:203–228).

As the riches of that empire flowed across the isthmus, the fortunes of its merchants, officials, and settlements improved dramatically and ensured the success of the isthmian highway. It was not until the opening of the silver mines at Potosí (in present-day Bolivia) in 1545 and the subsequent concentration of South American trade that the isthmus "became the most vital link in the transportation system between Spain and Peru, and the goal of West Indian pirates and buccaneers" (Haring 1918:181; Castillero 2008:77–100).

Great wealth crossed the isthmus (Castillero 2004b, 2004c), and as Ward (1993) notes, treasure shipped via Panamá between 1531 and 1540 totaled 2,694,693 pesos *ensayados* (a vast sum that is virtually incalculable in modern dollars); the amount of treasure increased dramatically with the conquest of Peru and the addition of the silver mines in South America. By 1660 treasure equal to 278,272,076 pesos *ensayados* had crossed the isthmus, a tenfold increase from the first decade of the route (Ward 1993:9). This was all part of Spain's tightly controlled system, the Carrera de Indias, in which overseas treasure flowed from select New World ports. This was all accomplished through a fleet system that worked on both sides of the isthmus, with ships from the south (the Armada del Sur) connecting Peru to Panamá City and the Tierra Firme fleet connecting Spain and its Caribbean ports to Nombre de Dios and later Portobelo.

All treasure that passed through Panamá from South America was amassed at Panamá City after the Armada del Sur sailed from Peru. Crossing the isthmus in controlled and guarded mule caravans to meet the annual Tierra Firme fleet, the treasure was loaded onto ships sailing from Nombre de Dios on the Caribbean shore (replaced by Portobelo in 1597). That fleet was joined by vessels from Cartagena, Veracruz, and Havana: from Havana all of these ships headed to Seville. After 1679, Cádiz became the port of entry into Spain (Ward 1993:19). In this fashion, the Isthmus of Panamá became a critical link not only for Spain's overseas empire but also for a vital part of an emerging global economy (Castillero 2008; Jaén Suárez 2014).

Panamá Viejo

Established by Pedro Arias de Ávila in 1519, Panamá City, now known as Panamá Viejo or Panamá La Vieja, was located at the site of a precontact fishing village of peoples who spoke the Cueva language, calling it "Panamá" (Castillero 2006; Patronato Panamá Viejo 2006). The name of this first European town on the American Pacific coast is therefore a transliterated survival of an indigenous name that persists to this day. Historians are perplexed by the selection of the site: "The Indian fishing village and its vicinity lacked resources, people and even a fair harbor" (Sauer 1966:280).

Although initially Panamá was nothing more than an outpost for further conquest, just as Santa María la Antigua del Darién had been previously, Panamá did adequately serve as a colonial outpost and capital until the inauguration of transisthmian trade. Then, despite its deficits as a site, the city consolidated its position as the principal settlement of the region.

The arrival of ships from conquered Peru to the south and Nicaragua to the north quickly exposed how inadequate the port was. The extreme tidal range of the bay (averaging 10 feet but at times nearly twice that), coupled with a gradual and muddy shore, forced large ships to anchor two leagues offshore. The port of the city was called "la Tasca," which literally means "the place where ships get stuck." A 1575 account noted how the "waters receded more than a league" twice a day on the tides, leaving ships and boats "high and dry" (Anderson 1911:276). To deal with this, the port was soon formally established in a group of four islands about 11 km to the southwest of the city. This area was known as the port of Perico, where small boats and lighters "loaded and unloaded the big ships, which lay in a sheltered and quiet haven . . . whence came each year more than forty ships" (Anderson 1911:276; Mena García 1992:61). Using this distant anchorage and bypassing the unusable port added to costs and risk to trade with an inefficient extra step in the process of offloading ships. Ships had to land and repack their cargoes a second time, and only then could they transport their goods across the isthmus.

The usability of the port nearest the city itself declined within decades. The settlement, which was perched on the edge of the beach and had unpaved streets, was nestled between two small rivers that deposited large amounts of eroded silt and human-generated trash into the harbor. The port was described in 1610 as a place "where for forty years had entered ships of 5,000 arrobas [60 tons] half laden . . . the river north of town emptied into the port, and with the wash of the streets was filling it up, so that barges could scarcely come in" (Anderson 1911:281; see also Castillero 2006:139–150; Hussey 1960; Mena García 1992:61–71).

Even with its problems, Panamá prospered and grew as an immigrant merchant class from Spain arrived in response to the maritime economy. The original Spanish plan for conquest and integration of the region had been the *encomienda*, in which the natives were distributed among the conquistadors or *encomenderos* who enslaved them mainly for agricultural work such as harvesting crops and raising cattle or for doing domestic chores (Castillero 1995:37–53). The virtual extinction of the indigenous peoples by 1530 and the abolition of the *encomienda* system in 1551 came just as the acquisition of Peru and the resultant flood of mineral wealth turned the city into an important transportation hub. Described in 1575 as a settlement of some 500 Spaniards, but with a population that was expected to grow to 800 men (counting women, children, and non-Spanish inhabitants), the city boasted 400 wooden houses (Anderson 1911:276; for an extensive discussion of sixteenth-century Panamá City see Castillero 2006; on its population see Mena García 1984:43–101).

By 1610 Panamá was a city of 548 Spanish male citizens, 303 women, 156 children, 146 mulattos, 148 free blacks, and 3,500 African slaves (Anderson 1911:278; Castillero 1994:68). They lived in a gridded city facing the beach with four streets running east to west and seven streets running south to north. Two small plazas and one large plaza (the first at the eastern end of the city near the beach) were surrounded by 332 wood houses with tiled roofs, 112 thatched shacks, 40 "small houses," government buildings, a cathedral, five convents, a hospital, and a slaughterhouse and meat market. The rivers at the north and south ends of the city had bridges over them (Anderson 1911:278; Castillero 2006:151–161; Mena García 1984:57–73).

Although ravaged by earthquakes, fires, and attacks by escaped slaves known as *cimarrones* (much like poorly situated Nombre de Dios had been), Panamá survived until its strategic vulnerabilities were demonstrated when Welsh privateer Henry Morgan arrived in 1671 and waged a successful overland assault, sacking the city, which subsequently burned down (Castillero 2006:961–996). Accounts vary as to whether Morgan and his men were responsible for burning the city or the Spanish burned it while retreating (Hanselmann et al. 2016). In 1673 the city was abandoned in favor of a new and better-protected site 10 km to the southwest and closer to the port of Perico. That site is now known as the Casco Viejo of modern Panamá City (Castillero 1999). Dismantling and reusing materials further removed traces of the old city, and the jungle overtook the remaining ruins.

Panamá Viejo: The Site

Nineteenth-century visitors commented on the ruins that lay beyond the walls of the Casco Viejo; these ruins attracted much attention from foreigners who poured in during the California Gold Rush. Their accounts sparked additional tourism during the early twentieth century as well as the construction of the Panamá Canal and the clearing of the jungle. The gradual growth of the city in time reached the old site (Abbot 1913). In the 1950s, to celebrate the fiftieth anniversary of Panamanian independence, the government decided to build a commemorative park on the plaza.

The construction of this park resulted in the almost complete disturbance of the provenience of colonial-era levels with two layers of modern fill, one of sand and one of earth, packed with a mix of colonial and contemporary artifacts. This activity not only disturbed the plaza itself, where it presumably erased most of the original occupation levels, but it also affected the colonial housing area to the west of the plaza. As these houses showed no above-ground remains, the modern architects probably did not think they would be disturbing anything. Thus, the houses were covered in sand and earth, and the new park covered the whole plaza and about 25 meters of the block of houses directly to the west. The park was completed by the addition of a surrounding paved street, in the form of a horseshoe.

Figure 21. The ruins of the original city of Panamá, destroyed by fire in 1671, today comprise the archaeological preserve of Panamá Viejo. The site contains elements of the precolonial indigenous settlement as well as the original sixteenth-century Spanish colonial settlement. The modern city stands where Panamá was relocated after 1671. Photograph by Félix Durán Ardila.

The subsequent creation of the Patronato Panamá Viejo, a mixed government and private enterprise foundation charged with managing the site, and the designation of the ruins as both a national and World Heritage Site, led to a successful effort to remove the park, the street, and commemorative statues. The ruins were stabilized, archaeological investigations were undertaken, and a museum was constructed (Arroyo 2010; Martín and Arango 2013; Mendizábal 1999; Osorio 2012).

Today the ruins of Panamá Viejo make up a historic enclave at the center of modern Panamá City. Documented by archaeological means since 1996, the site is somewhat L-shaped, with the main plaza and town center on the corner of the L, to the southeast. The calculated area of the original site was approximately 70 hectares. The site's borders are the Bay of Panamá to the south, the Río Matadero or the Río Algarrobo to the west, the Río Gallinero (today Río Abajo) to the east, and to the north, the modern neighborhood of Panamá Viejo. This neighborhood is standing where the ancient slums of the town stood, as the rich and middle-class people lived in and around the center. The poor whites, Indians, and blacks lived on the outskirts in two slums, Pierdevidas and Malambo, both to the northwest and north, respectively. All visible ruins above ground are what have survived of the stone and masonry buildings, which belonged to the colonial administration, the church, or the very rich. Among the more prominent (and photogenic) ruins are those of the cathedral and its tower is the highest surviving structure of the original city.

Everything relating to the Spanish colony is contained within the 1519–1671 period. However, it is also a multicomponent site; there is not only the colonial settlement but also the earlier pre-Columbian village underneath the Spanish ruins, with evidence of human occupation at the site going back as early as the middle of the first millennium of our era (Biese 1964; Mendizábal 2004; Martín 2002b, 2002c). The multivariate nature of the evidence and the sheer size of the site have provided work for a host of specialists, from anthropologists and archaeologists to restoration architects, physicists, and biologists.

Panamá Viejo had been limited to sporadic archaeological studies until the mid-1990s, when the Patronato Panamá Viejo was formed. What followed was, in the beginning, an archaeological project to uncover and restore the original layout of the Plaza Mayor (main square) and its environs, including the buildings around it (Campos Carrasco and Durán Ardila 2006). Research has uncovered evidence from the colonial occupation in the sixteenth and seventeenth centuries as well as pre-Columbian remains. In three field seasons since the beginning of 1996, most of the area around the square was excavated, while the 2013–2014 season was dedicated to exploring its southern flank. A broad range of material culture, with a large proportion of imported materials including ceramics, glass, and other manufactured goods, speaks to the city's location as a hub for Spanish overseas trade. However, in the years since, many other areas of the site have been explored, and a veritable wealth of colonial and pre-Columbian material culture has been recovered that has enriched our knowledge of the lives of Panamá Viejo's ancient inhabitants (Martín 2002a, 2002d, 2003, 2009)

Portobelo

During Columbus's fourth voyage in 1502 the site of Portobelo was named "a beautiful harbor" (*porto bello*). Closer by one day's sail to the Río Chagres, the port was superior to the one at Nombre de Dios (Ward 1999:56).

By land, the distance to Panamá City was 18 leagues, which meant a one- to two-week trip "depending upon the level of the river and strength of the current" when the Camino de Cruces was used (Ward 1999:56). The superiority of the harbor was noted because of its proximity to the Chagres as well as being more easily defended. Spanish Royal Engineer Juan Bautista Antonelli, tasked with fortifying the isthmus, wrote to the king of Spain in 1586 and recommended that the "city of Nombre de Dios be brought and built in this harbor" (Anderson 1914:310).

The official order to move was acted upon in 1597 (Mena García 1992:229–264), and despite an initial attack and seizure of the incomplete port and its fortifications, it soon rose to become "the region's international economic center" (Ward 1999:68). The amount of silver that poured out of the New World tripled the amount of the metal in the global economy, and 60 percent of that New World silver passed over the isthmus and then through Portobelo to the holds of Spanish ships (Ward 1999:71).

The annual arrival of the Tierra Firme fleet brought tons of silver across the isthmus on the backs of mules that had labored slowly over the cobblestones and deeply cut tracks that wound through mountains and river valleys. In Portobelo, the "trade fair" lasted for a few weeks as goods were exchanged and the treasure was loaded into the fleet for transport back to Spain. The fair of 1637 was described by one visitor, Englishman Thomas Gage, whose description captures the essence of this isthmian entrepôt:

> [W]hat most I wondered at was to see the recua's of mules which came thither from Panamá, laden with wedges of silver; in one day I told, two hundred mules laden with nothing else, which were unladen in the public market-place, so that there were heaps of silver wedges . . . in the street. . . . Within ten days the fleet came, consisting of eight galleons and ten merchant ships. . . . It was a wonder to see the multitude of people in those streets which the week before had been empty. . . . It was worth seeing how merchants sold their commodities, not by the ell or yard, but by the piece and weight, not paying in coined pieces of money, but in wedges which were weighed and taken for commodities. This lasted but fifteen days, whilst the galleons were lading with wedges of silver and nothing else; so that for those fifteen days, I dare boldly say and avouch, that in the world there is no greater fair than that of Portobelo, between the Spanish merchants and those of Peru, Panamá and other parts thereabouts. (Gage 1677:446)

Figure 22. The Portobelo fair in 1637, as depicted in Thomas Gage's *The English-American His Travail by Sea and Land; or a New Survey of the West Indias*, London 1648.

Portobelo: The Site

Very little archaeological work has been carried out at Portobelo except for a few very punctual interventions at the San Juan de Dios hospitaliers church, the Concepción convent, and San Geronimo battery (carried out by Alvaro Brizuela and Tomás Mendizábal between 1999 and 2000). The only extensive excavations at the site were those undertaken by Beatriz Rovira (1994) at the customs building and by Loreto Suárez at Casa Rodríguez (1994). Rovira documented the architectural changes that the customs building went through during its lifetime: from the early seventeenth century until its last modifications in the late eighteenth century following its destruction by Admiral Vernon in 1739. These excavations formed part of an integral government intervention called *Plan de Acción de Portobelo* that in 1990 sought to create a master plan for the conservation and management of the site's cultural heritage—a plan that saw limited success. Although the restoration of both Casa Rodríguez and the customs building was achieved, very soon the plan was abandoned.

Erratic government policies undertaken by several agencies at the national and local levels have tried to solve the Portobelo problem with punctual but ultimately failed interventions. Some of these interventions were carried out by the Tourism Institute, which managed to construct a parking lot on the ruins of the Concepción nuns' convent and the Museo del Cristo Negro in the San Juan de Dios hospital church (the museum has since

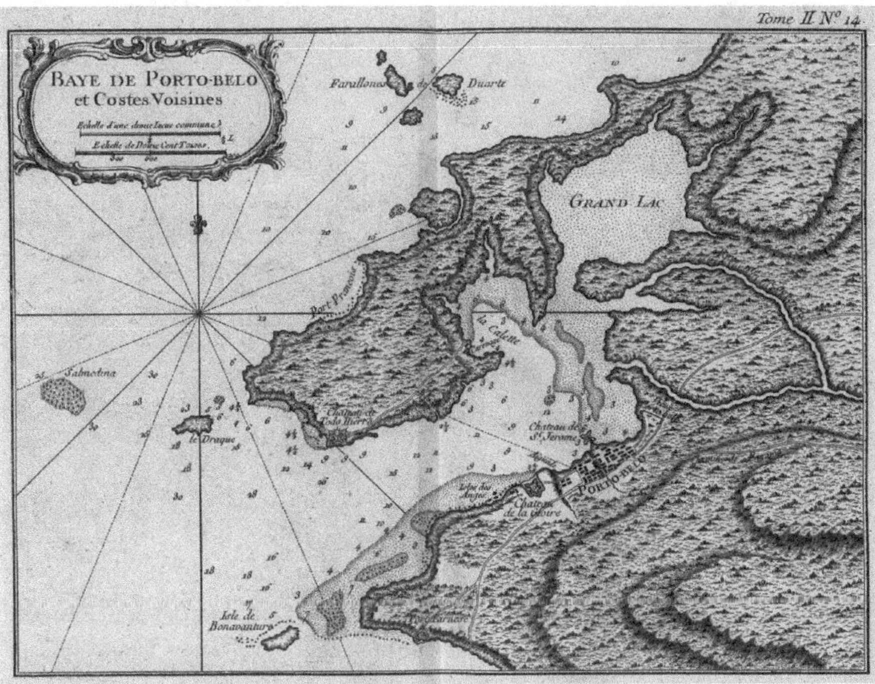

Figure 23a–b. The maritime landscape of Portobelo is evident both in this eighteenth-century chart and in this aerial view showing the peninsula, the harbor, and the shallow shore lined by the town and the Spanish fortifications. *Baye de Porto-Belo et Costes Voisines*, Jacques Nicolas Bellin, 1764, David Rumsey Historic Map Collection, list 6903.131. Aerial photograph by Jonathan Kingston, National Geographic Creative, 2014.

Figure 24. The *aduana* at Portobelo is a dominant architectural feature and a museum. Photograph by James P. Delgado.

closed). The Housing Ministry paid for a study of the urbanism of Portobelo in 2006, but the plan was never executed. More recently a Patronato de Portobelo y San Lorenzo was created, which was another multipurpose institution emulating the Patronato Panamá Viejo. But this institution received little government support until 2014 and has not been able to create the master plan for the city and ruins: in fact, it hasn't achieved much more than to prevent the many colonial-period structures from collapsing. In the end, the lack of a well-planned state policy for the management and care of the property has resulted in Portobelo and San Lorenzo being included in the World Heritage Endangered Sites list in 2013.

Camino de Cruces and Camino Real

The road between the coasts was an imperfect solution for linking Panamá and Nombre de Dios. While it was clear that no one river could be navigated entirely across the isthmus, the Trinidad and the Río de los Lagartos, soon to be renamed the Río Chagres, did penetrate far into the interior, while the former spilled into the latter, which empties into the Caribbean coast. In 1527 pilot Hernando de la Serna explored the Chagres.

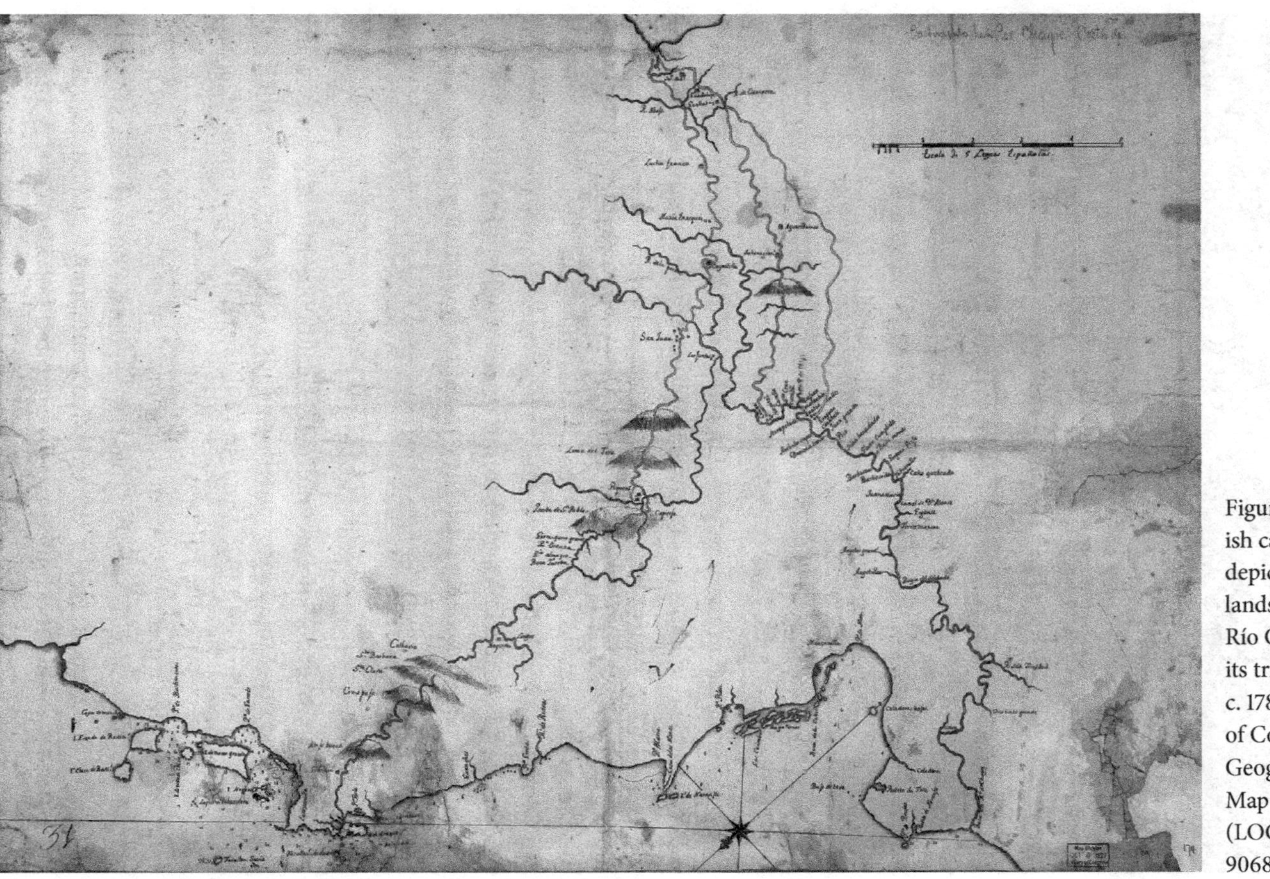

Figure 25. Spanish cartography depicts the landscape of the Río Chagres and its tributaries, c. 1780. Library of Congress, Geography and Map Division (LOC catalog no. 90680519).

Figure 26. Bongo navigating the Chagres, 1748. From Jorge Juan y Antonio de Ulloa, *Relación Histórica del viaje a la América Meridional*, Madrid 1748. Tomás Mendizábal Collection.

De la Serna used canoes to travel upriver and determined that the river was navigable. De la Serna's recommendation to the Spanish Crown was that a road from Panamá City be constructed to link to a local trans-shipment point at Las Cruces. This road was built in 1519 (Anderson 1911:302). In 1528, acting on de la Serna's report, merchants in Panamá petitioned the Crown to fund an alternate route across the isthmus for trade, arguing that goods could be carried to the upper reaches of the Chagres and floated down the river in boats. They recommended that a group of slaves could clear the fallen trees and other obstructions in the river (Haring 1918:181–182).

In February 1534, after two subsequent surveys of the river, the Crown ordered the Governor of Panamá to spend 1,000 gold pesos on clearing the river and erecting a warehouse for goods at the point where the river met the sea (Haring 1918:182; Anderson 1911:302). The river then became a partial highway across the Isthmus of Panamá (Ward 1993:57–58). The Río Chagres became a means for water transportation of goods to and from Panamá City on the Pacific side and that port's connections via the Caribbean Sea to South America, New Spain (Mexico), and Spain's distant outposts in the Philippines. Flat-bottomed barges operated between Cruces and Río Chagres, with one account noting that by 1579 as many as thirty of these craft were used on the river. Henceforth, during each rainy season, from

Figure 27. The Río Chagres, as depicted in the illustrated manuscript *Histoire Naturelle des Indies*, c. 1586. The original caption, in French, translates as "This river has been recently discovered by the Spaniards. It serves their shipping and carries gold and silver from the port of Panamá distant by three leagues over land from Cap La Cruz in Panamá and is the beginning of said river. When the fleet of ships from Peru arrives in Panamá laden with gold and minted silver, they carry the gold and silver on mules over land to the Port of La Cruz in order to ship it in barges on said river to Nombre de Dios, thus avoiding the danger from the runaway negro slaves, commonly called thieves, from the port of La Cruz to the entrance of the sea which is the end of the river, a distance of approximately nine leagues. The barges do not take long at all to come down to the sea and to be on the way to Nombre de Dios on account of the river's strong current. The barges are all laden with gold and silver and have only eight to ten negro slaves who swim when there is no proper wind, and one Spaniard, called Major-domo, who commands them. Having arrived in Nombre de Dios and unloaded the gold and silver, they take on merchandise meant for delivery to Panamá and from there to Peru, having to leave half of their merchandise at the grange, a place close to said Chagres River, because the barges—unless they are lightened—cannot go upstream on account of its violent current and swiftness. To this end they have to be pushed with poles so that laden with the treasures mentioned above, they need only six to seven hours to come downstream, while, on the other hand, it takes them four to five days to go back upstream." Pierpoint Morgan Library, New York, MA 3900, folio 106 recto, Bequest of Clara S. Peck, 1983.

Figure 28. The Puente del Rey, Panamá, is the colonial-era stone bridge on the edge of Panamá Viejo that marks the beginning of the Camino Real across the isthmus. Photograph by Ayaita, 2012.

May to December, the Chagres became a seasonal water route, and another way station, the Venta de Cruces, was established at the head of navigation in 1536 (Brady 1999:137; Castillero 2004c).

As Brady (1999) notes, this pattern of seasonal transport flows emerged in response to the local geography and climate. Mule trains laden with cargo left Panamá and followed the road for five leagues. At Venta de Cruces, the break in bulk point, "goods, especially those with a relatively low unit value, were transferred to boats" (Brady 1999:138) and followed the river for eighteen leagues to the mouth of the river and then up the coast to Nombre de Dios in a trip that lasted anywhere from 3 to 12 days. In the dry season the Chagres was too low to use, so the mule trains used the Camino Real: this overland route was a more arduous and expensive trip marked by high rates of mule mortality (Brady 1999:138).

The Camino Real was a shorter route but much more expensive than traveling along the Camino de Cruces—the cheaper, longer, safer, more comfortable, and historically better-known route—which connected the same destinations but through a mixed terrestrial and fluvial way along the Río Chagres. They were both used from the third decade of the sixteenth century onward, when the Camino Real was simply an open path through the jungle until it was partially paved (Mena García 1992:208). In time the route saw the flow of a vast amount of treasure, especially over the Camino Real, which was designated as the only possible route for the royal treasure in 1587 (Castillero 2004c:361).

Camino Real and Venta de Chagres: The Sites

The *caminos*, while declining in use with the end of the annual treasure shipments and trade fairs (the last one held in 1739), remained open and were used through the nineteenth century despite the building of the railroad. The *caminos*, after all, were the only means of communication between both coasts. The construction of the canal in the early twentieth century reportedly destroyed and flooded significant portions of the old routes and their way stations, but visible portions would remain on both coasts.

Along each of the two *caminos*, there were many small towns and way stations that provided opportunities for shelter, rest, and commerce for travelers. One of those was Venta de Chagres, a town on the Río Chagres that intersected with the Camino Real.[1] Francis Drake, who pillaged the town in February 1571 (Nichols 1653), describes the town as having

> forty or fifty houses, which had both a Governor and other officers and some fair houses, with many storehouses large and strong for the wares, which brought thither from Nombre de Dios, by the river of Chagres, so to be transported by mules to Panamá: beside the Monastery, where we found above a thousand bulls and pardons, newly sent from Rome. (Nichols 1653:64–65)

In town for about an hour and a half, long enough to impress "three gentlewomen"—Spanish ladies on their way to Nombre de Dios—with Drake's charm, the pirates got "some good pillage," leaving just before dawn (Nichols 1653:64–65).

Little is heard again of the story of Venta de Chagres in the documentary sources. One of the last Spanish maps to show it as an occupied site is that of Juan López in 1785 (Carta Marítima del Reyno de Tierra Firme ú Castilla del Oro). Its importance waned after the Panamanian route was abandoned in 1739 for the Cape Horn route to deliver the silver and gold train to Spain. Although the Camino Real continued to be used as a local transportation route, it was completely abandoned after 1855 when the Panamá Railroad was built.

The Camino Real and Venta de Chagres "disappeared" with the flooding of Lake Alajuela following the construction of the Madden Dam to impound more water for the Panamá Canal between 1931 and 1935. Like a number of sites associated with the early maritime cultural landscape of the isthmus that were originally "dry land," much of the *camino* and the *venta* are now submerged cultural heritage. During the dry season, lake levels are lower and, as a result, some of the sites are exposed above the water line. Recent (2008, 2010, 2012) surveys of the exposed portions of the road and the site of Venta de Chagres have been undertaken by archaeologists, including Delgado and Mendizábal (see Strassnig 2010; Mendizábal and Theodossopoulos 2012). Earlier work included a 1973 survey by Francis Drake historian Edwin Webster (Webster 1973).

From their fieldwork with the native Emberá, Mendizábal and Theodossopoulos (2012) have reported on a variety of sites, as the Emberá are the most recent successors to, and guardians of, this land. Acting on their advice, Theodossopoulos visited a site known to the Emberá as Isla Roja (Red Island), which was covered with broken ceramics when it emerged from Lake Alajuela. This site, surveyed first by Theodossopoulos, later joined by Mendizábal, is distinguished by an extensive field of ceramic roof tiles (which give it the red color of its name) and several other types of sixteenth-century wares, such as tin enameled earthenwares (like Panamanian *majolicas* and the type known as "Columbia plain"), stonewares, and olive jars (see Deagan 1987; Rovira 1984, 1997, 2001; Rovira and Mojica 2007; Rovira et al. 2006).

Isla Roja is the site of Venta de Chagres, which is immediately south of the ancient course of the Chagres and on its eastern bank along what was once the route of the Camino Real. As surveyed in 2012, there are no above-ground structural remains left in Venta de Chagres, although there is the surface scatter of roof tiles and (to a lesser extent) pottery that covers a somewhat V-shaped area of about 1400 m^2, with each leg of the "V" measuring up to 60 m. In April 2012, up to 8800 m^2 of the former hill (now an island) where Venta de Chagres stood could be seen above the waters of Lake Alajuela.

So there is evidence of a sizable and long-established habitation. And the fact that the roof tiles are still there—the upper layers of a stratified collapsed house—indicates that although the varying water levels of the lake have probably eroded much of the town's outskirts, its core could still be relatively intact. Mendizábal and Theodossopoulos found evidence of recent looting in the form of pits dug by treasure hunters, which negatively impacts the archaeological and touristic potential of the site.

The Emberá took Mendizábal and Theodossopoulos to one of the northeastern banks of the lake, where a portion of the Camino Real can be seen in good condition. Here can be seen its fully paved width of between 1.2 and 1.5 m, aligned by master stones—larger slabs of rock buried on their sides—that guide the trail and provide "walls" for its inner fill of irregularly

Figure 29. The maritime cultural landscape of the colonial isthmus included the mule and foot roads that crossed the isthmus and served as the main points of transit in addition to the Río Chagres. Ironically, these "maritime" elements were submerged during the construction of the Panamá Canal and later the Madden Dam's hydroelectric Lake Alajuela. Fluctuating water levels occasionally expose the sites of Venta de Cruces and Venta de Chagres and sections of the Camino Real shown here. Photograph by Tomás Mendizábal.

shaped boulders of the same stone. Strassnig noted this in 2010. At this point the Camino divides into two stone paths just before the top of a small hill, which may very well be the town of San Juan, located approximately 120 meters from the northern edge of the bank and on the southern flanks of San Juan Hill. The main (and wider) trail continues northeast, probably toward the Caribbean coast, and the narrower path (between 60 and 90 cm) heads northwest to an old riverbed. As Strassnig (2010) notes, other portions of the road emerge from various places along the lakeshore, one section being approximately 1.5 k from the Venta de Chagres site.

The Río Chagres and its Fortifications: 1534–1680

As the fluvial part of the Camino de Cruces, the Río Chagres was both a strategic asset and liability. In 1534, Filipe II, King of Spain, realized this weakness and ordered construction of a fortification at the mouth of the river. However, the river remained unprotected. Francis Drake's use of the river in his attack on the town of Cruces in 1571 served as the catalyst for the construction of a fortification. The first phase of construction (1597–1599), consisted of the building of a water-level battery. This construction was based on plans prepared by military engineer Bautista Antonelli. Though the battery was a necessary first step in the erection of the fortification, a major weakness in the defense still existed, because there had been no efforts made to fortify the elevated promontory overlooking the river's mouth (Ward 1993:166, 169). Construction continued, and in 1626 the fortress was christened "El Castillo de San Lorenzo el Real de Chagres" and fitted with guns. In 1656 these structures were ruined and subsequently abandoned after falling into enemy hands during a pirate attack.

This fortification was replaced with a star-shaped earthen feature and a wooden palisade constructed atop the *morro* or cliff (Ward 1993: 170). This fort fell during the 1671 attack by forces under the command of privateer Henry Morgan. Rebuilt as a three-tiered stone fortress between 1677 and 1680, it was during this phase of construction that the small village of Chagres was established beside it. In 1739 the fortress was again destroyed, this time by Admiral Vernon's forces: this led to the final construction phase of the fortifications in the 1760s. The fortifications from this final phase are still standing.

Shipwrecks

The ebb and flow of shipping from Panamá left indelible marks on the maritime cultural landscape—not only on isthmian shores but also farther afield. Among those wrecks are two vessels, *Nuestra Señora de Atocha* and *Santa Margarita*, both from the 1622 Tierra Firme fleet. These ships were laden with goods and silver that had been loaded in Portobelo and lost in the Florida Keys. Both vessels were recovered by treasure-hunting operations. A third 1622 Tierra Firme shipwreck, the wreck of *Buen Jesús y Nuestra Señora del Rosario*, has been identified by Odyssey Marine Explorations and was discovered in the Florida Straits in 1989 in 405 meters of water.

Historical accounts suggest a number of documented losses, many of them in the harbor or vicinity of Nombre de Dios and later Portobelo. These include vessels scuttled in 1544 at Nombre de Dios, an unidentified *nao* of the Tierra Firme fleet of 1551 lost on the coast 25 leagues from Nombre de Dios, seven unladen ships from the Tierra Firme fleet of 1563 lost in a storm in Nombre de Dios harbor, and a merchant *nao* from the 1567 fleet that sank while entering the harbor. Two merchant *naos* from the 1584 fleet were supposedly lost entering Nombre de Dios. A Portuguese caravel was reported lost north of Acla in 1609 but was salvaged.

At Portobelo, two unnamed merchant *naos* were reported lost in 1634 but were salvaged, while the galleon *Santa Ana María*, from the 1635 fleet, was reported stripped and scuttled at Portobelo that year.[2] On the Pacific coast, *patache Margarita* was reported lost at Isla Del Rey in 1632 but was completely salvaged.[3] A year earlier, the most famous treasure-laden wreck of the region, the galleon *San José*, *Almiranta* of the *Armada de Mar Del Sur*, was reported lost forty leagues from Panamá City near the islas Garachiné and La Galera. Some treasure and guns were recovered, but the rest of the wreck, with a reputed treasure trove of silver, was covered by sand. The aforementioned treasure hunting company IMDI (Investigaciones Marinas del Istmo), S.A., still in operation after its Playa Damas project, located the wreck in 2012–2013 and removed ceramic artifacts and a sizeable gold coin collection. Efforts to locate and salvage the 1631 wreck of *San José*, a longtime goal of treasure hunters, seem to have been realized in 2015 according to press reports.[4]

This is by no means a complete list of all vessels lost on either coast of the Isthmus of Panamá: a number of undocumented losses most certainly occurred, and no comprehensive inventory of Panamanian shipwrecks has been completed to date.[5] Wrecks associated with the 1671 attack of Henry Morgan and the abortive 1699 Scottish attempt at colonization will be discussed in the next chapter, as there has been archaeological work done there. The only colonial-period shipwreck in Panamá to have been archaeologically documented is a partially looted vessel from the 1681 Tierra Firme fleet. That fleet's vessels were scattered by a storm and saw losses that included the galleon *Nuestra Señora de la Soledad* (lost at Punta de Brujas), the *nao La Boticaria* (lost near the Isla de Naranjos), and the ship originally known as *Chaperón*.

When first discovered by sport divers in 1993 near the mouth of the Chagres at Punta Morillo, the site was known as the "Sword Wreck" (Lusardi 1998:114). The site may have been known to US military divers earlier, and in the 1980s divers Lucius Taylor and Barry Clifford located what may have been the wreck and noted the ship's five iron guns. Around this time, a variety of artifacts, including "double-headed Hapsburg eagles and rectangular decorative plates, lead textile seals, and pewter screw-on lids from square, green-glass gin bottles," were recovered (Lusardi 1998:115). In 1993 Dr. José Santiago found the wreck in nine meters of water. Santiago,

Figure 30. The wreck of *Nuestra Señora de la Encarnación*, showing the bow after excavation, 2012. Photograph by Jonathan Kingston, National Geographic Creative.

working both with Cornell University and independently, investigated the site from 1993 to 1995, and a more detailed (although still preliminary) investigation took place in 1997. The investigation found that "the site has been extensively looted by treasure hunters and amateur divers" who removed many artifacts, including edged weapons that had been packed in cases (Lusardi 1998:116). Lusardi (1998) studied blades recovered from the wreck and found them to be typical Spanish rapier blades of the last quarter of the seventeenth century. These blades had been packed in seven rectangular crates and were also found on the site in three bundles (Lusardi 1998:117–119).

No other professional or scholarly archaeological work was done on the site until work led by Hanselmann commenced in 2011. Hanselmann's project has documented the wreck more extensively and has recovered artifacts that are now in the hands of the government and undergoing conservation at Panamá Viejo (Hanselmann et al. 2011, 2016). The site is definitely *Chaperón* of the 1681 fleet, but research has provided a more definitive identification and context for the vessel than just its historically recorded nickname. This work makes the site of *Chaperón* one of only two shipwrecks in the maritime cultural landscape of Panamá to be archaeologically documented in any detail.

El Chaperón of 1681: The Site

The site examined here was clearly a wooden-hulled sailing vessel whose remains have settled into the soft sand and mud matrix resulting from the outflow of the Río Chagres. Scant marine growth is visible on the hull's remains, and the area itself is largely devoid of fish and other marine life. The hull's preservation is impressive and oriented along a north-south axis, with the bow facing true north. The vessel remains are upright with a slight list to the port side. Archaeologists documented extant hull structure, including ceiling planking, lower elements of what are considered to be the first futtocks, outer hull planking, possible remains of cant frames in the bow, a section of what may be a stringer, and numerous iron fasteners and lead strapping in the stern. The overall site measured approximately 20 m (65.62 ft) by 8.55 m (28 ft). The remains of the vessel itself measured 19.47 m (62.87 ft) in length with a beam of 4.90 m (16 ft). Clear evidence of salvage activity was documented with the observation of exposed ceiling planking where boxes once existed, although it was not clear whether the salvage

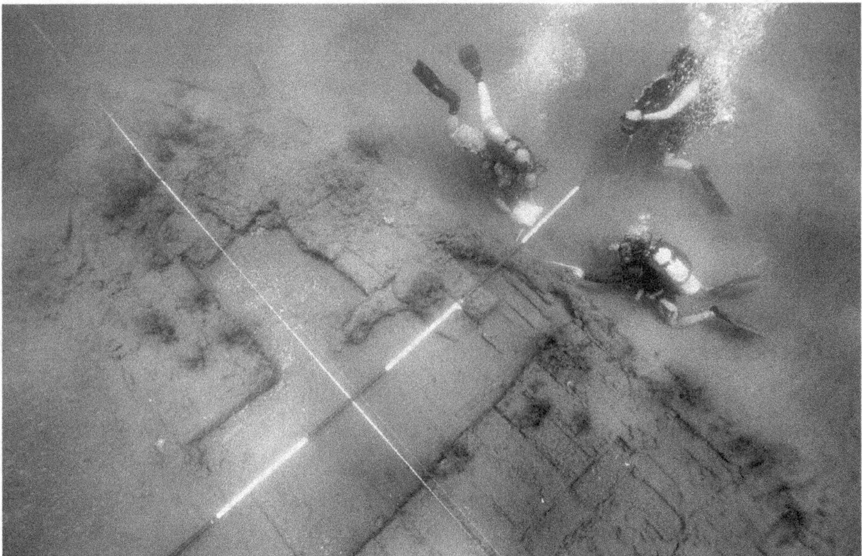

Figure 31. Archaeologists Juan Martín and Chris Morris and videographer Jason Sturgis mapping and documenting the wreck of the *Nuestra Señora de la Encarnación* in 2012. Photograph by Jonathan Kingston, National Geographic Creative.

Figure 32. Archaeologist Frederick Hanselmann takes notes and documents the characteristics of the hull of *Nuestra Señora de la Encarnación* in 2014. Photograph by Sam Meacham. Frederick Hanselmann Collection.

occurred during a single site visit or several. Local sources suggested that many years prior to this project, US military personnel could have been involved in the removal of items from the site. These activities, along with the constant outflow of the river, have uncovered a number of artifacts in recent years.

Cargo

Excavations during the 2011 field season documented 65 small boxes and 12 large boxes. Observation of the contents of these boxes indicated that the vessel was carrying a variety of utilitarian items, including nails or tacks as well as horseshoes and mule shoes. In addition, 12 larger boxes were also documented, one of them containing nails or tacks. During the 2012 field season, the extensive excavation of the site revealed a total of 122 boxes as well as one wooden barrel and two additional boxes located along the port side and buried in the sediments. Along the vessel's starboard side, two wooden barrels were found buried in the sediments. In addition to the boxes, 16 lead cloth or bale seals were found during the excavation of the sediment overburden. Many of the seals have markings impressed on the face and may provide insight into the kinds of cloth or textiles that were carried to and from the New World. Research is ongoing to identify the individual merchants' commodities associated with these markings.

One interesting pewter artifact was found in the bow section of the vessel. The artifact consists of two pieces, one fitting within the other. The smaller of the two pieces has what seems to be a small handle that could have been used to remove it from inside the larger piece. Both pieces are hand turned as evidenced by the lathe markings on the interior face of each object. The larger piece has a fairly substantial groove on its exterior. At this point, it is impossible to know what this object is or what its function was. One suggestion comes from a Sedgewick auction house catalog that has the same piece listed as an olive jar lid. To date, no olive jar necks have been identified on this site, and it seems highly unlikely that a pewter object would have served as a lid or plug for an olive jar. In addition, archaeologist Kathleen Deagan was consulted regarding this unique artifact, and she too indicated that it would not have been used as a lid or plug for an olive jar (personal communication, 13 July 2013). Body sherds from middle-style

Figure 33. Lead textile seals recovered from the wreck of *Nuestra Señora de la Encarnación*. Photograph by Jonathan Kingston, National Geographic Creative.

olive jars are ubiquitous throughout the site. These sherds present a unique problem in that archaeologists originally thought they might be former contents of a ship's cargo. However, as stated earlier, no examples of rim sherds have been found at the site. The lack of olive jar rim sherds suggests that these body sherds may have been used as packing material.

Conclusion of 2012 and 2014 Fieldwork

Due to weather delays and budget constraints, it was impossible to complete the mapping of the bow of the vessel in 2012. Although the area was somewhat exposed during the initial dredging of the site, the area was quickly filled in, which made it impossible to get an accurate depiction of the forward section of the vessel. The photomosaic provides tantalizing information about a site that must be further documented in order to fully understand it. The conclusion of the 2012 field season began with the recovery of one box with unknown contents plus a barrel and a sword. These artifacts were transported to Panamá City and are currently undergoing conservation. The collection of these artifacts may provide additional information regarding the name of this vessel. Small artifacts were documented in situ and left on site for future investigations. The brief 2014 field season sought to finalize the site map and resulted in a largely successful effort to map a large portion of the bow. Upon completion of each field season, the site is buried again so as to protect and preserve it from environmental deterioration and potential looting.

Potential Identification and Ties to Overland Trade

After completion of the two-month field season in 2012, questions remained about the identity of the shipwreck. Currently, research continues in the Archivo General de Indias in Sevilla to find out more about this site. A few observations can be made that provide an approximate date and possible identification of the nationality of the vessel now known as the "Horseshoe Wreck." First, the outer hull remains did not exhibit any metal sheathing. This trait suggests that the vessel predates the introduction of copper sheathing, which came into use in the mid-to-late eighteenth century. Second, lead strapping found in the seams is consistent with the construction techniques found on the Portuguese *nao* known as the "Pepper Wreck" (Castro 2005:140) and is indicative of Iberian ship construction techniques. Third, data collected during the 2011 and 2012 field seasons suggests that the horseshoes (or, more likely, mule shoes) are consistent with

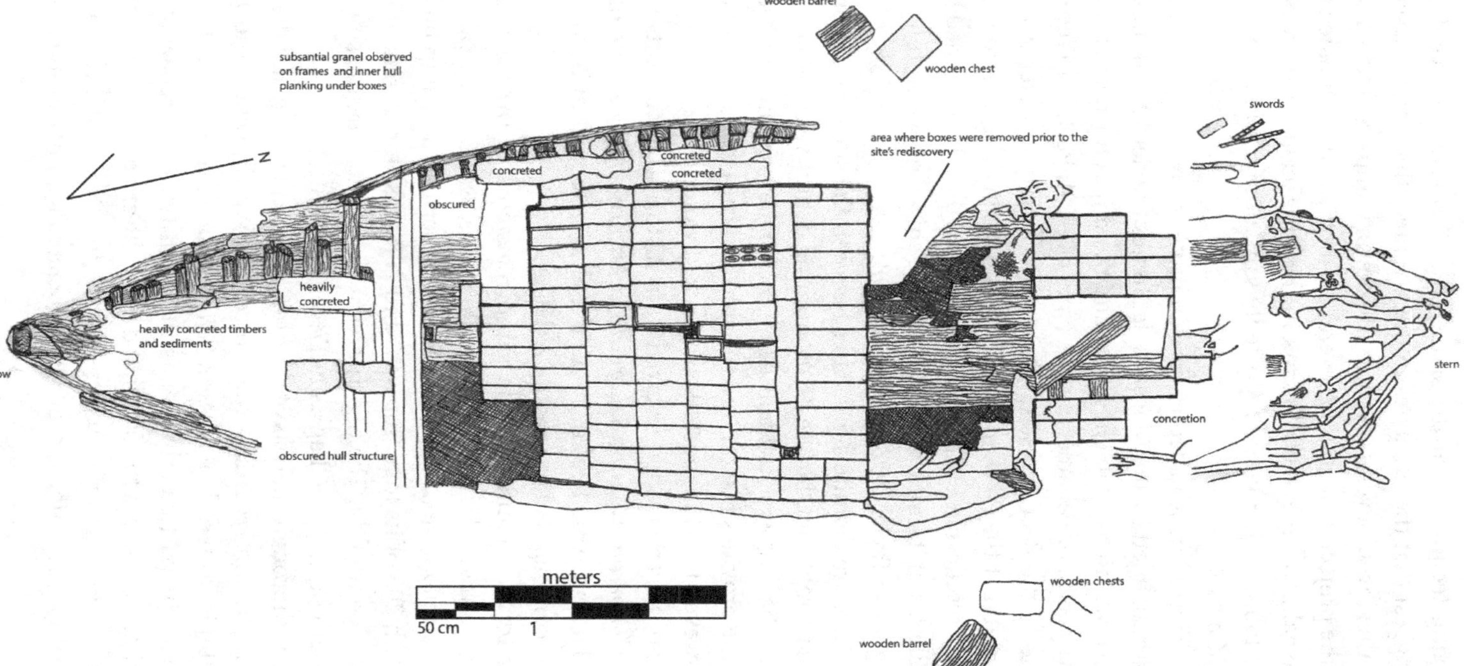

Figure 34. Site plan of the wreck of *Nuestra Señora de la Encarnación* in 2014. Map prepared by Frederick Hanselmann, Christopher Horrell, Melanie Damour, Bert Ho, and Andres Diaz.

Spanish ferrying techniques of the sixteenth and seventeenth centuries. These data suggest that the site dates to the seventeenth century. Research suggests that there were several seventeenth-century shipwrecks, including Morgan's, in the project area. In 1619 several flat-bottomed boats laden with goods for the galleons in Portobelo sank in the Río Chagres (Marx 1987). In November 1681 another vessel reportedly sank not far from the mouth of the river (Marx 1987).

In 1681 the Tierra Firme galleons were en route from Cartagena to Portobelo and commanded by the Marqués de Brenes (Tayler 1993 in Lusardi 1998). The fleet was hit by a violent storm, and the ships ended up scattered along the north coast of Panamá. On December 1, 1681, Portobelo received news that one of the fleet's vessels, *Chaperón*, was taking water near the Río Chagres and that the crew and passengers were in danger. Two vessels were sent to the rescue, but by the time they arrived the *Chaperón* had been abandoned. Eleven of its crew drowned, and the ship sank with a full cargo of European goods (Tayler 1993 in Lusardi 1998).

Although there are definite similarities between the site descriptions of the alleged *Chaperón* from the late 1990s, nothing definitive could be stated with regard to the shipwreck's identification. Further research in the archives in Seville provides insight into the ship and the events surrounding its wreck. However, the ship most likely wrecked would have been *Nuestra Señora de la Encarnación*, often referred to in historical documents by its nickname of *Chaperón*. *Nuestra Señora de la Encarnación* was one of the ships in the Tierra Firme fleet of 1681. The ship belonged to Nicolás de Zarra and was commanded by Juan de Arbelaiz.

According to the manifest of the cargo registered at the Casa de la Contratación, however, "Arvelaez," a Seville native, was both captain and owner. *Nuestra Señora de la Encarnación* was described as a ship built in Campeche, with 205 of its tons "for war" and 208 tons "for merchant" service and with a crew of 44. The registry went on to state that the ship was lost at the mouth of the Río Chagres in December 1681.

With a more thorough analysis of the archaeological record and the historical documentation regarding the Horseshoe Wreck, we can now hypothesize that it is the wreck of *Nuestra Señora de la Encarnación*. One line of inquiry that was particularly interesting from both an archaeological and historical perspective is the fact that during the excavation, no features were found that any relation to masts and rigging. No mast step was observed on the hull, and artifacts typically associated with masts and rigging were strangely absent. It is the historical accounts of the ship being "treeless" or "de-masted" that provide further circumstantial evidence of the ship's identity. Despite all the attention given to this particular shipwreck in 2012, further study and analysis should be completed, as this site could very well be the best-preserved Spanish *nao* ever found.

4

Buccaneers, Pirates, the Morgan Attack, and the Scottish at Darién

The Isthmus of Panamá includes a number of sites that provide a more intense focus on European challenges to Spanish control of the region. In this context, the maritime landscape also includes areas that would prove to be strategically vulnerable for Spain. These problematic aspects are looked at in terms of the complexity of the numerous islets, cays, and islands on the northern (Caribbean) coast that served as havens for bands of roving buccaneers, privateers, and pirates preying on coastal shipping and occasionally gathering sufficient strength to assault settlements and ports. Not surprisingly, Spain's strategic vulnerability with regard to this aspect of the maritime landscape proved to be a tactical strength for the marauders who took advantage of the landscape's defensive shortcomings. It was also, importantly, a key strategic strength for the surviving indigenous peoples of the isthmus who inhabited its isolated areas and developed a more pronounced maritime culture as a result of the landscape's duality of connectivity and isolation: for example, the Guna migrated from riverside communities on the mainland to the islands of the archipelago of San Blas to avoid colonial Spanish encroachment.

In addition to the archipelagos of Bocas del Toro and San Blas (Guna Yala), the areas of the maritime cultural landscape that were most important in facilitating the aforementioned activities are, firstly, the mouth of the Río Chagres, which was the site of a number of piratical and military attacks, culminating in the disastrous 1671 assault by Henry Morgan and the 1740 destruction of the fort there by Admiral Edward Vernon. Other major sites of conflict were the often-raided and occasionally ransacked Nombre de Dios and Portobelo, the ruins of Panamá Viejo, the locales that Oxenham and Drake attacked, and the still-unrecovered ships they scut-

Figure 35. Aerial view of the Castillo de San Lorenzo, Lajas Reef, and the mouth of the Río Chagres. Photograph by Jonathan Kingston, National Geographic Creative.

tled, sank, or abandoned. In all these cases, the maritime cultural landscape retains powerful archaeological aspects, both on land and underwater, that directly relate to this nexus of challenge and Spain's response (Castillero 2004e). The responses included a complex of fortifications that were built at Portobelo and San Lorenzo—those forts were later destroyed and replaced—and the relocated city of Panamá, now known as the Casco Antiguo. Pirate attacks and raids helped England to challenge Spain's control of the isthmus: the maritime cultural landscape also includes the site of the short-lived late seventeenth-century Scottish colony of New Edinburgh (in the Darién) and at least one shipwreck associated with it.

Drake and the First Attacks on the Isthmus

The rise of the Isthmus of Panamá as a transit hub for Spanish treasure and the repetitive pattern of sailings of the Tierra Firme fleet inspired a rise in piratical activity off Panamá's Caribbean shores. And in time, the same scenario could be found on its Pacific coast. Initial piratical forays were small, yet attacks on the treasure barges sailing down the Chagres to the Caribbean or land-based attacks on the *recuas* or mule trains were persistent, often somehow involving the Cimarron population of escaped slaves and their descendants. Attacks by English freebooters included Francis Drake's raid on Nombre de Dios in July 1572 as well as another raid on the isthmus in March 1573, in which he and his men successfully robbed a treasure-laden *recua*, capturing 15 tons of silver and carrying off all they could before escaping the isthmus and returning home to England by August (Anderson 1911:355–357). The first Englishman to see the Pacific, Drake vowed he would return to that "Spanish Lake" to plunder it. The pirate attacks also took advantage of the Cimarron wars, a long and ferocious conflict that saw its worst violence between the years 1549 and 1582 (Mena García 1984:400–427; Jaén Suaréz 1998:360–361). The corsairs allied themselves with these escaped slaves, who collaborated as guides and soldiers to fight their common enemy: the Spanish Crown (see also Fortune 1958; Tardieu 2009). This bloody conflict would not end until around 1600, after Spain and certain Cimarron groups negotiated a peace that resulted in the first settlements of free black peoples in the Americas.[1]

Although he was the first to "see" that ocean, Drake was not the first Englishman to sail the Pacific. The subsequent crossing of the isthmus in 1575 by Drake's associate John Oxenham, who like Drake allied himself with the Cimarrones, resulted in a change in Oxenham's plan to emulate Drake and attack a mule train laden with silver. Finding the *recuas* too well guarded, Oxenham, guided by the Cimarrones, went to an isolated part of the Pacific coast of the isthmus. On the Pacific shore, Oxenham built a small pinnace and plundered shipping in the Islas de las Perlas. His concealed ship and cached arms on the Caribbean, betrayed by some of his men who had been captured, were confiscated by the Spanish. Stranded and taking refuge with the Cimarrones, Oxenham and his remaining men, weary and diseased, were finally captured and ultimately executed (Anderson 1911:351–353). Drake began his journey in the Pacific in 1578 with a small fleet, which was eventually reduced to one small vessel: *Golden Hind*. After successful raids at Valparaíso and Callao, Drake captured and plundered the galleon *Nuestra Señora de la Concepción* just 150 leagues from Panamá on March 1, 1579, but he did not enter the bay or attack Panamá City. He and *Golden Hind*, accompanied by a pinnace they had captured, vanished from Spanish view into the Pacific, ultimately reaching England in September 1580 having made a voyage in which the world was "encompassed" (Anderson 1911:358–362; Castillero 2004e:491–494; Sternbeck 1930:41 ff.).

Drake returned to the Isthmus of Panamá in December 1595 and made an abortive attempt to cross it and take Panamá City. He retreated to Nombre de Dios after being badly beaten by Spanish forces in the hills of Capirilla at the battle of Fuerte San Pablo. After burning Nombre de Dios to the ground in January, Drake and his fleet made for Portobelo, where the great admiral died and was buried at sea on January 28, 1596 (Anderson 1911:370–372; Caro de Torres 1620:70–74). The site of his burial (in a lead-sheathed casket) has yet to be discovered but is still a notable and sought-after part of the maritime cultural landscape of Panamá.[2]

Constant War

From the time England took control of the island of Jamaica from the Spanish Crown in 1655, the relationship between the two countries and their respective Caribbean colonies remained contentious. England utilized bands of privateers to protect its burgeoning island colony from the continuous threats of Spanish reprisal. During this period, Captain Henry Morgan emerged as one of the most profitable privateers in the region, establishing a rapport with both the local authorities and officials back in England. From 1664 to 1670, Morgan led daring raids throughout the Spanish Main, including major incursions on Villahermosa, Mexico; Trujillo, Honduras; Granada, Nicaragua; Puerto Príncipe, Cuba; Portobelo, Panamá; and Maracaibo, Venezuela. These raids generated riches for the privateers while exposing the fragility of the Spanish Empire in the New World.

Morgan's raid on Portobelo came as part of a larger attack on Spanish shipping and ports in the Caribbean. Initially equipped with a fleet of 10 ships and 500 privateers, Morgan set out for Cuba, raiding and eventually seizing Puerto Príncipe in March 1668. Even after losing nearly half his force, who left disappointed by their lack of plunder, Morgan nonetheless persevered, raising additional ships and men to resume his forays against Spanish commerce. Arriving off Costa Rica, Morgan announced that the fleet's target was Portobelo. Mindful of Drake's failure to capture the well-defended port in 1596, some of Morgan's fleet—mainly the French contingent—abandoned the venture. Morgan pressed on, aided by intelligence that the town was lightly defended. And in fact, Portobelo *was* poorly armed as the result of budget constraints and lethargy that had set in in the decades since the last freebooter had attempted to take it.

Instead of direct assault by the fleet, Morgan and his men approached the port in canoes. They landed three miles off the coast, hiked through the jungle, overpowered sentries, and took Portobelo on July 11, 1668. After ransacking the city in search of loot (but not finding much), Morgan settled there for two months but ultimately departed without completely destroying Portobelo. He received a ransom of 100,000 *reales* in exchange for departing and returning the city to the Spanish. This was a lesser sum than originally sought, but in the face of disease and discomfort, the inadequate amount was accepted (Talty 2005; Earle 1981). The ransom, loot, merchandise, and slaves added to a total take of some 215,000 pesos, which enriched Morgan and his men and allowed them to return home heroes for having taken the "impregnable" Portobelo (Earle 1981:77, 79; for a description of its military defensive complex see Castillero 2004f and especially Alba and Trute 2003).

Morgan's Sack of Panamá, 1671

With his appetite for plunder stimulated and now conscious of the weakened state of the defenses on the Isthmus of Panamá, Morgan amassed a fleet of 36 vessels and 1,846 men in 1670. It was the largest fleet of privateers and pirates in the history of the Caribbean. Their target was one of the richest cities in the western hemisphere, situated in the heart of the Spanish colonies: Panamá City. Morgan's subsequent sacking of Panamá City not only served as a pirate victory but also dealt a blow that continued to loosen

Spain's grip on the New World (for detailed accounts and analyses see Earle 1981; Exquemelin 1969; Castillero 2004g, 2006:961–998; 2014:19–36; Talty 2005).

After capturing Santa Catalina Island (modern-day Isla Providencia in Colombia) Morgan acquired more provisions before he dispatched 470 men in three ships under the command of Joseph Bradley. They were to take the Castillo de San Lorenzo, the guardian of the Río Chagres, "understanding ye Castle of Chagres blockt our way" (The National Archives of the United Kingdom [TNA], Colonial Office [CO] 1671: 1/26 no. 51, p. 140). After the capture of the Castillo de San Lorenzo, Morgan and the rest of his fleet arrived on January 12, 1671, "whereupon I gave orders for ye fleete to follow mee into ye harbour but had ye ill fortune to cast away ye ship that I was in and 4 more but saved ye men" (TNA CO 1671: 1/26 no. 51, p. 140). Morgan and his flagship, *Satisfaction*, were the first to run aground on Lajas Reef, hitting the landmass so hard that the force of the collision brought down the masts and yards and caused sailors to fall overboard into the sea (Exquemelin 1969). Three to four other vessels were also grounded before the rest of the fleet was warned to keep back from the reef. The ships caught on the reef "were shattered to pieces," as "the wind was blowing hard across the reef" (Earle 1981:182). While Morgan wrote that no one perished, historian Peter Earle writes that 10 men drowned, "the sea running very high," and the only woman in the fleet, a *bruja*, or witch, who Morgan kept with him, also drowned (Earle 1981:182).

Accounts vary on whether the stores of the ships were salvaged, but it is clear from the historical records that none of the vessels were ever seaworthy again. Morgan's flagship *Satisfaction* was originally a 14-gun French pirate ship from La Rochelle named *Le Cerf Volant* (TNA CO 1669: 1/33 no. 103a). Captured by one of Morgan's privateers, Edward Collier, with the ship *Oxford*, the vessel was taken to Port Royal, where it was added to Morgan's fleet and renamed *Satisfaction* (TNA CO 1669: 1/33 no. 103a). Following the explosion and sinking of *Oxford* off Isla Vaca (Ile a Vache) in 1669, *Satisfaction* sailed to Campeche. *Satisfaction* then spent 18 months at sea (TNA 1670: 1/25 no. 51), during which time Morgan attacked and took Maracaibo. Upon his return to Port Royal to rendezvous with the rest of the privateer fleet, Morgan designated *Satisfaction* as his flagship for the voyage to Panamá. At that time, *Satisfaction* was reported to weigh 120 tons and carry 22 guns, which was the largest in Morgan's fleet of 38 ships until the subsequent grounding.

After the capture of the Castillo de San Lorenzo, 200 of Morgan's men repaired and refortified the fort, while he salvaged what he could from the wrecks. Then he continued up the Río Chagres with the rest of his crew to attack and take control of Panamá. The force traveled light to quickly cross the isthmus and take the city by surprise (TNA CO 1/26, No. 51). In the meantime, news of the fall of San Lorenzo had already reached Panamá City. A small force of 150 men sent to ambush Morgan was overwhelmed by superior force and had to retreat. The invaders, however, faced a grueling hike in the heat, plagued by insects and hunger and traveling without many provisions (Exquemelin 1969). Every Spanish outpost they reached, including Venta de Cruces, was desolate or had been burned to the ground in order to hinder their advance. It was not until nine days after setting out from San Lorenzo that they finally stood on the mountains overlooking the Pacific and Panamá.

After slaughtering cattle for food, eating, and then resting, on the tenth day of their journey Morgan and his men advanced on Panamá. The city was in panic, with many inhabitants fleeing with their valuables, while ships in the harbor loaded up the riches of the city and set off to sea. A Spanish force of 1,200 men, led by the city's president, Don Juan Pérez de Guzmán, met the privateers in battle outside the city gate. Spanish cavalry attacks were hindered by swampy conditions, and Morgan, dividing his forces into three groups, met the Spanish charges with musket volleys.

The actual battle for Panamá City was short-lived: "After two hours' hard fighting, the Spanish cavalry were thoroughly routed; most were dead or wounded, and the rest had fled" (Exquemelin 1969:195). The Spanish infantry retreated, leaving some 600 men dead and Morgan unimpeded. Entering the city on January 28, 1671, the privateers took it within three hours of fighting—in the city streets, block by block, and in the trenches and barricades erected by the defenders. The hardest fight took place in Playa Prieta, the harbor of the town, where the locals tried to burn any remaining vessels to avoid seizure by the pirates. According to Morgan himself, his men had found only half as much treasure as they had seized earlier in Portobelo (Castillero 2006:981). Accounts vary as to who started it, but a fire raged through Panamá. Chronicler Exquemelin repeats a Spanish charge that Morgan and his men set it, but Morgan wrote that the retreating Spanish forces had set fire to parts of the city to impede his advance, a charge confirmed by local sources. Artillery Captain Baltasar de Pau y Rocaberti states that he was ordered by Don Juan Pérez de Guzmán to blow up the powder stores and set out barrels of gunpowder at strategic points in the city and then ignite them if the enemy entered (Castillero 2006:964). The city was not completely destroyed, since Morgan's men managed to keep the fire from spreading. Soon after the battle, Morgan and his men maintained control of the city for a month, all the while venturing into the countryside to rob refugees, take hostages for ransom, and raid the neighboring islands where fleeing Panameños had taken refuge with their treasure. Morgan was well aware that a greater force from stronger Spanish garrisons, either in Cartagena or Lima, would likely arrive to try and take back the city. So Morgan left with the equivalent of some £30,000 (or so he reported) as well as some 400 slaves to be sold for the benefit of the expedition on the return to Jamaica (Earle 1981:229–230).

On March 6, 1671, following Morgan's triumphant return from the Pacific, "Wee fired the Castle, spiked ye guns and begun our voyage for Jamaica" (TNA CO 1671: 1/26 no. 51, 142). Spanish prestige had taken another tremendous blow, and its control of the isthmus had not only been challenged but also temporarily interrupted. This was not forgotten, and in the aftermath of the sack of Panamá, the Spanish government took steps to reinforce its garrisons, build new fortifications, and relocate Panamá City to a new, more easily defended location in 1673 (Castillero 1999, 2014).

Seeking Archaeological Traces of Morgan in Panamá Viejo

Archaeological evidence of the events of 1671 remains elusive despite years of excavation. One possible trace emerged in the 1996 excavations of the area around the city's biggest plaza, the governmental and religious center of town. The most prominent ruin at the site facing the old plaza is the standing four-story bell tower of the Catedral de Nuestra Señora de la Asunción. Close to it, excavators encountered the ruins of the *cabildo* (city hall). The excavation revealed the remaining patterned stone floors (*canto rodado*) and the wall and column foundations of the original two-story masonry building. A flight of stone steps leading to an upper floor (later destroyed) was also discovered under modern levels (Brizuela 1996a, 1996b).

Upon removal of the steps for restoration, the fill of the structure was revealed, and a rich collection of "sealed" material came to light, possibly from the 1640s when the stairway was originally built or perhaps from the last construction phase of the building. On these steps, a stratum of soil, ash, bricks, broken roof tiles, and iron nails from the destroyed upper portion of the building overlay a thick pocket of ash. This deposit and an iron sword found in the level with the ash, as well as foremarked masonry flooring and segments of the surviving wall, point to the last days of Spanish oc

Figure 36. Excavations of the Panamá Cabildo at the base of the iconic bell tower yielded the only possible archaeological evidence of the destruction of the city during Morgan's raid. Reproduced by permission of Patronato Panamá Viejo.

cupation when Morgan's pirates overran the city's defenses and the *cabildo* and other buildings were torched.

After fifteen years of continuous archaeological excavation, the *cabildo* site remains the only direct evidence of the events of January 1671 in Panamá Viejo. The lack of evidence of fire destroying other areas has been noted in excavations of private homes on the western side of the plaza (Mendizábal 1996), where ash-free strata intermixed with roof-tile fragments and nails have been found without ash directly overlaying unmarked

Figure 37. A sword uncovered during the excavations of the Cabildo may also date to Morgan's raid and the destruction of the old city. Photograph by Tomás Mendizábal, reproduced with permission from Patronato Panamá Viejo.

cobblestone floors. Excavation of the houses of the Terrin family at the north end of the plaza in 1997 also found no trace of fire, only evidence of abandonment and collapse (Mendizábal 1997). The fire may have only been confined to the *cabildo* and cathedral, places that were highly symbolic and seen in the bell tower's status as the tallest structure in the city and a strategically vulnerable spot. With no archaeological evidence of a widespread fire, archaeological findings at Panamá Viejo may tell us that Morgan's account of his men fighting fires set by retreating Spanish forces

Figure 38. Traces of fire on the excavated steps of the Cabildo. Reproduced by permission of Patronato Panamá Viejo.

was accurate: any suggestion that Morgan burned down the entire city was a gross exaggeration.

Archaeological Evidence of Morgan at the Río Chagres

The waters off the Castillo de San Lorenzo, as well as the associated land sites, have attracted professional archaeological attention as well as interest from treasure hunters. A 1993 report by Dr. Kathleen Deagan of the University of Florida outlined a recommended archaeological plan of action for San Lorenzo (Deagan 1993). Another assessment (Lange 1999) recommended archaeological excavations in and around the fort and exploration of the coastal waters and the waters of the Río Chagres near the fort.

In 2003 a permit was issued by the Panamanian Ministry of Economy and Finance for underwater survey and commercial recovery of shipwrecks in the vicinity: as of this writing, this permit has not yet been put to use in the area.[3] In addition to previously authorized recovery attempts, much unauthorized activity has reportedly taken place. This ranges from casual recovery of artifacts during the American occupation of the site as part of Fort Sherman (1909–1999), to more recent activities that have resulted in private collections such as Internet-advertised sales of materials apparently illicitly taken from the waters off San Lorenzo.

Treasure hunter Robert F. Marx reported in 2004 that he had discovered the remains of Morgan's ships in 1954 and had recovered materials from them. However, in 1970 he returned to find the wrecks had been removed.

> In 1954, when I was a diver and salvage expert in the U.S. Marine Corps, I was in Panamá for a short time and looked for the *Oxford*. I had, as a guide, a copy of an old manuscript with a chart showing the position where all five of Morgan's ships were wrecked in 1670. The reef, with waves breaking over it, was easy to find and so were vestiges of the pirate wrecks embedded in it. . . . I spent an exciting five days digging in the reef and discovered many artifacts from Morgan's ships. . . . Eighteen years passed before I was able to return to Panamá with a salvage vessel to explore Morgan's wrecks further. Anticipation turned to disillusionment when I found nothing but deep holes in the coral reef where salvors had used explosives to dislodge the cannon and anchors. (Marx 2004:136)

Reports and discussions with locals document the removal of a large number of artifacts from the waters off the Castillo de San Lorenzo and

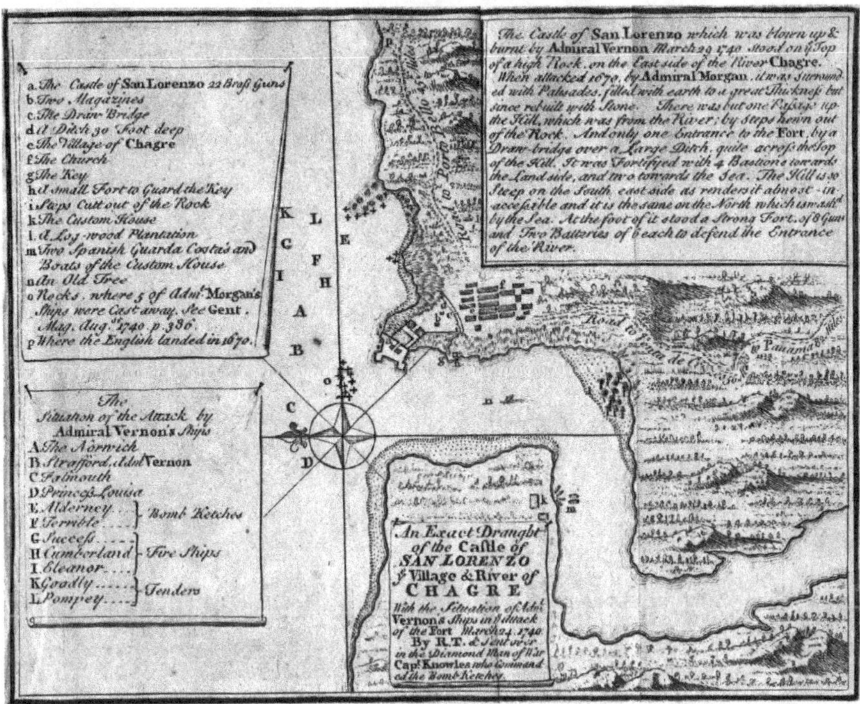

Figure 39. A number of elements in the maritime cultural landscape of the mouth of the Río Chagres are illustrated in this eighteenth-century map from Vernon's 1740 attack. The fort, settlement, and anchorage are noted, as is Lajas Reef, the site of the wreck of several of Morgan's ships in 1671. *An Exact Draught of the Castle of San Lorenzo, the Village and River of Chagres*, originally published in *Gentleman's Magazine*, August 1740. James P. Delgado collection.

taken abroad for sale to collectors. Discussions with local residents confirmed that materials including bottles, ceramics, and coins were recovered from the beaches and shallow waters off the Castillo and Chagres town sites during the period of the American military occupation, especially after the introduction of scuba diving in the 1950s.

In 2008 a collaborative effort between the Institute of Nautical Archaeology and the Waitt Institute for Discovery resulted in the first-ever archaeological reconnaissance and survey of the submerged cultural resources in the mouth of the Río Chagres and its approaches. The 2008 survey located and documented numerous artifacts, including eight cannon that could be from Henry Morgan's ships that wrecked on Lajas Reef in 1671 (Delgado et al. 2009; Hanselmann et al. 2010).

During dives on Lajas Reef, a number of areas were observed where the reef surface had been subjected to fairly recent blasting and digging. The

Figure 40. An in situ image of one of several iron cannon discovered on and adjacent to Lajas Reef from the 1671 wrecks of Henry Morgan's attacking fleet, a significant element of the maritime cultural landscape and significant maritime archaeological sites. The guns were archaeologically recovered and are undergoing conservation at Panamá Viejo prior to museum display. Photograph by Frederick Hanselmann.

extensive nature of the destruction to some of these areas confirms accounts of treasure-hunting activities here and hints at still-undetermined damage to the archaeological sites of the apparent sixteenth- to seventeenth-century shipwrecks on and near the reef. The reef may have had yielded smaller iron artifacts, and tight crevices between rocks may have hosted deposits of smaller artifacts. There may have been additional cannon exposed on the reef, as suggested by the accounts of the various treasure hunters. The survival of the iron guns and the anchor on the reef is not surprising. Although they have considerable cultural value, conservation of these items is expensive and they are difficult to sell. Furthermore, many treasure hunters ignore large iron artifacts.

What this reef damage indicates in regard to the wreck of *Satisfaction* or other wrecks on Lajas Reef is that accounts of the presence of these vessels and the recovery of artifacts from them is accurate and that there has been considerable disturbance to these sites. However, the exposed artifacts and a cluster of magnetic anomalies in the sand at the southwest end of the reef, in close proximity to the exposed cannon noted during the survey of 2008, indicate that a shipwreck (or wrecks) probably remains just off the reef. As noted in the final report on the 2008 survey, "Given the temporal range of the guns, it is also likely that the wreck is a contemporary (seventeenth century) vessel and therefore could represent the wreckage of one or more of the ships from Henry Morgan's fleet" (Delgado et al. 2009:52). The final survey report recommended the immediate recovery of the guns on the reef due to a recent history of looting, salvaging, and weather-related site alterations (Delgado et al. 2009:74). In 2010 an excavation permit was issued in order to recover the guns from the reef. That work was carried out in the same year, again with the support of the Waitt Institute (Hanselmann et al. 2010).

Although in 2010 eight cannon were initially located, only six were found and recovered, and these were immediately placed in passive desalination tanks provided courtesy of the Smithsonian Tropical Research Institute (STRI). And as of this writing these cannon are at the conservation laboratory of the Patronato de Panamá Viejo, where conservators Jacinto Almendra, Marcelina Godoy and team have commenced the cleaning and analyzing of the guns. During this process, with the assistance of cannon scholar Ruth Brown (formerly with the Tower of London), what has begun to emerge is that these cannon are associated with Morgan's 1671 wrecks, either jettisoned on the reef or scattered on it during the wrecking itself (Hanselmann et al. 2016:157–160). While only eight guns were visible in 2008, other guns once observed are no longer present (Marx 2004:136). Additional cultural materials exerting a magnetic influence lie immediately inland on Lajas Reef and likely consist of a shipwreck and additional cannon buried beneath bottom sediments.

The initial characterization of the exposed (and recovered) guns, while at that time heavily concreted and with details obscured, was that they were small deck guns of the sixteenth to seventeenth centuries and likely breech-loading swivel guns firing ammunition that weighed less than a pound. Rail mounted, these were antipersonnel weapons that could be loaded with normal ammunition or grapeshot for close-quarter fighting. This style of weapon was developed in the sixteenth century and remained in use on both naval and merchant vessels through the seventeenth century. Although Lavery (1987) notes that these guns were obsolete on English vessels by the eighteenth century, the 1707 wreck of *Association* included French-manufactured guns of this type, indicating ongoing French use of

Figure 41. One of the Lajas Reef guns with concretions removed. Photograph by Jonathan Kingston, National Geographic Creative.

swivel guns (Lavery 1987:104). This type of gun reentered British service later in the eighteenth century (Lavery 1987:104). Tucker (1989) states that the typical swivel gun of the eighteenth century was usually between 34 and 36 inches in length, 1.5 to 1.75 inches in bore, and utilized shot that weighed either .50 or .75 pounds (Tucker 1989:98).

The guns from Lajas Reef fit within the previously mentioned ranges. Gun #2 is within a few inches of the normal-sized swivel gun but may be a slightly larger deck gun. The sizes and shapes of the other guns suggest smaller weapons, perhaps in the three-pounder range or less, and of types that in English use were termed "murderers," "minions," "falcons," "falconettes," and "port-pieces." These sixteenth- and seventeenth-century guns were considered obsolete by 1635 in England, although some may have stayed in use later into the century (Lavery 1987:103). Cannon numbers 1, 3, 6, and 8 all appear to be heavier guns that would have been in position on the gun deck, just below the main deck (Hanselmann et al. 2010, 2016).

Work on the guns had progressed by 2014 to reveal the details of three of the guns after the concretion covering them was removed. Two are falconets that exhibited markings that proved they were of English manufacture, and they date to the mid- to late seventeenth century (Brown 2012; Hanselmann et al. 2016). Another gun was found to be of French manufacture from the same period.

> Guns in these small calibers were cast in their hundreds for export and use by merchant ships from the late sixteenth century through

> to the early eighteenth century. They were the smallest, lightest and cheapest ordnance, were easy to move and took up the least space aboard ship. Their production and sales were less regulated by government regulations than the larger caliber guns. However they were always difficult to cast because of the problems of removing a core from such a small gun and they had poor rates of passing proof. (Brown 2012; Hanselmann et al. 2016)

The mix of small guns found on the reef, in addition to the date and place of manufacture are what would be expected in a non-naval privateer or pirate fleet. A shipwreck from a naval force of any one nation would be characterized archaeologically by uniform gun types but of varying caliber. When a privately outfitted force arms itself for an attack, it would be expected that any and all weapons gathered through various means—including those of different sizes, places of manufacture, and even different and, at times, divergent periods of manufacture—would be assembled.

The small size of the three guns[4] thus far treated suggests that they were indeed deck mounted and perhaps even bulwark mounted. Forged iron rings around the cascabel of one of the falconets indicates it carried a yoke so that a gunner could swivel, aim, and then fire. Interestingly, the gun is still loaded with a cannonball in the muzzle and, as the deconcretion commenced, a fabric sash or belt was found wrapped around the gun, covering the wick. This, on examination, would be something usually found with a fleet of vessels coming into an ostensibly hostile environment (the Chagres, in this case) and past a Spanish fort that may or may not have been completely subdued.

The small size of the guns, as opposed to larger weapons, may support the hypothesis that the deck guns were thrown overboard to lighten the ship as *Satisfaction* struck Lajas Reef. Conversely, they could have been mounted on the upper deck and thrown overboard because of the collision with the reef. However, extensive looting and loss of other guns to parties unknown and the resultant damage to the archaeological record make it difficult to offer these scenarios as anything more than a possibility. What is clear—despite the ravages of looters, treasure hunters, and souvenir collectors—is that these guns (and what lies buried nearby) are direct archaeological evidence of Henry Morgan's 1671 attack (Hanselmann et al. 2010, 2016). Once treatment is complete, the guns will be exhibited in the museum of the Patronato Panamá Viejo.

The Scots at Darién, 1698–1700

Spurred by the accounts of Morgan and other adventurers, and bolstered by a sense of Spanish weakness, incursions by other buccaneers and "soldiers of fortune" continued in the aftermath of the destruction of Panamá City. In what became known as the "South Seas Expedition," in 1680 a force of 330 buccaneers, led by John Coxon, sacked Portobelo. Later, in an attempt to assault Panamá City, Bartholomew Sharp and his men crossed the isthmus that same year with the help of local natives, only to falter and fail due to illness, death, and desertion. However, Sharp and his men did block the port and raided towns and shipping in the vicinity (Marley 2010). Two of Sharp's crew, William Dampier and Lionel Wafer, published detailed accounts of their adventures. These journals joined those of other buccaneers who had operated with near impunity on the coast of the isthmus and also served to perpetuate the idea of the inadequacy of the colonial Spanish, as Patrick Chassé points out: "On the whole, buccaneering journals faithfully repeated the popular trope that the Spanish were incompetent sailors, their territories vulnerable to attack, and their dominions haunted by the spectre of Indian rebellion" (2005:12). This was not an inaccurate impression since Spanish dominions in the Americas were too vast and included too many large stretches of uncolonized lands to be effectively controlled.

A number of buccaneers, especially French buccaneers, hid and hunted in the San Blas archipelago off the Darién coast of the isthmus, which was the domain of the Guna people. The archipelago, with its 378 islands and cays, was a relatively safe haven. William Dampier, sailing through the archipelago in 1681, explained that his native guides

> told us that there had been a great many English and French ships here which were all gone but one *barcolongo*, a French privateer that lay at La Sounds Key or Island. This island is about 3 miles from the mouth of the river Concepción, and is one of the Samballoes, a range of islands reaching for about 20 leagues from Point Samballas to Golden Island eastward. These islands or keys, as we'll call them, were first made the rendezvous of privaters in the year 1679, being very convenient for careening, and had names given to some of them by captains of the privateers, as this La Sounds Key particularly. (Dampier 1699:22)

Dampier noted that while in the islands, at a site he called Springer's Key, eight privateer vessels lay at anchor: and from these the buccaneers launched regular raids with men in *canoas* on Spanish coastal shipping. They seized a small boat laden with flour at the mouth of the Chagres and took its crew hostage during Dampier's sojourn with them (Dampier 1699:26–27).

Dampier noted that another isolated archipelago, Bocas del Toro, a group of some 260 islands, islets, and cays further west (but like the San Blas also on the north coast of the isthmus) was another privateer haven and

> a place that the privateers use to resort to as much as any place on all the coast, because here is plenty of green tortoise, and a good careening place. The Indians here have no commerce with the Spaniards; but are very barbarous and will not be dealt with. They have destroyed many privateers, as they did not long after this to some of Captain Pain's men; who, having built a tent ashore to his goods in while he careen'd his ship, and some men lying in there with their arms, in the night the Indians crept softly into the tent, and cut off the heads of 3 or 4 men, and made their escape; nor was this the first time they had served the privateers so. (Dampier 1699:38)

The indigenous people of the Darién, having had good interactions with the English, and with an English sea captain having married into the community, proved to be friendlier than the Indians Dampier had previously encountered. Dampier reported that the people of the Darién had invited the privateers to cross through their territory between the seas, and in 1684–1685 a large number of them did so (Dampier 1699:197, 261). The location of the Darién made it the second most easily transited place on the isthmus other than the route between Portobelo and the Ciudad de Panamá. The Darién had been the site of the early settlement of Acla, deserted by the 1540s in the face of the rise of Panamá City and the city's control of its own transisthmian route.

It was through accounts like these that William Paterson, a Scottish emigrant to the Caribbean, learned of the Darién. Living in Port Royal, Jamaica, from 1673 to 1681, he would have heard much about the region, perhaps even from veterans of Morgan's and Sharp's assaults. Eager to capitalize on the Darién as an unguarded gateway to the Pacific, Paterson returned to Scotland and there, as well as in England, sought to raise money to build a colony on the Darién to serve as an entrepôt for transoceanic trade in direct competition to Spain's control of the isthmus. Paterson was unable to raise money in England because his scheme was a challenge not only to the Spanish, with whom the English were no longer at war, but also to the English-chartered and English-owned East India Company. So Paterson turned to his native Scotland, and there he found success. The Scottish Parliament chartered the Company of Scotland Trading to Africa and the Indies in 1695:[5]

> The interest of Scotland was the main purpose of the undertaking, and one of the conditions of the grant was that at least half of the stock was to be held by Scotchmen residing in Scotland, and that inalienably. The remaining half was to be allotted to Scotchmen residing either in Scotland or else-where or to foreigners. Many favorable conditions were granted to the company, and its officers were empowered to plant colonies in any parts of Asia, Africa, or America which were not possessed by any European power, and to which possession the natives did not object. The ships were to return with their cargoes to Scotland, without breaking bulk, on pain of forfeiture, and the company was to have the sole right of trading from Scotland to these three quarters of the globe, right of seizure and forfeiture being granted against all delinquents. (Parlane 1888:9)

The charter for global trade notwithstanding, the goal was the Darién. It was "the most famous isthmus in the World" (Parlane 1888:22). The transshipment of goods had been proven profitable to Spain, but "if it were possible to cut a channel from sea to sea, capable of shipping, it would facilitate the navigation of the world two parts in three, but it is next to an impossibility, for it is almost a continued chain of mountains, of which some are as high as any of the Alps" (Parlane 1888:22–23).

Having raised sufficient capital, the company ultimately sent two expeditions to the Darién between 1698 and 1700. The first, with five ships, left Leith on July 18, 1698, arriving on the isthmus on October 31 of the same year. Their destination was "Golden Island," a buccaneer outpost familiar to Dampier and others. It was known to the Spanish as the Isla de Oro and to the indigenous Guna as Sulatupo. Just past the island was a coastal inlet bordered by a narrow peninsula. Named Caledonia Bay by the colonists, this body of water is today known as Puerto Escocés (or "Scottish port"). This was to be the setting for New Edinburgh: much like the new name for the bay, Scotland's onamastic marks were appearing on the maritime landscape. A settlement arose, fortified at the entrance to the harbor by an earthwork battery named Fort St. Andrew. The climate proved deadly, however. And troubled by the loss of the first ship to attempt to trade, *St.*

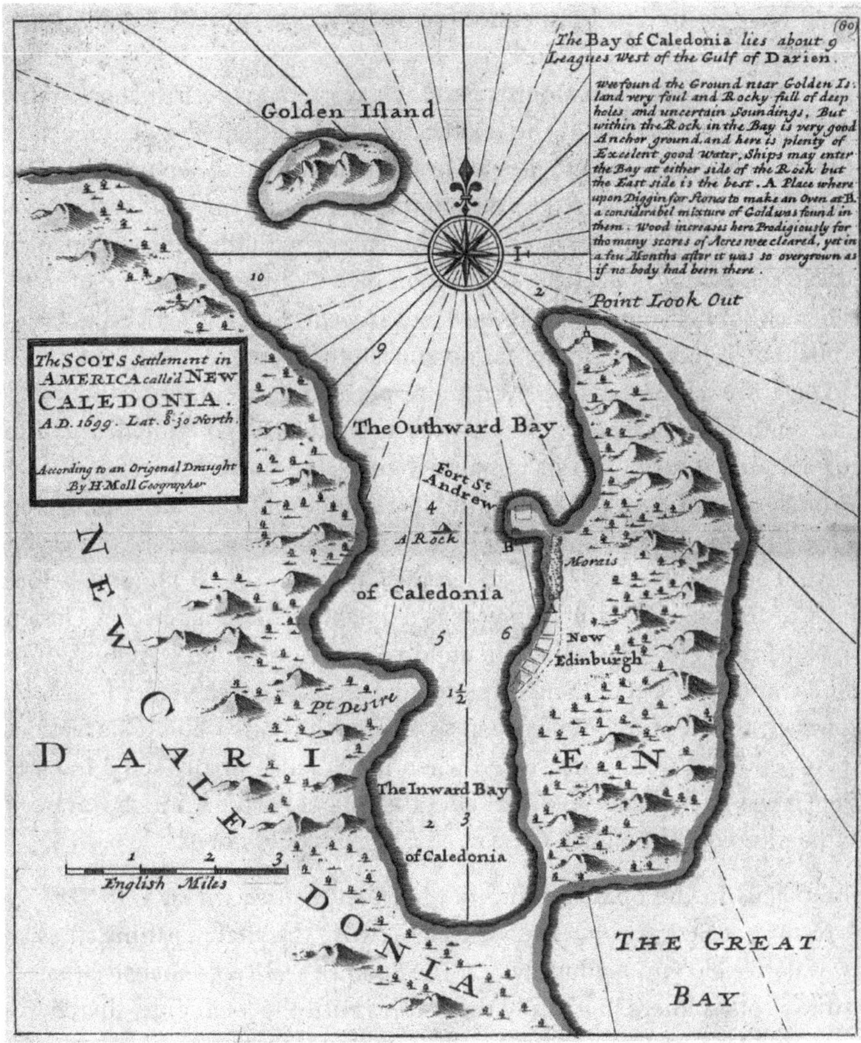

Figure 42. The ill-fated Scottish settlement of New Edinburgh at Darién is depicted in this eighteenth-century map. Although the archaeological traces of the settlement remain part of the landscape, the place names placed on the maritime cultural landscape have for the most part disappeared. *The Scotts Settlement in America Called New Caledonia*, Herman Moll, London 1729. David Rumsey Historic Map Collection, list 5580.060.

Antony,[6] the colony faltered. The fatal blow, however, came when the English Crown forbade its subjects to trade with the new colony, as they wanted to avoid another war with Spain. A series of royal proclamations issued in Jamaica, Bermuda, New York, and Boston in the summer of 1699 led officials to note that "his Majesty has of himself done all that the Spaniards could have desired of him, either for the preventing or defeating of this expedition (Chassé 2005:16).

On the isthmus, the colonists and their work fared poorly. Heavy rains eroded the earthworks of the fortifications; cleared areas faced constant reencroachment by the jungle; and fever, malaria, and dysentery led to increasing numbers of fatalities. Within months of arriving, half of the colonists were dead. In the face of these woes, along with the threat of Spanish attack, the colonists decided to abandon New Edinburgh in June of 1699. When two relief ships, *Olive Branch* and *Hopeful Binning*, arrived in Caledonia Bay in July 1699, there was no one left to rescue.

Olive Branch became an even more permanent element of the maritime cultural landscape when spilt brandy from its cargo ignited. The ship burned until it sank, and its remains were visible above the water when a second group of colonists arrived at New Edinburgh. They also discovered some 400 graves amid a number of disintegrating huts. The second group of 1,300 colonists and sailors had left the Clyde on August 18, 1699, before news of the failure of the colony reached Scotland and arrived in Darién on November 30. They settled in, building new houses and warehouses for goods, and they strengthened the fortifications. Like their predecessors, however, the new colonists began to suffer from disease and starvation. Their problems were exacerbated when the Spanish finally acted in early 1700. It was after all, only 30 years after the sack of Panamá, which was fresh in the mind of the Spanish Crown. As Chassé (2005) notes,

> Officials in the Spanish Empire took the Scottish threat very seriously. The Scots colony was wedged between the vital maritime cities of Portobelo and Cartagena. . . . The Spanish were apprehensive that the Scots soldiers might ally themselves with the local Tule, thereby yoking local aboriginal discontent to the resources and ambitions of a European nation. Moreover, Spanish officials feared that this allegiance would allow the Scots to improve upon the example set by the buccaneers during the 1680s. (Chasse 2005:18)

An earlier attack by Spanish land and sea forces in February 1699 had been routed by 170 Scottish troops in the colony. A year later, Spanish officials took no chances. A 1,600-strong force landed on the peninsula in February, and their ships blockaded the harbor. Initially routed, the Spanish troops did not retreat: within days they had encircled the colony to begin a protracted two-month siege. The Scots, along with some eighty Guna warriors, dug into Fort St. Andrew, adding colonists to their ranks as they expanded the defensive perimeter.

Weakened by disease and facing up to sixteen fatalities a day (Parlane 1888:38), the Scots refused the demands of the Spanish commander, the governor of Cartagena Juan Díaz Pimienta, and told him during negotiations that they were all prepared to die to uphold their honor (Chasse 2005:19). Impressed, Pimienta agreed to a ceasefire and gracious terms of capitulation for the Scots:

> The Spanish general did not exact hard terms; all he wanted was to get the colonists away as quickly as possible. The guns and most of the ammunition were given up to him, and there was a provision made that any reliefs arriving in the course of two months should be allowed to wood and water, and then depart in peace. (Parlane 1888:39)

Gathering the survivors and what supplies they could, the Scots sailed from the Darién on April 12, 1700. Most of them never reached home: they became the victims of shipwrecks en route, which left them stranded far afield. The failure of the Darién colony was an unmitigated disaster: it suffered a loss of nearly £400,000 while nearly 1,500 out of 2,800 colonists died. The colony also saw the abandonment, capture, or wrecking of 11 of the 14 ships[7] involved in the venture (Horton 2009:131). The economic blow to Scotland was such that historians consider it to be a causal factor in the Scottish union with England in 1707 to form Great Britain (Prebble 1968:313–314).

Archaeological Traces of the Darién Colony

The site of the ill-fated colony was not forgotten. Spain, changed the name of the bay to Puerto Escocés while the Guna temporarily occupied the site and removed one of the cannon from the abandoned fort. This cannon is now displayed in the village square at Mulatupu (Horton 2009:146). Archaeological investigation at the site began in 1979, when archaeologist Mark Horton (1979) surveyed it. Horton's work was part of Operation Drake (Blashford-Snell 1981), a British youth leadership initiative that conducted excavations at the site of the Scottish Fort St. Andrew and the Spanish siege camp. Operation Drake also was responsible for locating and investigating the wreck of *Olive Branch* in the bay. These efforts were followed up in 1985 in a second expedition called Operation Raleigh (Higgins 1986).

After locating magnetic anomalies with a proton magnetometer, probe surveys and trenches revealed evidence of a ship structure over an area 30 m x 10 m, oriented north to south. Removal of sediments revealed ship's timbers (some joined together), including part of a rudder, under a considerable depth of mud. There was evidence of fire damage in both the hull and deck timbers. The most diagnostic finds were clay pipes that had identical stamps and form to those found in the excavations at Fort St. Andrew. The excavation raised a cannon and, from a hull deeply buried in silt, recovered "iron objects, lead piping, stoneware, slate, Scottish clay pipes," and a large quantity of animal bone, "possibly [from] salt beef that was stored in barrels" (Horton 1979:11). All these artifacts were taken to the Museo del Hombre Panameño in Panamá City.

The remains of *Olive Branch* are of particular interest: the ship's manifest survives, as do the receipts for the supplies of the various commodities. This allowed for a correlation between the archaeological and documentary evidence (see Horton 1979:10–11; Horton 2009:134,145). The ship was armed with 14 cannon and was practically rebuilt for this voyage. She had a crew of 32, including Captain William Jameson, and a complement of 21 land officers, soldiers, and tradesmen. The cargo included much flour in addition to cartridge paper, weapons, medicaments, garden seeds and candles, four pipes for tobacco, as well as the tobacco itself, and other stores packed in barrels. Horton thought the site had potential, saying that the ship's structure may partially be intact. The stores packed in the lower decks may be in position, but it is not known what kind of attempt was made to salvage the wreck (Horton 1979:11).

Horton returned to the site in 2003 as part of a television documentary that supported more extensive survey and test excavations: he worked together with a team of young archaeologists and Panamanian government officials that included Mendizábal (2003). Horton was surprised by the survival of a more extensive archaeological record than one might imagine in an aggressive jungle environment and for a colony that was only around for twelve months (Horton 2009:135).

Horton was particularly interested in assessing the failure of the colony within the context of its setting, as few firsthand accounts survived from the colony that documented the colonists' experiences. There were detailed records, however, of materials shipped, including the previously mentioned manifests of ships like *Olive Branch*. Archaeology "provides the geography in which to understand the documentary record . . . the archaeological approach is based on understanding the whole landscape of the Scots colony"

(Horton 2009:134). Horton realized that the success of the colony outside of political forces (that is, the English Crown's blocking of support) also depended on local factors, namely the colony's interactions with the environment, the indigenous population, and the Spanish (Horton 2009:135).

Horton's excavations outlined the fortifications, located surviving postholes from structures at New Edinburgh and inside the fort, representing the second colony's last stand. Horton also uncovered the remains of what may have been the two warehouses constructed in late 1699, with associated trade goods such as brandy bottles and beads, a unique and evocative personal object, a portable bronze sundial as well as twenty dress buckles, a bronze bowl stamped "Nurnberg," and a [silver?] coin dated 1693[8] (Horton 2009:144; Mendizábal 2003). A substantial quantity of clay pipes was also excavated, as they had been left over from the wreck (Horton et al. 1987; Horton 2009:143).

A range of ceramics was also recovered, most of them being Spanish olive jars and majolicas as well as indigenous pre-Columbian-style pottery that indicates either earlier settlement or reuse by the Scots of ancient pottery. These were attributed both to the Spanish occupation of the site after the Scottish withdrawal in April 1700 as well as to post-abandonment occupation by the Guna. Horton believes that the Spanish occupation "may have lasted less than a year," leaving the site to the Guna, who "presumably [took] advantage of the cleared ground" for agricultural purposes and then abandoned it to clear and work new areas to maintain a sustainable crop yield (Horton 2009:149). The excavations also yielded twelve sherds of Scottish pottery, sherds of German Westerwald and Frechen stoneware, and a sherd of Staffordshire trailed slipware (Horton 2009:144).

In assessing the failure of how the "dream of a Scottish Central American entrepôt never came close to fruition," Horton claimed that although the interactions with the Guna were cooperative and friendly, the fear of Spanish intervention led to desperate efforts to fortify and defend the colony at the expense of more permanent dwellings. However and more importantly, defensive work in response to fears of the Spanish was detrimental to maintaining the "fields and plantations that would have enabled them to survive" (Horton 2009:149). This led to food shortages. As Horton notes, "archaeological evidence of only rare bone-finds from occupation levels, despite the quantities of salt beef on board the ships" indicates that such shortages were "a constant problem" (2009:149). Furthermore, no effort was spent in overland exploration or in reaching the Pacific shores of the isthmus. The selection of the harbor itself was a mistake; it was narrow, easily blockaded, and it proved difficult to navigate as the loss of *St. Antony* on the first trade mission to New Edinburgh indicated. Although a part of the maritime cultural landscape that represents a colonial challenge to Spanish control, the Darién colony is also an example, like Nombre de Dios before, that European-imposed settlements on the isthmus did not work as well as the longer-lasting (and still thriving) indigenous settlements in the same landscape.

The Landscape of Response: New Forts and a New Ciudad de Panamá

Also known as the Casco Antiguo or Casco Viejo, the resettled Panamá City was founded in 1672 under the guidance of a new president, Antonio Fernández de Córdoba, following a vote on October 24 of that year to relocate the city to a point some six miles to the southwest of the original city to a hill known as the Cerro del Ancón. This spot was also closer to the better anchorage off Isla Perico. The new site was a rocky peninsula (or *ancon*), surrounded on three sides by the bay that could be more easily defended, especially when at low tide the seas withdraw at least one mile to expose the entire rocky base, which made amphibious assaults nearly impossible (See Castillero 1994, 1999, 2014; Tejeira 2001, 2013). Work began on a series of bastions and a wall that would surround the city on all sides (seafront and landfront). This project would be in addition to new fortifications at Portobelo and at the mouth of the Chagres with the new Castillo de San Lorenzo. The Castillo had a lower gun platform and an upper walled castle. Protected from land assault by a stone hornwork, it was now "one of the strongest in the Indies" (Castillero 2004f; Ward 1993:176; Zapatero 1985). A stronger coastal naval force was also created (Ward 1993:175).

Orthogonal in form, the stone walls of the Casco Viejo encompassed an urban grid layout of streets surrounding a central plaza, in which about 300 lots were handed out, which was a number very similar to the amount of white families that had survived after Morgan's attack. Inside, only the rich, the church, and the government would enjoy the best protection. For the walls had not only the purpose of defending the city against foreign attack but also would defend against local internal revolts by the poor, nonwhite population (who were always in the majority). Thus the social barriers between the haves and the have-nots, between white Spanish and nonwhites, took on a physical expression through the city walls. The division became so pronounced that society became almost formally divided into "the insiders" and "the outsiders" (or *los de adentro* and *los de afuera*) (Castillero

Figure 43. The Ciudad de Panamá as relocated to its second (modern) site in 1673. *Plano de la Ciudad de Panamá*, 1673, Archivo General de Indias, Seville, Spain. Tomás Mendizábal Collection.

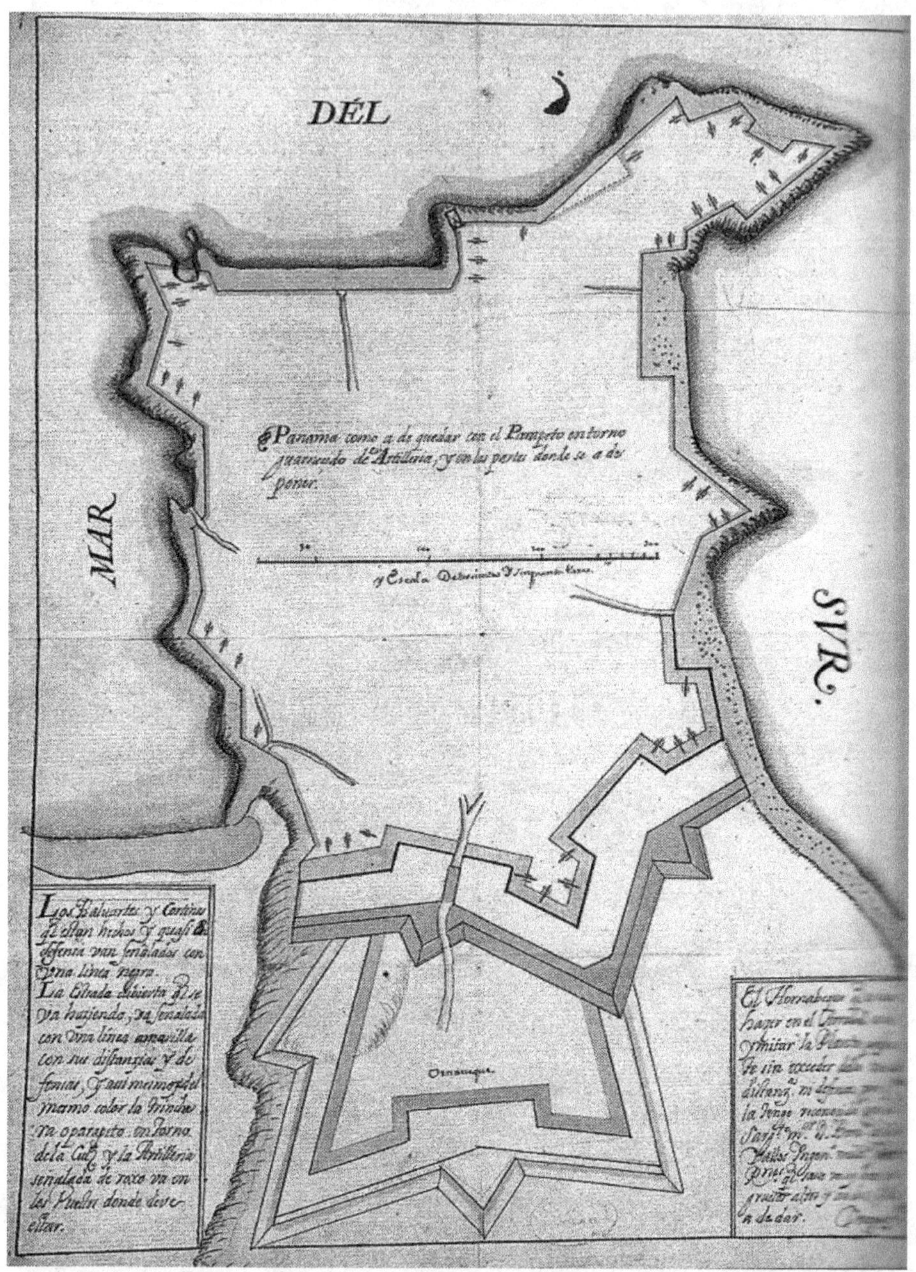

Figure 44. The Ciudad de Panamá's fortifications as drawn by Luis Veñegas Osorío, 1680. Archivo General de Indias, Seville, Spain. Tomás Mendizábal Collection.

1994:204). The formidable defenses of the new city comprised a wall on the three sides of the seafront and a landfront (Frente de Tierra) that included a wall with bastions (armed with artillery) and gates, a moat, a counterwall that ringed the moat, and an esplanade or no-man's land where building was forbidden. The esplanade served as a buffer zone between the defenses and the suburbs and allowed for an unimpeded view and clear shots from the walls (Castillero 1999:43–47; 2014:59–101).

Therefore, the suburb for "the outsiders," called Santa Ana, lay outside the perimeter of the walls and the esplanade (or no-man's land) around them, which was an "arquebus shot away" (Castillero 1999:47). This suburb was irregularly laid out and, for a time, it was forbidden to build masonry buildings in order to prevent possible assailants from converting them into defensible positions to attack the city (Castillero 1999:43–47).

Construction began on the walls in 1672 under the direction of the Royal Engineers, and they were officially completed in the 1680s. However, the poor quality of the work and changes in design and layout meant that the construction was never fully completed until the 1790s. The defenses were so formidable that they effectively discouraged any attacks on the walled city. By 1856, the feared attack had still not taken place, and the National Assembly of Colombia (of which Panamá was a part) deemed the defenses unnecessary and had the landward wall defenses demolished and the land sold for real estate (Castillero 2014:59–101).

William Dampier described the city in 1684:

> New Panamá is a very fair city, standing close by the sea, about four miles from the ruins of the old town. . . . It is encompassed on the backside with a pleasant country, which is full of small hills and valleys, beautified with many groves and spots of trees that appear in the savannahs like so many little islands. This city is all compassed with a high stone wall; the houses are said to be of brick. Their roofs appear higher than the top of the city wall. It is beautified with a great many fair churches and religious houses besides the president's house and other eminent buildings; which altogether make one of the finest objects that I did ever see, in America especially. There are a great many guns on her walls, most of which look toward the land. They had none at all against the sea when I first entered those seas with Captain Sawkins, Captain Coxon, Captain Sharp, and others; for till then they did not fear any enemy by sea: but since that they have planted guns clear round. (Dampier 1699:178–179)

The move was expensive and involved the construction of new and more elaborate public and religious buildings, including convents, cathedrals, and the houses for the elite. Most of these structures were made of masonry (Castillero 2004g:351–356; Castillero 2004h; Castillero 2014:219–270). Archaeological, architectural, and historical evidence shows that residents removed stone and other materials from Panamá Viejo to the new site. However, in the eighteenth century the closed quarters of the walled compound would fall prey to catastrophic fires, which laid waste to most of the settlement. The Big Fire of 1737 destroyed 95 percent of the buildings, followed by the fires of 1756 and 1781, which resulted in an urban space mostly consisting of vacant, overgrown lots (Castillero 2014:285–311). During the nineteenth century more conflagrations affected the city, but these were not as major although they were more frequent.

A number of landmark buildings from the mid-eighteenth century survive: these are mostly churches, the walls, and a few private residences, all of which maintain their ancient masonry structures hidden under more recent renovations and adornments. The Casco of the twenty-first century embodies an urban center that evolved through the eighteenth, nineteenth, and twentieth centuries. In fact, most of the buildings still standing today were erected or remodeled during the days of the French canal construction effort, which gave the city its present-day look.

Inscribed as a World Heritage Site by UNESCO in 1997, the Casco Antiguo is currently undergoing considerable redevelopment and renovation (Martín and Mendizábal 2009) with a concomitant gentrification process (Espino 2009; Tejeira 2001, 2013). It is also at the center of a heritage controversy, as UNESCO is in the process of deciding whether the property remains on the World Heritage Site list. UNESCO responded to concerns over a lack of planning as well as to the 2014 construction of the highway viaduct of the Cinta Costera Phase III, which rings the historic city and compromises the integrity of its setting (see Osorio 2012).[9]

The Archaeology of the Casco Viejo

Initial archaeological work in the Casco Viejo dates to the last quarter of the twentieth century. In the 1980s a project to restore certain prominent sections of the Casco Antiguo took place in which excavations were carried out at the ruins of the Convent of Santo Domingo, the Jesuit Convent, and the area around Las Bovedas (Vaults) of the Plaza de Francia. At Santo Domingo and the Jesuit complex, investigations uncovered structural remains and thousands of artifacts that documented changing social and economic conditions, the "demise of the peninsular trade monopoly, the Industrial Revolution," and international rivalry in the postcolonial period (Cooke and Rovira 1983:52–53).

Beginning in the first decade of the twenty-first century, and due to the establishment of new legislation, cultural resource management and salvage archaeology investigations have taken place in the midst of the real estate boom of Panamá City (Martín and Mendizábal 2009). As the Casco Antiguo is a protected area, the law states that every restoration project for properties in the area must be complemented by an archaeological excavation. In the last decade, this has led to an extensive documentation of the urban archaeology, especially of the interior or walled city.

Most of these excavations take place in residential buildings, offering a glimpse into the material culture and way of life of the city's ancient inhabitants. One notable case reported in 2012 was one in which excavations were carried out in advance of the restoration project of La Casa de Rosa. This excavation project uncovered a massive masonry foundation near the edifice's façade. The structure proved to be a fragment of a wall that ran in a northwest-southeast direction and was similar in form and manufacture to the ancient defensive wall of the city. Due to its location, constructive technique, sheer size and volume, alignment and associated material culture, the excavators believe it represents the remains of a new hornwork for the land front of defensive walls proposed by Spanish military engineer Manuel Hernández in 1765. No material evidence of this project had been found until the excavation, which was unexpected as available historical documentation indicates that it was never finished (Mendizábal and Martín 2012:55). In other instances public or public-use buildings have also been explored, in some cases repeatedly, like the Metropolitan Cathedral (Martín and Mendizábal 2010), the church of Santo Domingo, the Jesuit Convent (Mendizábal and Martín 2013), the church of La Merced, and also the famous Hotel Central.

More important, all these excavations generate reports submitted to the authorities while adding to collections of excavated materials, which are slowly but surely building up in local museums' storage facilities. These reports (gray literature) are most often descriptive, and their material analyses are mostly counts and proportions. But taken together, these contextualized collections constitute future resources for myriad studies on the material culture of the last three centuries of Panamanian history, studies that can begin with a comparison of the changes in that material culture between the old and new cities. Other interesting subjects for study would be the building of a ceramic taxonomy and chronology of Criolla Ware (also known as Loza de Tierra) and the domestic use of ordinary pottery found in large quantities in the colonial period from the sixteenth to the early twentieth century. Faunal assemblages are also being collected and studied, complementing historical sources on the gastronomical history of Panamá (Castillero 2010).

5

The Isthmus in "Decline," 1739–1848

The late eighteenth and early nineteenth centuries saw the decline of Spain's treasure fleets and their eventual abandonment of the isthmian route. With this, Panamá was relegated to lesser status in the waning period of the Spanish Empire. This did not stop the development of a major new series of fortifications in response to growing interest and challenges from Great Britain, and the landscape includes sites where British attacks in the mid-eighteenth century destroyed older fortifications that were then replaced by new forts—all of which continue to stand in the twenty-first century.

Unfortunately a detailed assessment of every local port on both shores—and each port's own particular maritime cultural landscape—is beyond the scope of this book. However, the maritime cultural landscape of the Chagres is analyzed here as a microcosm of the larger isthmian landscape during this period of change. It was around this time that centuries of Spanish trade and domination came to an end and when other major powers, especially those vying for economic opportunity and control of global patterns of shipping, began to take an economic interest in Panamá: Britain, France, and the then-new nation of the United States all saw Panamá as a vital link between the Pacific and Caribbean if trade were revived via the isthmus.

Decline of the *Trajín*

The period from 1681 to 1739 has been marked by historians as the time of the "final collapse" of regular transisthmian trade (also known as "el trajín" [the toils]) and use of the Tierra Firme fleet (Ward 1993:152), although its deterioration was evident at least as early as 1654 (Castillero 2004j; 2008:144–155). The attacks of the buccaneers played a role, as did contraband trade with the English: this was a threat to Spanish economic control of trade that intensified in opposition to high taxes and resulting high prices for goods.

In 1680 royal permission for Portobelo to join Havana and Cartagena in open slave trading with Jamaica opened the door for widespread smuggling. With the English shipments of slaves "came hundreds of thousands of pesos worth of cheap European goods . . . given these circumstances, there was really no hope for resurrection of the carrera of old" (Ward 1993:152).

The number and quality of the trade fairs at Portobelo began to falter in the mid-seventeenth century. Demand from Peru slipped as overland routes through the Andes and up rivers, coupled with easier access to cheaper goods, saw ebbing Peruvian demand for the goods at each *feria* (Ward 1993:153). Trade fairs were held at Portobelo in 1682, 1686, 1691, and 1698, and after that "what was left of the already failed fleet system began to break down rapidly" (Ward 1993:153). Fairs took place in 1708, 1713–1714, 1722, and 1726, with the last one in 1731. The planned 1739 fair was canceled due to the War of Jenkins' Ear—a marked departure from the heyday of the route with more or less annual arrivals of the Tierra Firme fleet (Castillero 2008:148). The restrictive trade regulations and high duties that allowed Spain to monopolize commerce with its colonies encouraged the contraband trade, one of the many factors along with piracy and constant war that doomed the Tierra Firme fleet system, which was canceled by royal order in 1754. In 1778 the monopoly system was relaxed by Spain's new royal house, the Bourbons; however, the changes came too late (Castillero 2008:154).

The flourishing of a black market through contraband trade was aided by official indifference and corruption as well as by the nature of the maritime landscape, which aided smuggling to various coves and harbors that had also served as bases for the buccaneers (Jaén Suárez 1998:300–303). Spain's imperial weaknesses were exacerbated by problems in Europe. The death in November 1700 of the last Hapsburg ruler of Spain, the weak and ineffectual Carlos II, and his designation of his French grand-nephew, Philip of Anjou, as his heir led to more than a decade of global war. A so-called grand alliance, which included England, fought to keep the French from gaining a political foothold in Spain. The War of the Spanish Succession ended in 1713 with the Treaty of Utrecht, signed on March 23, 1713, in which Philip kept his new throne and renounced any claim to the French Crown and Spain made humiliating concessions to the British, including the ceding of Spanish territories in Italy to Austria, the relinquishment of Gibraltar to England, and the granting of the *asiento*, which gave Britain exclusive rights to trade slaves in the Spanish colonies (Castillero 2008:151).

The *asiento* granted Britain's South Sea Company (The Governor and

Company of the Merchants of Great Britain, Trading to the South Seas and other parts of America, and for the Encouragement of Fishing) the right to enter into trade with Spain, supplying its American colonies with 4,800 slaves per year and launching a single voyage each year with a ship. This was known as the annual *Navío de Permiso*, which brought 500 tons of duty-free merchandise to the *ferias* of Cartagena, Portobelo, and Vera Cruz.

Portobelo was selected as one of the ports, and it was the only isthmian port to participate in the *asiento* trade (Castillero 2004d:468–472; 2008:151–152). *Asientos* were nothing new to Spain or the colonies. The Spanish Crown had granted *asientos* to bring slaves to the New World starting in 1528, and after 1601 foreigners were allowed to participate (Sorsby 1975:7). What the *asiento* of 1713 did was facilitate widespread British access and smuggling from Jamaica. The arrival of a British ship *Royal George* (*Real Jorge*) at Portobelo undercut the Spanish merchants and their higher-priced merchandise and ultimately led to the collapse of the trade fair system.

Illicit trade between English slavers and merchants and the isthmus predated 1713, and it utilized the same rendezvous points favored by buccaneers, privateers, and British entrepreneurs who illegally logged the isthmus' logwood, a valuable trade commodity. Logwood (*Haematoxylon campechianum*) is a native tree that was used to make purple textile dyes. Ranging from the Yucatan down the Central American coast to Panamá, logwood was a major Caribbean trade commodity from the sixteenth through the twentieth century. A number of the buccaneers also worked as loggers in that trade. As Sorsby (1975) notes, the maritime landscape favored this illegal and highly profitable activity:

> There were several places on the Spanish coast favoured by British traders for making rendezvous with Spanish merchants. Naturally they preferred secluded spots to principal ports. A small uninhabited island named Bastimentos near Portobelo was one such place. Another was the bay near the river leading to Santa Marta. They met the merchants of Cartagena at a place known as Fellow, a small fishing village about 35 leagues southwest of the city. The Mosquito Coast was also favoured for the introduction of slaves and goods because of the presence of British settlers and the protection afforded by the Mosquito Indians. (Sorsby 1975:10)

Spain's control of remote coastal regions was maintained by small garrisons and a fleet of Guarda Costa customs vessels. The Spanish military on the isthmus, however, was weak, plagued by lack of pay and diminished numbers and debilitated by the concentration of available resources on the strategic points that had been fortified: Portobelo, the Chagres, Panamá City, and a few earth and wood forts that stretched along the Camino Real. Throughout the eighteenth century, for example, the military was unable to halt Miskito Indians raids into the Bocas del Toro area and the Laguna de Chiriquí from what is now Nicaragua:

> During these raids, villagers were captured to be sold as slaves to British colonists in Jamaica. In 1722, Spanish authorities complained that the Miskito had captured over 2000 Indians within the Caribbean coast of Costa Rica and Bocas del Toro combined. . . . Miskito "slave-hunting" raids in the Talamanca region of Costa Rica near the border of Panamá are thought to be a major contributor to the depopulation of this region (Conzemius 1932). These raids likely also diminished the indigenous population in coastal Bocas del Toro during the eighteenth century, although to a lesser extent. (Cramer 2013:13; see also Castillero 1995:367–384, 2004e:503)

Incidentally these actions, while also indicative of Spain's relative military weakness outside of its fortified ports and garrisons, also reflected on the indigenous maritime cultural landscape. The Ngöbe people of the region had successfully resisted Spanish incursions, and while occasionally trading with merchants and buccaneers they had also kept those Europeans out of their territory. By the early nineteenth century, however, the Ngöbe were largely gone: they had either succumbed to disease or, as Gordon (1982) posits, possibly retreated from the coast to avoid European and Miskito aggression (Roberts 1827; Cramer 2013:13; Heckadon Moreno 2011).

Spanish weakness on the isthmus was also readily apparent on the Darién. The Guna maintained their independence throughout the period, as evidenced by the Spanish withdrawal in 1700 after ousting the Scottish colonists. But Guna control persisted throughout the century, even when the Spanish military attempted to "pacify" and fortify the region to ostensibly thwart British ambitions from the 1760s onward. Fortifications in southern Darién were built, such as the forts at Yaviza and El Real, but hostilities continued until a major massacre of Spanish soldiers by the Guna in 1782 led to a change in royal policy toward an extermination war (Castillero 2004e:505–510; García Casares 2008:393–408). Five *presidios* (fortified settlements) were built between 1785 and 1786 in the isthmus down to the

Figure 45a–b. Graffiti inside a powder magazine at Fuerte San Gerónimo depicts a typical Spanish coastal sloop of the late eighteenth to early nineteenth centuries. Photographs by Tomás Mendizábal.

modern border of Colombia; however, the Guna proved resilient. By 1789, facing pressures in Europe and ongoing Guna resistance, Spain abandoned its presence in the Darién and razed its forts (Weber 2005:174–176).

Whether through decline in the annual trade fairs and the Tierra Firme fleet or through a lack of control of the entire isthmian coast and much of its "unpacified" interior, the fortunes of Panamá waned in the eighteenth century. Loss of political authority followed. Ciudad de Panamá lost its Audencia's independence from 1718 to 1722, and in 1751, the Audiencia was suppressed by the Crown: Panamá then went from being a powerful independent province to being part of a new province, Nueva Granada. The problems of the isthmus were magnified by the incessant commercial assault by British interests, friction between Spain and Britain occasioned by seizures of British contraband, and by the closing of the British "factories" of the South Seas Company in response to tensions in 1718, 1727, and 1739. These factors ultimately led to war and the destruction of the fortifications of Portobelo and those at the mouth of the Chagres. The events of 1739–1740 adversely affected more than the annual *feria* at Portobelo.

In response to sturdier ships now able to sail directly to and from the Pacific via Cape Horn and the Straits of Magellan, via overland waterways, and through the Río de la Plata, a government decision was made in 1740 to allow Spanish colonial ports on the Pacific to trade directly with Spain (Jaén Suárez 2014:266). The *trajín* ended after little more than two centuries' existence, and the isthmian route ceased to be a major conduit in the global economy.

The Village and Port of Chagres, 1680–1848

The small riverine settlement in the lee of the Castillo de San Lorenzo and its harbor are instructive in assessing a smaller, more focused aspect of the maritime cultural landscape of the isthmus. Rebuilt as a three-tiered stone fortress in between 1677 and 1680, the Castillo de San Lorenzo gave rise to an associated village, Chagres, in the 1680s. Visiting English buccaneer Lionel Wafer, who lived among the natives of Darién from 1680 to 1688, described the importance of the river as a marine highway: "The River of *Chagre*, which runs into the North Sea . . . on the South-side of it, at no great distance from *Panamá*, is *Venta de Cruces*, a small Village of Inns and Storehouses; whither Merchandises that are to be sent down the River *Chagre* are carried from Panamá by Mules, and there embark'd in Canoas and pereagoes" (Wafer 1699:88).

During the active period of Spanish control of Chagres and its port (1680s through 1740), the government maintained a custom house and moored Guarda Costa vessels at the port, which served as Caribbean coastguard headquarters. A 1760s map of the mouth of the river also shows a logwood plantation near the village of Chagres: this was a logical enterprise, since the logwood trade with Britain via the West Indies was one of the few potentially lucrative trades available to locals—especially after goods were no longer coming down the river from Panamá City. Undoubtedly a number of similar (and, at times, more or less temporary) plantations had existed up and down the coast beyond consistent Spanish control in the seventeenth and early eighteenth centuries. The establishment of one of these plantations at Chagres is a striking example of the end of effective Spanish control at the century's end and the opening of the coast in the post-*trajín* period. After 1740 Chagres served largely as a backwater port and a point for illicit smuggling carried on by British mariners from Jamaica collaborating with Panamá City merchants (Bancroft 1887:491). Jamaica had dominated British West Indies trade with Central America throughout the eighteenth century and was the only major link between Chagres and the world outside the Caribbean after 1780 (Hinckley 1963:109).

After illicit trade declined, regular trade continued through the early nineteenth century although at a greatly diminished scale, declining further following Panamá's independence from Spain in 1821 as part of Bolivar's Gran Colombia—and later as part of New Granada (Colombia). The idea of the Chagres as a potential route to the Pacific maintained interest in the river, however, which was described in an 1818 British account:

> The river Chagre [*sic*] is the principal stream in this province, and may be called the high road of Panamá, being used as a means of communication between the eastern shore and the capital. It takes its rise in the mountains near Cruces, which is about five leagues from Panamá; the Chagre has a considerable descent, but is nonetheless navigable for boats up to Cruces; its velocity is about three miles an hour; therefore the ascent from the coast is rather fatiguing. . . . It is by means of this river that a communication between the two oceans has been argued to be possible. (Bonnycastle 1818:231)

Chagres, as a backwater port, saw little trade other than from ships arriving from Jamaica and the occasional American trader. In 1822 an American visitor recorded his less-than-favorable impression of Chagres:

> On doubling the high and jutting promontory at the base of which the town is situated, you are, in a few minutes, at the anchorage opposite. . . . What a prospect! A few wretched hovels constructed of reeds, and indiscriminately located on a low marshy plain—no wharf—no street—no any thing. . . . Nearly all the houses are built of cane, and thatched; most of them are without any flooring except bare earth." (Morrell 1832:234)

The port remained unchanged for the next two decades and up to the California Gold Rush. An 1845 British account briefly described Chagres:

> Chagres . . . has a good harbour, but vessels drawing more than 12 feet water cannot enter it, on account of a ledge of rock which runs across its entrance. It is also an unhealthy place. The town is a mere collection of huts, which in 1822 contained 856 inhabitants of mixed race. By means of this harbour the town of Panamá carries on some commerce with Jamaica. (Long 1845:117)

A more detailed account, in a letter from the British Consul in Panamá dated March 23, 1845, described the bar and port of Chagres and also a shipwreck:

> The bar of Chagres is divided into two narrow channels by a bed of rock, upon which the sea generally breaks at low water, and during gales of wind (from the Westward and Northerly to N.N.E.) the surf is so heavy at all times of tide, as to render the passage of the bar, in open boats or canoes, both difficult and dangerous. . . . The rise and fall of the tide upon this bar vary from one and a half to two feet, as the wind prevails on or off the shore. In the eastern channel I found a depth of 13 feet at low water, spring tides, but that although the deepest and best of the two channels is so narrow as to render it perilous for a steamer, drawing 9 or 10 feet water, to attempt it during a fresh gale with a heavy sea; as, in addition to risk from the "heave and set" of the sea, the least deviation from the deepest part of the channel would cause her to strike, and incur serious damage, if not total wreck. Sailing vessels, bound into the port of Chagres, generally enter by the eastern channel, and they require a brisk leading wind to carry them through it, (the set of the current being in the direction of the rocks); for were the breeze to fail (which it sometimes does under the castle point), they would be in imminent danger of striking upon them. Shipwrecks are not uncommon in Chagres Roads.

> Whilst I was there, and American schooner, (the "Rocket"), dragged her anchors, was driven ashore, and lost. The Port of Chagres is essentially an inconvenient port, it is from five to six fathoms deep in some parts, but very shoal in others; the anchorage, moreover, is so narrow, that a steam vessel of moderate length could not swing there at her moorings; to be always "water bourne," she should "moor stem and stern." In the rainy season, however, large trees are sometimes swept down the river by the current, and carried "athwart hawse" of vessels moored off the village, thus they are liable to be driven from their anchors, and if they drift upon the bar they probably go to pieces. (Liot 1849:18–19)

The inconvenience of Chagres as a port notwithstanding, events in California in 1848 would soon change the port's fortunes and reopen it as a gateway to transisthmian and transoceanic trade.

Chagres: The Site, 1680–1848

Off the Castillo de San Lorenzo, and directly in front of the original site of Chagres, a wide variety of material culture sits in waters ranging from one to three meters deep. This area was noted in the map of the river mouth in Thomas Jefferys's *West-India Atlas* (1775) as being the site of the logwood plantation. A curving mud bank, discernible by sonar, roughly approximates the outer boundary of the plantation as delineated in that map. As indicated on the map, in the middle of the logwood plantation there is a noticeable gap.

The position of this gap is the approximate location of a rock feature documented in 2008. This is likely the original "embarcadero" of the settlement of Chagres, and at some point the rocks were placed into the water to facilitate the access of vessels anchored or moored in the river channel to the settlement. That access was accomplished by spanning the shallows just offshore from the town, which would variably be an exposed mudflat at low tides and, at best, covered by less than a fathom (two meters) of water at high tide.

The majority of material culture spotted in the shallows appears to be from the California Gold Rush (1849–1855) period. However, two fragments of majolica, two ceramic *botijas*, and fragments of what appear to be eighteenth-century bottle glass were noted in a snorkel survey. None of these materials were recovered. The first and more substantial *botija* lies top

Figure 46a–b. The village of Chagres, at the mouth of the Río Chagres, was a long-lasting element of the maritime cultural landscape of the isthmus from the seventeenth century through the early twentieth century, when the U.S. Army relocated its inhabitants from the newly imposed American Canal Zone. The village survives as a partially inundated archaeological site. These early twentieth-century postcard views document the village in an almost timeless state, as it changed little in appearance in the four hundred years it lasted. Historic postcards, photographs by Underwood & Underwood, New York, c. 1910. James P. Delgado Collection.

down in the mud, and in form it appears to be a Type A olive jar of the seventeenth to eighteenth centuries (Marken 1994:132). The second example, also found in the mud, is lying on the surface and is also missing its bottom but retains its top and rim. It is a rounder form and is either a Type B olive jar dating from the late eighteenth century or the very top of a tapering Type C jar of the same period (Marken 1994:135–136).

Two additional glazed ceramic fragments were also noted in the survey of the shallows along the former embarcadero. These represent the remains of hand-painted majolica vessels. The first majolica fragment is a fairly intact base from a deep-sided vessel such as a bowl. The terra cotta body and the thick white enamel glaze are common to majolica ceramics. The central design consists of three flowers surrounded by arching stems and tendrils. This floral motif also appears in a band further up the inside of the bowl. This floral band is flanked top and bottom with bands in a repeated "v" pattern.

Hand painting is evidenced by the pooling of paint seen at various places and, in particular, at the points of the "v" in the bands discussed above. In addition to this pooling, the pattern itself is very irregular, indicating the object was painted by hand rather than subjected to the transfer print process, which would have yielded a more standardized pattern. The second majolica fragment is the rim of a shallow vessel, such as plate, with a hand-painted linear design. The style of the two fragments suggests its origins were in the eighteenth century. No other remains of the early settlement were discerned, but excavation of the site, both above and below the river, would doubtless yield archaeological evidence of it. Archaeological survey of Chagres has yielded visible evidence of the British assault and destruction of the Castillo de San Lorenzo.

Vernon's Attack During the "War of Jenkins' Ear," 1740

The 1739–1740 War of Jenkins' Ear was the final blow to the isthmus as a major point of transit. It was the culmination of decades of economic decline driven by protectionist trade policy, a not-so-covert British campaign to undermine that policy, and by the efforts of privateers, buccaneers, and others eager to plunder the isthmus. The conflict was popularly named for British captain Robert Jenkins, whose ear was purportedly cut off by a Spanish Guarda Costa official who had caught him smuggling on the Florida coast in 1731. The real cause of the war, however, was Spain's revocation of the *asiento* (Spain's contract permitting the British to sell slaves in its colonies) in 1737. In Spain, it is known as the Guerra del Asiento. After negotiations broke down, Britain decided to go to war. As the British Parliament debated what course of action to take, Vice Admiral Edward Vernon was said to boast that he could prevail with a small force. The boast got him the job.

Vernon's orders, issued on July 16, 1739, sent him to the West Indies to conduct a punitive expedition against Spain's trade. Instead of attacking galleons off the coast of Spain or in Havana harbor, Vernon ultimately decided to seek out Spanish ships in either Cartagena or Portobelo. Learning that Cartagena was heavily defended, Vernon decided to strike at Portobelo. Attacking on November 20, Vernon succeeded in taking Portobelo two days later. In three weeks Vernon and his men demolished the port's fortifications before withdrawing to Jamaica (Castillero 2004e:503–504). As a result of this action, another onomastic landmark, Portobello Road in London, was named to commemorate the victory.

After refitting in Jamaica, Vernon's squadron was joined by "bomb ships" (heavyweight craft that carried sea mortars for firing shells into harbors and forts). Then Vernon headed to Cartagena, where he bombarded the port in early March 1740. The bombardment failed to achieve Vernon's goal of drawing out the Spanish fleet, commanded by Don Blas de Lezo, to fight. Famously defeated at Cartagena, Vernon decided to strike at Chagres, with its customs house, the Castillo de San Lorenzo, and the Guarda Costa boats. Arriving off Chagres on March 22, 1740, Vernon's ships opened fire with mortars and cannon. After a seven-hour bombardment, the garrison at the Castillo de San Lorenzo surrendered. Vernon's troops seized goods, sank the Spanish vessels in the port, and demolished the Castillo (Zapatero 1985:164).

In a letter to Sir Charles Wager, dated April 5, 1740, Vernon gave a detailed account of his actions at Chagres, including how the ships were sunk:

> Two *Guarda Costa* Sloops in the river were sunk just above the Customs House, but their masts and booms were of great service to us, to make out stage for shipping off the cannon [bronze guns taken from the Castillo], and I ordered carpenters to break up their decks and entirely destroy them, and these conclude the pleasure of destroying all the *Guarda Costas* they had in these parts. (Vernon 1740, qtd. in Ranft 1958:82)

An illustrated broadsheet, published in London in 1740, depicted the assault on San Lorenzo and the position of the two sloops off Chagres, anchored near the custom house on the opposite bank.

Vernon's letter noted that he sent men ashore to set mines at the base of the walls. He personally inspected the work, which he described as settling on "what mines should be prepared for destroying the works" as well as giving the orders "for the embarkation of the brass cannon from the fort and rendering unserviceable the iron cannon" (83). On March 29, after loading the brass cannon, "which were but eleven guns and eleven patereros . . . the mines were sprung under the lower bastion, which entirely demolished it as effectually as could be desired" (83). As the English fleet left the river to anchor by the fort, they "sprung two mines to blow up some of the upper part of the works, and afterwards set fire to all the inner buildings of the castle, which made a glorious and beautiful bonfire for all the 29th at night" (83).

By the time Vernon and his squadron sailed back from Chagres on March 30, 1740, the damage to the Castillo de San Lorenzo was so severe that a complete rebuilding of the fort was required.

Vernon's 1740 Attack in the Archaeological Record

Although archaeological study has not found any direct evidence of the attack at Portobelo (only the rebuilt fortifications), survey activities directly off the current Castillo de San Lorenzo documented a variety of material in the shallows directly beneath the fort's walls. This included ceramic tile and brick, cut stone, cannon, balls and shells, ceramic sherds, and glass shards. The survey of the waters beneath the fort was not comprehensive: it was a two-day reconnaissance of the area intended to assess the presence and probable association of any material culture in the shallows.

Some of the cut stone and brick are attributable to fallen materials from the latest incarnation (1762) of the fort. This includes an intact section of the wall that matches a partially collapsed casemate facing the mouth of the river. However, other building material observed on the site appears to be from the previous fort, which was destroyed in 1740 during the English attack. This includes broken and loose brick and stone that lie compacted in layers in the shallows that are associated with iron concretions and damaged iron cannon, shot, and shell.

Some of the guns mixed with the rubble may have been from the most recent construction of the fort and deposited as the result of erosion, discard, or vandalism. Other guns, however, appear to have come from the destroyed fort. Three cannon were found at the tip of the point, close to the documented location of a water battery destroyed by Vernon in 1740. One of these weapons was 280 cm (9.2 ft) long with no cascabel, which suggests the weapon was purposely damaged to make it unusable or look battle damaged. The second was 225 cm (7.4 ft) in length, with a cascabel, and the third was 305 cm (10.1 ft) in length with a cascabel.

These guns lie at a considerable distance from the cliff, which suggests they were deliberately deposited as the result of the demolition of the water battery. There were also associated mortar shells, all of which appeared to be 13-inch shells, mixed into the rubble. Although some of these could be from Castillo de San Lorenzo's magazines, it is possible that some of these munitions had been fired by the English ships during Vernon's bombardment of the fort. Some of the shells were fragmented, indicating that they had been fired and had exploded near the fort. This suggests that the waters off Castillo de San Lorenzo hold more than discarded or fallen material from the fort. Instead, this material may represent a more or less undisturbed remnant of the naval battlefield of 1740. This is a logical assumption, given that the fort was so close to the water, which suggests additional material may lie beneath the 1740 level—that is, material from the 1670–1671 battle and subsequent destruction of Castillo de San Lorenzo by Henry Morgan's forces.

A final possible archaeological resource off Chagres would be the remains of the two sloops sunk by the British forces under Vernon's command in 1740. The map of the Vernon attack notes the presence of the two Guarda Costa vessels anchored near the customs house on the river's western bank. If the vessels were sunk in or near this location, this would place their wrecks in the channel above the modern-day location of the wharf (in this case, above the mouth would indicate a position up the river and below it would indicate a position in the small bay below the Castillo). This would be in accord with Vernon's notation that "The two *Guarda Costa* sloops in the river were sunk just above the Customs House" (Vernon 1740, qtd. in Ranfft 1958:82). A discussion with local fishermen noted the presence of what they called "three wooden shipwrecks" at the river's mouth.

Magnetometer and side-scan sonar survey of this area delineated a series of anomalies directly off the existing wharf and extending west across the river. One of the anomalies has the signature of a shipwreck, while another in conjunction with the side-scan has a possible ballast pile of rock but does not have a strong magnetic signature. Diver surveys of the anomalies indicate thick, loose mud and scattered timbers as well as a range of loose artifacts from the eighteenth and the nineteenth centuries. Worm-eaten and deteriorated wooden features observed in this area lay atop the river bottom's mud surface. They included timbers large enough to be structural members such as a keelson and corroded iron spikes imbedded in the remains of deteriorated wood. These features may represent remains of a sunken Guarda Costa sloop or one or more wrecks from the California Gold Rush period or foundation timbers and other structural remains associated with submerged portions of the settlement of Chagres. Without excavation, definitive assessment is not possible.

New Fortifications at Portobelo and at the Chagres

The dominant physical features of the Isthmus of Panamá in this period are the late eighteenth-century fortifications built by Spain to replace those Vernon destroyed at Portobelo and at the mouth of the Chagres. Ironically, these impressive works proved to be of little consequence. Nonetheless, they represent the most visible Spanish fortifications in Panamá's maritime cultural landscape.

The refortification of Portobelo commenced with the arrival of Royal Engineer Ignacio Sala in 1753 and his construction of forts to protect the harbor. San Fernando was built facing the entrance to the bay, as was a new Fuerte de Santiago. A third fort, San Gerónimo, was built on the waterfront in front of the custom house; it was built low and projected into the bay to protect the anchorage (Ward 1993:181–182). To protect against attacks by land, a wall and two *casas fuertes* were built (Castillero 2004f:45–51). The Portobelo forts were never modified or battle tested. In the twenty-first century, they continue to stand as prominent ruins and World Heritage Sites in the Portobelo maritime landscape.

The repairs at the ruins of the Castillo de San Lorenzo at the mouth of the Chagres started with reconstruction of earlier earth and wood forts upstream. These *fortalezas*, completed in 1749, stood at the junctions of the Chagres with the Río Gatún and the Río de la Trinidad (Ward 1993:183; Zapatero 1985:175–180). A new fort for the precipice above the mouth of the Chagres was built between 1761 and 1768 (Zapatero 1985:184–192). Comprising a moat-surrounded, stone-walled platform for guns, a fortified gatehouse, and an elevated platform for guns and troops to protect

a

b

c

d

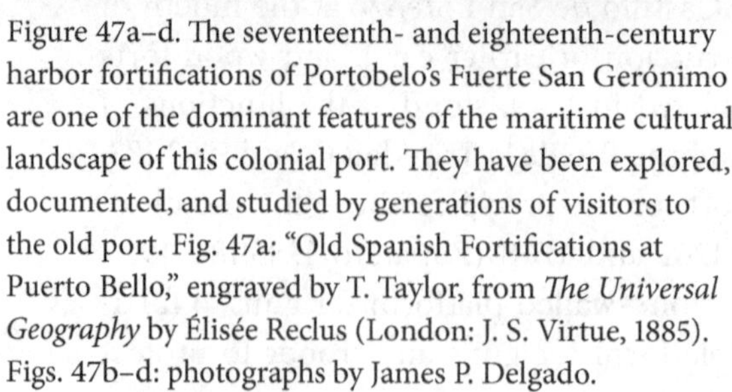

Figure 47a–d. The seventeenth- and eighteenth-century harbor fortifications of Portobelo's Fuerte San Gerónimo are one of the dominant features of the maritime cultural landscape of this colonial port. They have been explored, documented, and studied by generations of visitors to the old port. Fig. 47a: "Old Spanish Fortifications at Puerto Bello," engraved by T. Taylor, from *The Universal Geography* by Élisée Reclus (London: J. S. Virtue, 1885). Figs. 47b–d: photographs by James P. Delgado.

the landward approaches, the new fort was "the largest, strongest defense structure ever built on the isthmus, even grander in scope than the walls of Panamá City" (Ward 1993:184).

The Castillo was modified in 1779, with a second moat and a "massive, semicircular gundeck" and additional emplacements for musketeers (Ward 1993:184). The fort, which had been used as a prison during the early nineteenth century, was ultimately abandoned and is now a ruin; it is also a World Heritage Site with periodic renovation taking place (Zapatero 1985; Alba and Trute 2003). Like Portobelo, the Castillo is now overseen by a newly proclaimed *patronato*, which the Panamanian government has chosen to manage the site and to bolster its preservation and tourism potential.

Apart from small test pits and limited excavations that offered little information, no major archaeological excavations have been carried out at any of the fortresses on either site.

International Interest in the Isthmus, 1800–1848

South American patriots seeking independence from Spain attempted to use the isthmus as a political bargaining chip. Venezuelan General Francisco Miranda offered a Panamanian canal concession to Britain in exchange for support, but nothing came of it. When Panamá itself became independent from Spain in 1821, it joined Colombia in this regard; however, within the next twenty years, the Panamanians made three separate attempts to secede from Colombia (Lasso 2004). European critics maintained that the Panamá route languished because of these "frequent revolutions . . . and the consequent poverty and want of enterprise in the Spanish part of the population" (Scarlett 1838:285).

At that time, "the trade of the isthmus is . . . at a very low ebb. On the Atlantic shore it is maintained with Jamaica, by a British man of war, which sails every month . . . for the express purpose of carrying letters and specie, with Carthagena [*sic*], by government vessels, twice a month, and with the same, and a few other points, by independent traders, who bring freight to Chagres, and exchange them" (Lloyd 1831:96). On the Pacific, vessels sporadically called at "all parts of the coast, north and south, which find it in their interest to communicate with Europe in this way" (Lloyd 1831:96). An 1825 record of the vessels calling at Chagres—exclusive of warships, packets, and small coasters—included 1 large ship from Bordeaux; 7 brigs from Havre de Grace, France; 21 British schooners from the West Indies; 6 American schooners; and 3 schooners from Cartagena. Three years later, in

1828, the number of schooners had dropped to 11 West Indian, 6 American, and 3 Cartagena-registered vessels. For the same period, the port of Panamá saw 17 vessels arrive in 1825 and 24 in 1828 (Lloyd 1831:97).

In 1837 the Honorable Peter Campbell Scarlett published an account of his South American and isthmian travels, finding that there was demand for revitalized isthmian transit: "Although trade has languished at Panamá since the revolution, the greater part of the natives of the isthmus are still engaged in foreign commerce. Some are anxious for a railroad to Portobelo, others for a canal from the Pacific into the river Chagres, and all desire that some means or other should be discovered for restoring the prosperity of this neglected region" (Scarlett 1838:215–216). The answer, Scarlett reckoned, might come through the initiative of British and American entrepreneurs in Chile and Peru.

Scarlett included a prospectus for the company in his book. "The establishment of steam navigation along the southern shores of the Pacific Ocean, in connexion [*sic*] with the Passage of the Isthmus of Panamá to the Atlantic, has created much interest," the prospectus read, "since the trade of the countries whose shores are washed by that sea has been thrown open; and, as commerce and intercourse have increased, a still greater interest has been manifested" (Scarlett 1838:289). Indeed, Scarlett noted in approval, "the transit of merchandise from one ocean to the other, must produce an incalculable saving in time and distance" (1838:217).

After conferring with locals as to how it might be done, Scarlett felt that a ship canal through the isthmus "would never answer," but the isthmus, as the Spaniards had learned, could be utilized piecemeal with the novel benefits of steam technology. "It presents great facilities for effecting the transfer of merchandise by a river and canal sufficiently deep for steam-boats, at a comparably trifling expense between the two seas" (Scarlett 1838:239). Scarlett noted how, to make the link work, local entrepreneurs suggested connecting the Chagres to the Río Obispo, deepening it, and opening a canal to the Río Mandinga. Those plans never came to fruition.

International and transoceanic trade "revived," to a point, when two steamers, *Chile* and *Peru*, were built in London in the 1840s and sent to the Pacific by the Pacific Steam Navigation Company, which had been founded in Chile by expatriate businessman William Wheelwright. It was not until February 1842 that one of the steamers, *Chile*, finally reached Panamá City after a year and half of operation farther south. Regular connection with Panamá was not achieved again until 1846, however, when the company placed another ship, *Ecuador*, into service and received a contract from the British government to transport mail via Panamá.

By 1847 the company had placed a fourth steamer in service and was able to advertise joint sailings linking with Royal Mail steamers calling at Chagres on Panamá's Caribbean shore. It remained in service for several years. This route "revitalized isthmian transit," according to the company's most recent historian (Duncan 1975). It also attracted renewed American interest, which coincided with the recent conquest of California by the United States during the Mexican War. The only site on the isthmus and in the maritime cultural landscape that reflects this inaugural steam line is the Isla Taboga, in the Bay of Panamá, which served as the Pacific Steam Navigation Company's base in Panamá (see Castillero 2004k:53–54).

The prescience of William Wheelwright in part reflected rising American interest in the isthmus. While initial US interests in the isthmus dated to the 1780s, it was not until 1842 that the US position was clearly enunciated by acting secretary of state, Fletcher Webster, to US consul in Bogotá, William M. Blackford: "It is of great importance to the United States that the railroad or canal . . . should be constructed, and that we should have free use of it upon the same terms as the citizens or subjects of other nations" (Manning 1935:354).

In 1845 Secretary of State James Buchanan instructed Benjamin Bidlack, *charge d'affaires* at Bogotá, to collect information about any foreign schemes for a railroad or canal across the isthmus, since the United States had "strong motives for viewing with interest any project which may be designed to facilitate the intercourse between the Atlantic and Pacific oceans," also noting that it was important that "no other nation should obtain an exclusive privilege or an advantage," and that "you will use your influence . . . with the government of New Granada, to prevent it from granting privileges to any other nation which might prove injurious to the United States" (Manning 1935:357).

A treaty implemented to put these policies into effect was signed at Bogotá on December 12, 1846. Secretary of State John M. Clayton wrote to Thomas M. Foote to inform him that, according to the *charge d'affaires*, the rights it gave the United States were laden with responsibilities—not the least of which was a guaranty of neutrality and sovereignty (Manning 1935:362). Speculating that British financial interests on the isthmus might lead the British government to "seize the isthmus of Panamá" to settle debts, Clayton felt that this might bring "an inevitable war" between the

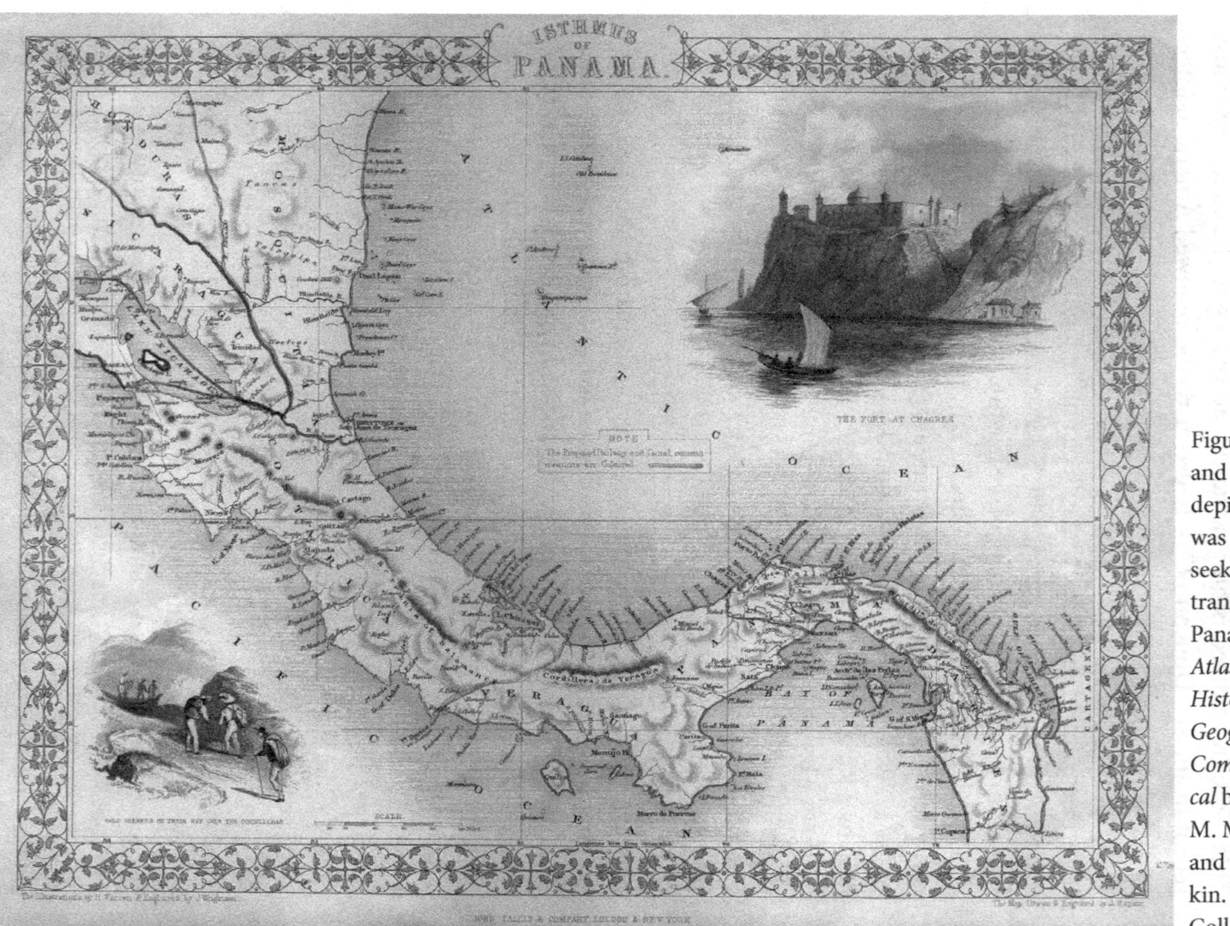

Figure 48. The Tallis and Martin map of 1851 depicts the isthmus as it was known to gold-seeking travelers who transited it. "Isthmus of Panama," *The Illustrated Atlas, and Modern History of the World Geographical, Political, Commercial and Statistical* by John Tallis and R. M. Martin; map drawn and engraved by J. Rapkin. James P. Delgado Collection.

United States and Britain. That war never came. Instead, America's hold on Panamá was strengthened by the 1848 discovery of gold in the newly conquered American territory of California. The resultant "rush" quickly created demand for Panamá as a fast and efficient means to get to California. In doing so, American interests in collaboration with Colombian and local Panamanian officials reopened the Isthmus of Panamá as a global link in maritime trade. A century of disuse and backwater status was seemingly over for Panamá.

6

The Isthmus during and after the "Fiebre del Oro," 1849–1861

The discovery of gold in California in 1848 had global consequences. The global economy benefited from the introduction of hundreds of millions of dollars in gold equal to many nations' economies. Individual fortunes were made, and the patterns of global shipping were diverted in response to the California market (Delgado 2009). This was dramatically underscored in the Gold Rush's impact on Panamá. The isthmian route abandoned by Spain was appropriated without military struggle by the emerging nation of the United States. The transisthmian zone in Panamá—as a strategic route for the flow of gold, high-value freight, passengers, and mail essential to the development of the expansionist ambitions of the United States—became a de facto American colony (McGuiness 2008). This rapid development (1848–1855) is reflected by profound and major developments in the maritime cultural landscape of the isthmus.

At first focused on preexisting elements of the maritime landscape—the Chagres, the Camino Real, and Panamá City as the main transit hubs—the maritime landscape evolved with intensive capitalization evident in the creation of the first transcontinental railroad in the Americas: the Panamá Railroad. Built between 1849 and 1855 at great cost in lives and capital, the railroad became a major link in maritime trade. With it, the Camino Real was finally abandoned. Panamá City shifted to resemble a more "American" city, and that is reflected in the economic restructuring of parts of the Casco Viejo in a "Yankee" enclave. The historical archaeology of the Casco reflects the influx of global trade and new commodities from the Fiebre del Oro, the time of "gold fever." New infrastructure arose, and the islands of the Bay of Panamá became the depot of the newly formed Pacific Mail Steamship Company. On shore, the principal port on the Pacific quickly shifted from inadequate Chagres to Limón Bay, where a "Yankee" city called Aspinwall (known locally as Colón) arose. In Panamá City, the waterfront was now the setting for a major new industrial hub: the terminal and shops of the Panamá Railroad.

All of this was reflected by a fundamental shift in the maritime cultural landscape as manifested in the change in the centuries-old transportation system, from a "locally controlled network powered primarily by human beings, mules, currents and the wind" to the "more centralized and largely U.S.-owned network of shops and locomotives powered by steam" (McGuiness 2008:9). It was also part of a new era that would reshape Panamá physically, economically, and politically over the next century: this was known as an American "technological imperative" that historian Michael Adas terms "dominance by design" (Adas 2006).

The mid-nineteenth century's American revival of the isthmus as a part of the global economy also reintroduced another element to the broader maritime cultural landscape of the Panamá route: namely, shipwrecks off isthmian shores and those farther abroad. There are Panamá-related shipwrecks from the nineteenth century spread along the Pacific coast of North America from Mexico to British Columbia, as well as a notable wreck off the Carolinas on the Atlantic coast. There is even a Panamá route–related shipwreck in Australia.

The Panamá Route Reopens via the Chagres, 1848–1850

American interest in Panamá was heightened by the conquest of California during the Mexican War of 1846–1848. With its new Pacific possessions firmly in hand in 1847, Congress subsidized the creation of two steamship lines to operate on the Panamá route and link the eastern seaboard with California and Oregon. Chartered in 1848, the United States Mail and the Pacific Mail Steamship companies built steamers to connect New York with Chagres, on the isthmus' Caribbean shores, and Panamá City with San Francisco. Both companies expected to lose money on passenger and freight service, but the discovery of gold in California in 1848 and the resultant "rush" brought hordes of eager gold seekers to Panamá's shores (McGuiness 2004).

For the first time in U.S. history, large numbers of Americans went abroad, many of them temporarily settling in a foreign land. Their presence intensified American desires for the Isthmus of Panamá, and by the 1850s, Panamá became the first American "colony"—a status it would "enjoy" until 1870. The demographics of the rush were phenomenal. Between 1848 and 1869, some 372,615 people crossed the isthmus to get to California, and 223,716 crossed in the opposite direction (Kemble 1943:254). Between 1849 and 1869 the total amount of California gold shipped back to the United States and to European markets totaled $710,753,857.62 (Kemble 1943:255).[1]

The Gold Rush revived the fortunes of Chagres. It was reopened as a port and in the coming years would be busier than it had been in its previous three centuries of existence. The Mallarino-Bidlack treaty between the United States and New Granada (Colombia) guaranteed Americans tax-exempt passage across the isthmus and its political neutrality: this all served to boost Chagres' fortunes (Delgado 1991). A new customs house was built that year in anticipation of the imminent new era of trade.

The U.S. Mail Steamship Company and the Pacific Mail Steamship Company, established by New York entrepreneurs before the California Gold Rush, were set to commence operation carrying passengers, baggage, and mail between New York and San Francisco via Chagres and Panamá City

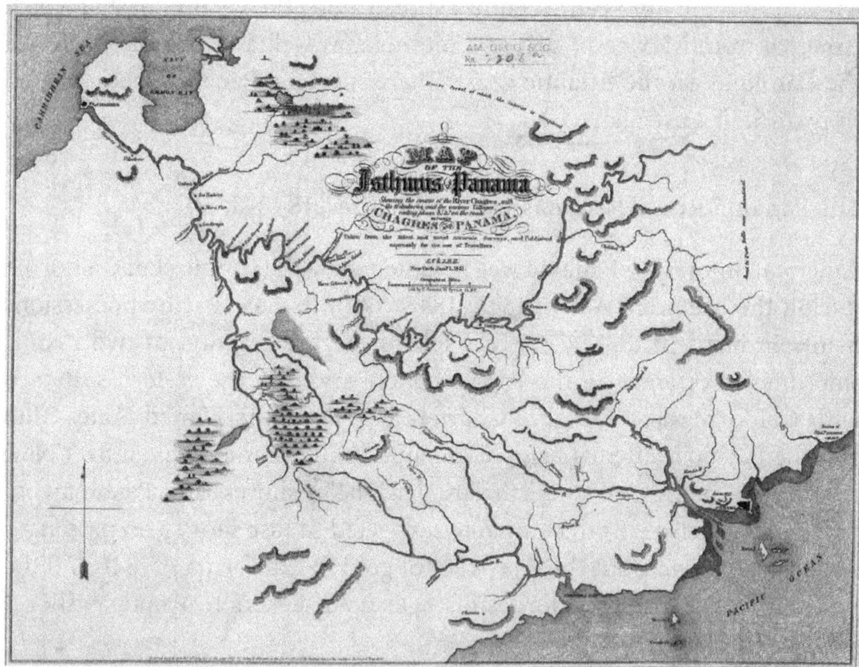

Figure 49. The Gold Rush maritime landscape of the isthmus is captured in this 1851 map, with the Chagres highlighted as a water highway for traveling to Panamá City. Courtesy of American Geographical Society Collection, Meier Library, University of Wisconsin–Milwaukee (digital file no. AM012707).

Figure 50. "The way they wait for 'the steamer' at Panamá," 1849. The frustration of American gold seekers delayed in Panamá waiting for ships to take them to California—a key factor in reviving dreams of a canal across the isthmus—is depicted in this satirical Gold Rush broadside. Drawing by John Cameron (New York: N. Currier, c. 1849), Library of Congress, Prints and Photographs Division (LOC catalog no. 2002698191).

in January 1849. However, the sheer numbers of passengers eager to use the 5,500 nautical mile route, the fastest to California, prompted the steamship line to commence operations in late 1848. Other ships also joined in, sailing to Chagres to disgorge their passengers.

An early guide offering advice to those using the Panamá route to California noted, "The passage across the isthmus from Chagres to Panamá is now made by water forty miles, in canoes, and twenty miles by mules, and occupies, on the average, two days." It went on to describe Chagres as a "miserable, sickly mud village" and advised, "It is generally practicable, and is by far the best way, to step on board a canoe from the ship, and not to touch at Chagres at all" (qtd. in Thornton 1864:348). Another set of "Practical Directions to Persons about to cross the Isthmus of Panamá" told passengers the following:

> Upon your arrival at Chagres, take your baggage at once to the custom-house, where you will experience but little delay. Then hurry out of the village, which is pestilential. Hire your canoe, which, for expedition, ought to be of small size. This is called a "piragua," is about 25 feet long, and navigated by a steersman and two rowers. The cost

> of the boat-hire, and men to Cruces ought not to exceed $12, unless, indeed, an increased traffic may have had the effect of raising the prices. (Thornton 1864:353)

By late 1848 steamers that had advertised sailings from Panamá to San Francisco for departure in January and February 1849 were already fully booked, and "the steamers *Crescent City*, *Isthmus*, and *Orus*, are advertised for Chagres, and are nearly all full. The *Orus* is intended to navigate Chagres River. Besides, there are some forty-five or fifty vessels, of all sizes, up for Chagres or San Francisco direct" (Thornton 1864:357).

On January 18, 1849, the *New York Tribune* reported that *Falcon* and *John Benson*, which were the first steamers full of gold seekers to sail for the isthmus, had arrived at Chagres with 251 passengers: "The natives about Chagres were much astonished at the irruption [*sic*] of these Northern Argonauts, and much more especially at the quantity of luggage they carried. . . . 1,700 trunks and 100 tons of other baggage." Within a few days of *Falcon*'s arrival, the steamer *Crescent City* and several sailing ships arrived and landed nearly 1,500 passengers.

The initial rush brought 59 vessels to Chagres between December 1848 and May 1849. They disgorged some 4,000 passengers (Kemble 1943:48). On February 24, 1849, the inaugural issue of the *Panamá Star* newspaper reported that two steamers and six sailing vessels had arrived at Chagres "within the last few days," with "about one thousand passengers in all." The initial arrivals, mostly from the sailing vessels, approached the reef and stayed close to shore. In the strong northerly winds, or "Nortes," however, they lost their anchors and wrecked at the river's mouth (McCollum 1960:49). They were still visible in February when gold seeker J. M. Letts arrived:

> We remained outside until the 17th, when we weighed anchor and passed into the mouth, making fast to the right bank, now called the American side of the river. We found an abundance of water in the channel, but at the entrance several dangerous rocks. As this coast is subject to severe northers, it is an extremely difficult port to make. The steamers still anchor some two miles out. We found several vessels near the mouth, beached and filled. (Letts 1852:13–14)

This report of wrecks near the entrance of the river is verified by another California-bound gold seeker, German traveler Carl Meyer. Arriving at Chagres in 1849, he noted that

> both shores of the quiet river, which separates the town from the landing place of the ships, were thick with boats or *cayucas*. Several sailboats rocked on their anchor chains in the middle of the bay, which was 250 minutes broad. Several others lay wrecked on the rocky coast as proofs of the violent and dangerous storms which often assail these shores. A steamer which did duty as both hotel and hospital, was continually engaged in towing ships in or out. (Meyer 1938:9)

Many American impressions of Chagres were less than favorable. Theodore T. Johnson, passenger on the steamer *Crescent City*, arrived at Chagres in February 1849 and described his

> landing in the far-famed Chagres. Here were, indeed, Pluto's dominions, and here was the veritable Styx: Amidst hundreds of canoes, our boat was forced up on the low, sandy beach, and we jumped ashore to find ourselves surrounded by a host of Charons, whose dark visages and rude paddles belied not the comparison. As soon as we could escape from the yells of "Canoa! canoa! a Cruces! a Gorgona!" and the incessant demand for riales and pesos, we strolled into the town, which we found to consist of about two hundred and fifty bamboo huts, with high-peaked roofs of dried palmetto leaves, situated in a complete morass—the streets or lanes exhibiting the remains of a species of rough paving, and filled with a confused mixture of dogs, hogs, naked children, negroes and creoles. All was excitement, wonder, and amazement at the tremendous irruption of Americanos. (Johnson 1849:14)

J. M. Letts landed at Chagres on February 14, 1849, and had a more favorable first impression:

> We shorten sail, and on the morning of the 14th are standing in for the port of Chagres. A most beautiful scene is spread out before us; we are making directly for the mouth of the river, the left point of the entrance being a bold, rocky promontory, surmounted by fortifications. The coast to the left is bold and rocky, extending a distance of five miles, and terminating in a rocky promontory, one of the points to the entrance of Navy Bay, the anticipated terminus of the Panamá railroad. The coast to the right is low, stretching away as far as the eye can reach. In the background is a succession of elevations, terminating in mountains of considerable height, the valleys, as well as the crests of the hills, being covered with a most luxuriant growth of veg-

> etation, together with the palm, cocoa-nut, and other tropical trees of the most gigantic size. As we neared the port, we passed around the steamer *Falcon*, which had just come to anchor, and passing on to within half a mile of the mouth of the river, we rounded to, and let go our anchor. (Letts 1852:13–14)

The initial rush overwhelmed Chagres and its inhabitants. Despite raising their rates in response to the demands and relative wealth of the landing gold seekers, the port of Chagres still could not effectively handle the traffic. There are accounts of weary boatmen forced by gun-wielding 49ers to work for them. Charles Hotchkiss, crossing the isthmus in October 1849, noted that when his group's "patience became exhausted" in a dispute with his boat's crew, pistols were flourished and the boat and its crew proceeded up the Chagres at gunpoint: "Four Yankees, with each a pistol, on even ground, against two natives, stark naked, was considerable odds in our favor" (Hotchkiss 1878:86). Julius Pratt, crossing in April 1849, later reminisced about an exhausted boat crew that refused to work anymore: "At length we formed our company into a line behind the boatmen and drove them into the boats at the muzzles of our guns and revolvers" (Pratt 1891:904).

Soon Yankee entrepreneurs established steam navigation on the river with smaller, shallow draft boats. The first was the steamer *Orus*, a 158-foot-long sidewheel steamer registered at 247 tons. Built in New York in 1842, *Orus* ran between New York and Red Bank, New Jersey, via the Shrewsbury River. The firm of Howland & Aspinwall, owners of the Pacific Mail Steamship Company, purchased *Orus* in 1848 and sent it to Chagres with passengers on December 22, 1848. After arriving at Chagres, *Orus* remained, running passengers up river and working as a tug for the next year.

The arrival of *Orus* is also said to have spurred the development of a new town across the river's mouth from the original village of Chagres. It was variously known as "Yankee Town" or "Yankee Chagres" (Larson 2002:15). In January 1849 the agent for *Orus* built a wharf out from the bank on the opposite side of the river and then built a small wooden building behind it to use as an office. Other wood-frame structures and small wharves followed, including the two-story wood frame "Crescent City" and "Californian" hotels.

At the end of 1849 *Orus* was sold to Cornelius Vanderbilt for operations on the San Juan River in Nicaragua. However, *Orus*' departure did not leave the Chagres River without a steamer. In September 1849 the shallow-draft

Figure 51. "View of the City of Chagres," from *Gleason's Pictorial Drawing-Room Companion*, September 30, 1854. The scene depicts "Yankee" or "American Chagres." This Gold Rush settlement, quickly built across the mouth of the Río Chagres from the seventeenth-century village, was a short-lived but significant element of the maritime cultural landscape from 1849 through 1855. Much like the village of Chagres, only archaeological elements survive in the twenty-first century. James P. Delgado Collection.

sternwheeler *General Herrán* began daily runs between Chagres and Gorgona. *General Herrán* is said to have run for several months before *teredo* (marine worm) damage forced it out of action.

A huge new steamer, the 110-foot-long, 23-foot-wide *Raphael Rivas*, was built to carry up to 450 passengers and was sheathed in iron to protect the hull from *teredo* infestation. Originally designed to draw 12 inches of water, the extra weight of the iron dragged the hull down to a total depth of 30 inches. When *Raphael Rivas* first steamed out of Chagres in June 1850, the river was at low tide, and the steamboat could only reach Palenquilla, which was 28 miles above Chagres and 11 miles below Gorgona. In August 1850 another riverboat joined *Rivas*. This was a former Mississippi River sidewheeler steamer, the 46-foot-long *Henry Gleason*. A month later, in September, a third steamer, *Swan*, started running on the Río Chagres. In 1851 the steamer *Millie* joined the river fleet, and on February 6, 1851, the 400-passenger steamer *William H. Aspinwall*, built at Manzanillo Island near Aspinwall (Colón), was the last Chagres steamer to work the river (Kemble 1949:51–52).

Demand for passage up the river was sufficient to fill the steamers and still provide work for local boatmen. By early 1851 there were thirteen steamships running regularly to and from Chagres, carrying on average 5,000 passengers to and from the river port (Kemble 1949:49). The importance of the port was such that a U.S. Consulate opened in it in 1850 and remained there until it relocated to Aspinwall (Colón) in March 1852 (Kemble 1943:50).

The Rise of Aspinwall (Colón) and the Decline of Chagres

The imperfect nature of the Río Chagres as a water highway, if not already known to historically minded Americans, was soon apparent, and in 1849 plans to construct a railway across the isthmus were drawn up, capital raised, and a workforce assembled (McGuiness 2008:54–66). By 1850 work on the Panamá Railroad began with the establishment of an American town on the Caribbean shore where previously none other had stood: it was on a marshy coral flatland called Isla Manzanillo (or as renamed by the Americans, Manzanillo Island) in Limón Bay, also renamed "Navy Bay." The new transit hub, named by company officials in 1852 for the chief financier of the railroad (and, coincidently, the Pacific Mail Steamship Company), William Henry Aspinwall),[2] became a dominant new feature of Panamá's maritime cultural landscape (Tejeira 2011; Castillero Reyes 1962). It replaced Chagres and eventually surpassed its colonial predecessors of Nombre de Dios and Portobelo in terms of volume of trade in specie, merchandise, and passengers within a few decades. British essayist Frank Marryat noted that all of this was built "with American money and for American purposes," because in Panamá, "the advantages of the California emigration are entirely reaped by foreigners" (Marryat 1948: 27–28). This was an exaggeration to be sure, as fortunes were made both by local and foreign entrepreneurs, rich and poor, in the service economy: these entrepreneurs transported and accommodated the waves of travelers at least until the railroad was finished in 1855. The high demand that outstripped the available offer ensured a very profitable business for those involved in the transit of travelers through the isthmus on the way to California (McGuiness 2003:68–71, 2008:35–38; Pizzurno 2010:120–122).

Money was definitely required, not to mention plenty of labor, as there were many obstacles to building the railroad. Just as difficult was the creation of the Caribbean port. Aspinwall, as noted, was built on the western end of a marsh-surrounded coral islet, which on average stood a little more than three feet above sea level (Wagner 1861:8). Frequently wet and mosquito ridden (hence disease ridden), the settlement was principally an in-

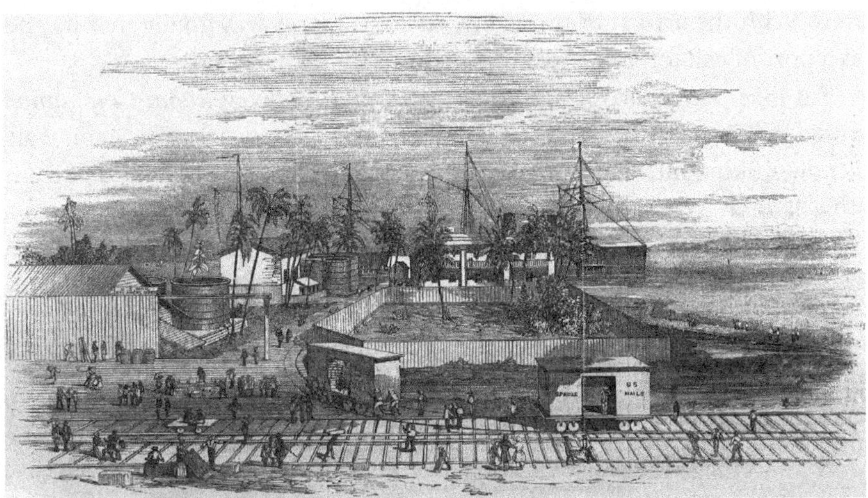

Figure 52. An artificially created element of the Gold Rush–era maritime cultural landscape was the land-filled swamp that became "Aspinwall" (Colón), the Caribbean port that bypassed the Chagres. From its rudimentary beginnings as a dock for U.S. Mail steamships adjacent to the station for the Panamá Railroad, it grew into a more substantial urban center. "The United States Mail Steam-Ship Company's Premises, at Aspinwall," *Illustrated London News*, March 31, 1855, 292. James P. Delgado Collection.

dustrial yard centered around the docks and the Caribbean terminal for the future railroad. It was surrounded by the unpaved streets and residences of its laborers and their white supervisors. Initial work drained part of the island to allow construction to commence and to facilitate the erection of a causeway to link the island to the mainland. The only factor that made the site ideal was the vastness of Limón (or Navy) Bay as a gathering place for ships. Chagres remained a favored landing spot for the next few years, however, as there was little to recommend landing at Aspinwall unless you were working on the railroad.

By late 1851 the construction of the Panamá Railroad had progressed to the point that the Chagres experienced a decline in popularity. Gatún, seven miles from Aspinwall (Colón), was reached by rail in October, and the following month "the steamers *Georgia* and *Philadelphia* were caught in a cyclone off Chagres, and were compelled to put into Navy Bay for refuge. This event gave the railroad its first business of any importance" (Robinson 1907:16). Construction of the railroad continued to reach farther into the jungle and closer to Cruces. In July 1852 the rails had reached Barbacoas, which was 23 miles from the Caribbean coast and halfway across the isthmus. With the arrival of trains in Cruces, Chagres was finally met its end as a port of call for gold seekers.

An 1854 account in *Gleason's Pictorial and Drawing Room Companion* noted that "Chagres . . . the ancient port, but nine miles west of Aspinwall, is now sinking into nothingness; the most of its business men and citizens now live at Aspinwall." (*Gleason's Pictorial Drawing-Room Companion*, September 30, 1854: 200). An entry in the *English Cyclopaedia*, written in February 1854 noted, "This small river was until lately of considerable importance," but . . . the Chagres river and town are now deserted" (Knight 1866:411). There was a brief but intense period of activity between 1849 and 1854 when Chagres hosted a transient population of approximately 250,000 people who were going to and from California. But eventually the port and village returned to the backwater it had been during the previous century. Chagres settled back into a daily existence of subsistence and coastal trading, quietly existing and occasionally visited by tourists until the construction of the canal and the U.S. military defense "needs" led to its abandonment in the early twentieth century.

Despite its imperfections, Aspinwall, as noted before, became the new terminus by 1854. When founded in early 1850 it was so uninhabitable that the company used the derelict hulks of a brig and steamer as floating bunkhouses. But capital and labor won out eventually. By 1855 Aspinwall was described as a settlement of some 800 inhabitants and a hundred or so houses. And with the depot and machine shops of the railroad as the only major structures, Aspinwall, the ostensible new gateway of commerce, was inadequate. It had a main street bordered on one side by a "meager row of houses facing the water" that "made up the rail road office, a store or two, some half dozen lodging and drinking establishments," plus it had "the railroad track, on its embankment of a few feet above the level of the shore" on the other side (Tomes 1855a:57). The town would flourish, despite its deficits, although floods, disease, and fire would erase most of its early presence above ground. Today the modern city of Colón bears no resemblance to the Gold Rush–era port it began as or to the "emporium of commerce of the Americas, or maybe for the entire world" that it was supposed to become (Tejeira 2011:46).

Chagres: The Site

Diver and snorkel survey of the waters at the river mouth, as well as isolated finds on Lajas Reef observed during the 2008 Institute of Nautical Archaeology/Waitt Institute survey, were not recovered but documented in situ. They date to the nineteenth century and most appear to relate to the Gold Rush activity at Chagres. The most prominent of these artifacts is a small single anchor of the admiralty pattern style, which is lodged on the western end of Lajas Reef. One palm, exposed on the reef, and the end of the stock along with its ring, are missing. This may be from erosion or the loss of the anchor on the reef. The anchor was not measured or drawn due to heavy surge conditions. The anchor is probably not from the same period as the guns described in chapter 5 and may be a snag from one of the many Gold Rush–era vessels said to have anchored off San Lorenzo and driven toward shore by the wind and heavy seas. Documentation and further analysis of the anchor was not possible, but it remains on the reef.

Additional Gold Rush–era material culture found includes an intact black glass bottle noted in a crevasse in the reef, broken black glass bottles, and two ceramic fragments observed off the Chagres town site. The concreted form of a bottle was noted and photographed on Lajas Reef but was not disturbed. The form suggests a heavy-bottomed champagne bottle. The ceramic fragments appear to have white, improved earthenware bodies and display blue-on-white transfer print patterns. The first fragment is the rim fragment of a shallow vessel such as a plate. This fragment has a heavily inked floral design around the rim and a central design that is too fragmented to discern. The second fragment is a base fragment from a deep-sided vessel such as a bowl. This specimen is more minimally inked and depicts two deer in a pastoral setting. These ceramic fragments with transfer print patterns are likely associated with the Gold Rush or immediately post–Gold Rush activities at Chagres.

While a number of broken black and green bottle glass specimens were noted, one black bottle glass base was selected for documentation and discussion. While black glass bottles are by no means absent in later nineteenth-century deposits, they are much more common and found in greater proportions in Gold Rush–era contexts. Black glass is olive-green or olive-amber glass that is so dark as to be nearly opaque (Fike 1987:17). Although some mineral water bottles were manufactured from black glass, this kind of glass was most commonly used for alcoholic beverages such as stout, ale, and wine prior to 1870 (Fike 1987:13). The black glass bottle base is from a cylindrical bottle and displays a high-domed "kick up" or "push up." As the fragment was left in situ, the bottom of the base could not be examined for signs of manufacturing technique. Black glass bottles with cylindrical morphologies such as these have been found in association with

Gold Rush deposits in San Francisco at the Hoff Store Site (Pastron et al. 1990) and of the store-ship *General Harrison* (Delgado et al. 2007), both of which date to May 1851. In the latter collection, analysis of contents from a bottle of this type indicated an alcoholic beverage with characteristics typically associated with beer.

Doubtless more of Chagres and Yankee Chagres may survive on both banks of the river, and various modern accounts by souvenir hunters and bottle collectors note the recovery of artifacts from the area. However, no archaeological excavation or detailed study of this short-lived moment when Chagres was a major hub in revived isthmian transit—and when the river was used as a major highway—has been undertaken. The authors did a short pedestrian survey of both coastlines in 2012 that (at least on the Chagres side) documented primarily nineteenth-century artifacts along the shoreline, principally ceramics like cream, pearl, and stoneware. Also the remains of one masonry building were found along the shore that could date from colonial times. The survey on the Yankee Chagres shore revealed no archaeological finds whatsoever, and a preliminary review of the copious cartography of the Chagres mouth suggests that both sites may now be mostly underwater. As noted, most of what would be considered to have archaeological value from Chagres today was plundered long ago.

Panamá City during the Gold Rush

Panamá City did not change physically after construction of the sea walls was finished in the 1790s. Change came only with the construction of the railroad and its associated infrastructure on the waterfront in 1854–1855. However, the character of the city changed dramatically, mainly as a result of the influx of foreigners. Names of businesses changed, and the city was "remapped" and conceptualized as a center of commerce suited to the new (albeit temporary) vastly transient population. The indigenous population was eventually marginalized and excluded from most maritime business in the city (and on the isthmus) by Yankee drive and industrial developments underscored by racism, as most Americans denigrated the isthmus' "dark-skinned" and non-English-speaking population. A new element also entered the maritime cultural landscape in the city, namely a cemetery for non-Catholic foreigners who died while crossing the isthmus or awaiting transit from Panamá to California. The Cementerio de los Extranjeros (foreigner's cemetery) predated the Gold Rush, but it filled up quickly as in-

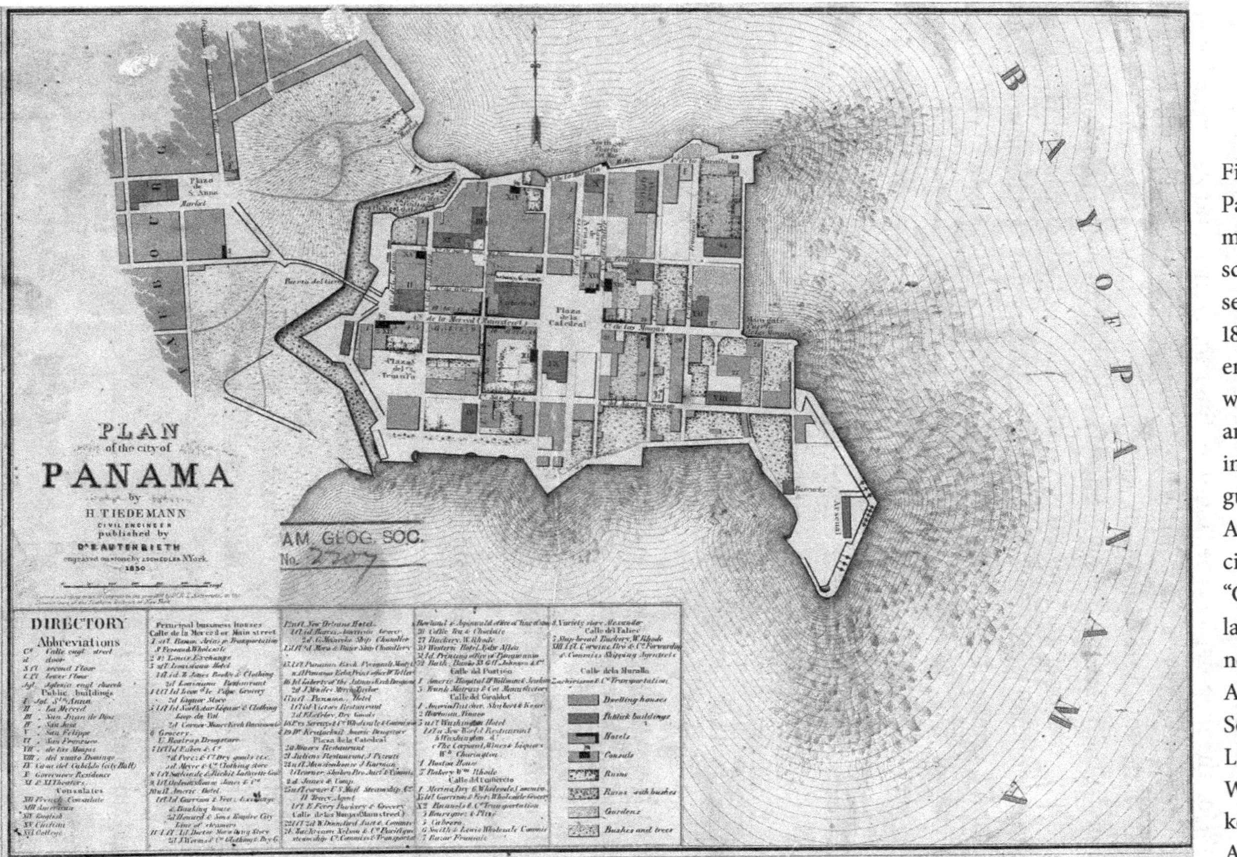

Figure 53. The City of Panamá's urban and maritime cultural landscape as known to gold-seeking foreigners in 1850. This map, drawn by engineer H. Tiedemann, was widely reproduced and was also published in an 1850 traveler's guide (New York: D. E. Autenreith). The old city was overrun by "Gringos," and English-language names for businesses were common. American Geographical Society Collection, Meier Library, University of Wisconsin–Milwaukee (digital file no. AM012723).

creasing numbers of people unused to the climate (and exposed to fevers and dysentery) began dying.

But the foreigners who arrived in the city did more than simply die and have their bodies buried in the cemetery. In 1850 an illustrated map of Panamá City, done by H. Tiedemann (a "civil engineer") and published by Dr. E. Autenrieth, showed the foreign occupants and businesses in the Casco Viejo. The map depicts the "Chilian, English, French and American" consulates, all representing countries with maritime interests in the isthmus (Chile being where Valparaíso, the major Pacific port at the time, was located). There are also a range of hotels, many with English names (the New Orleans, the Mansion House, the Western Hotel, the Washington Hotel and the Boston Hotel among them), exchange houses and restaurants (the Louisiana Restaurant, Meyer & Co. Clothing, Garrison & Fretz Exchange, G. Meinecke Ship Chandler, Harris American Grocer, American Drugstore, E. Ferry Bakery and Grocery, the New World Restaurant) all mixed in with local businesses such as Arias Transportation, Pérez y Cia Dry Goods, Henriquez y Plize and all on streets identified in Spanish and English such as the "Calle de la Merced (Mainstreet)" on the map (see p. 149).

Architecturally speaking, new buildings were built all around the city, and soon its urban landscape would no longer be dominated by the vacant lot, which was a frequent scene described by many visitors in the eighteenth and early nineteenth century. This was a result of the many fires that ran unchecked, especially within the walled city (Tejeira 2007:118; Tejeira 2013:44–60). The sleepy, decaying little town became a bustling entrepôt where money once again flowed to the joy of the local elite who saw their salvation in free commerce (Lasso 2004:64–5).

Strongly influenced by the maritime migration, the cultural landscape of the city had not been altered physically but rather had shifted demographically, architecturally, cognitively, and onamastically with a new language working to supplant much older place names. In a way, it was a recurrence of what happened centuries earlier when Spanish names began supplanting indigenous ones across the landscape. Unlike the earlier "invasion," however, this shift in names and language did not last, as the Gold Rush was a passing phenomenon whose impact on the landscape was more powerfully felt elsewhere on the isthmus, such as with the railroad, which was spurred and financed by Gold Rush traffic (McGuiness 2004).

The New Camino: The Panamá Railroad and Its Infrastructure

The Panamá Railroad was the first major industrial enterprise conducted by American interests outside of the United States (Castillero Reyes 1932). Heralded as an interoceanic railroad in its time, the Panamá Railroad was also ultimately hailed as the first intercontinental railroad in the Americas, albeit the "continent" was a narrow isthmus spanned by a 47.6-mile (76 km) rail line. The construction took five years, cost 8 million dollars, employed more than 6,000 laborers, and claimed thousands of lives by disease and accident. The length of the line rolled along a maximum grade of 60 ft to the mile (11.4 km)or 1.14 percent until it climbed to the summit, 37.38 miles (60.16 km)from Aspinwall and 10.2 miles (16.4 km) from Panamá City, which had a 258.64-foot (78.83 m) elevation (Nott 1867:36). In all, 26 stations marked the route, which was a single line of track "winding, generally taking the path of least resistance along the banks of the rivers," crossing 176 waterways, "most of which were less than ten feet wide" (Nott 1867:41). The waterway spans included 134 culverts, narrow drains and bridges, and 42 bridges "ranging from twelve to six hundred and twenty five feet in length (Nott 1867:41). Some were wood, and others were iron.

As noted at the time,

> The iron bridge across the Chagres at Barbacoas may be taken . . . as the type of all like structures on the line of the road. This bridge was composed of six spans of over a hundred feet each, built of boiler iron, with a top and bottom chord two feet in breadth and one inch in thickness, and joined together by a web of boiler iron nine feet in height at the centre and seven feet at the ends. The track was laid on iron floor-girders three feet apart, and the whole structure supported by five piers and two abutments of stone twenty-six feet wide and eight feet in thickness. (Nott 1867:41–42)

Regular repair, rebuilding, and improvement continued after the railroad was officially "completed." Smaller ravines were filled with crushed stone, lines were straightened, grades were reduced, and all of the rail ties were replaced with lignum vitae imported from Colombia.

Infrastructure for the railroad included machine shops, forges, a foundry, "a car-repair shop . . . a freight house and passenger depot at either terminus," as well as a 450-foot-long pier on Panamá Bay, originally built of wood and later rebuilt with iron, "which gave greatly increased facilities for embarking and landing passengers and freight," and hauled in separate

Figure 54a–b. Significant elements of the maritime cultural landscape of the Gold Rush period included elements of the Panamá Railroad that formed part of the transportation link across the isthmus. Shown here are the summit of the railroad at Culebra and the Camino Real wayside town of Gorgona transformed into a station on the railroad. Fig. 54a: "View of Culebra or the Summit, the Terminus of the Panama Railroad," lithograph by Charles Parsons (New York: Endicott, 1854). Fig. 54b: "Gorgona, Panama," *Illustrated London News*, date unknown, c. 1855. Both engravings are in the James P. Delgado Collection.

pieces a small iron steam tug across the isthmus by rail, reassembled it, and used it as a "substitute for the lighters and small boats which had previously been used for transportation between ship and shore, a distance of two and half miles" (Nott 1867:40). Furthermore, a telegraph line was strung along the rail line, opening up communication between the seas even faster than the transit of a rail car (Otis 1867:42). The company also shipped a cast-iron prefabricated lighthouse "sixty feet in height, and furnished with a Fresnel light" in Aspinwall (Colón) at the entrance to the port (Otis 1867:45).

The railroad officially opened on January 28, 1855. The new rail option ultimately cut the travel time across the isthmus to just four hours (while simultaneously ruining the service economy that sprung up along the route). Moreover, it opened the isthmian transit to freight that measured in the tons and brought in revenues that, within less than a decade, repaid the cost and brought substantial dividends to the company's officers and shareholders. The major emphasis, however, was more than the shipment of people, mail, and specie: it was also the intermodal movement of freight from ship to train to ship again—albeit bulk break (a shipper's term for the laborious practice of repetitive loading and unloading of cargo and freight). By the 1860s the company's backers could note with pride that the railroad was served on both coasts by eight steamship and four sailing-ship lines that connected to Australia, New Zealand, Japan, China, France, Britain, Germany, the West Indies, Mexico, California, Oregon, and the Pacific Northwest, as well as various Caribbean and South American ports (Otis 1867:148).

The Panamá Railroad again transformed the Isthmus of Panamá into a key transit hub that connected the North Atlantic's commercial and industrial centers with emerging economies and commodities in the Pacific. Now North American coastal ports as well as Asia, Australia, and the Pacific islands noted above could be accessed: "The impact of the Gold Rush was felt in many places beyond California, but perhaps none was transformed more dramatically than the Isthmus of Panamá" (McGuiness 2001:5).

The railroad, like the steamships of the Pacific and United States Mail Steamship companies, provided the means by which the United States seized control of the isthmus as a trade route. Prior to 1849 the majority of isthmian trade (80 percent) was controlled by Britain and its Caribbean colonies, while U.S. trade accounted for only 4.28 percent (Arauz 1994:96). The creation of the railroad also shifted the axis of trade across the isthmus from the Camino Real's centuries-old Portobelo-Panamá route and the Chagres-Cruces-Panamá route to an axis that would remain the dominant route in the twenty-first century, as the canal ultimately followed the railroad's course.

The Panamá Railroad of 1855–1903: The Sites

The railroad remained on its "original" (albeit somewhat straightened and strengthened) alignment for more than six decades until the construction of the canal rerouted parts of it, flooding the old alignment or erasing it through excavations of large tracts for the canal. Additionally, a number of specific elements (iron bridges, for example) were dismantled and track was pulled up. Standing structures were taken down, leaving only foundations and subsurface remains, all of which would eventually be submerged under water. Ironically, within the canal-period maritime cultural landscape, formerly terrestrial and now-submerged cultural resources passed into the archaeological record. The submergence of these resources did not necessarily guarantee their preservation. Continuous and ongoing dredging for canal maintenance for more than a hundred years, dumping of dredge spoil, and scuba-assisted bottle collecting beginning in the 1960s all had a significant impact on the submerged remains of the precanal landscape. Knowledgeable collectors knew where the old town and station sites were, including colonial sites, and began diving and digging. The *Panamá Canal Review*'s May 1968 issue reported, for example, that collectors were "rummaging" for early bottles on the Las Cruces trail, and that old town sites "are the most fertile grounds and have exposed many rare old bottles" (*Panamá Canal Review* 1968:6). The article interviewed Adrien Bouche, "who first began digging about 20 years ago," and whose collection included, in addition to bottles," . . . old wood and coal burning stoves, grates, coins, iron beds, springs, high-button shoes, spittoons, clay pipes and other objects of a bygone era" (*Panamá Canal Review* 1968:7). Another collector, J.P. McLaren, was reported to have a collection of approximately 500 bottles, while another, James Fulton, had a collection of approximately 1,500 bottles. Bottle hunting continues to this day but much more sporadically and at more relaxed pace.

In 1977 the final environmental impact report for the canal treaties (indicating what would happen to the canal's resources when they reverted to Panamá) noted, in a report by Richard Cooke (Department of State 1977) the condition of and probable impacts to cultural resources. Cooke noted that a number of former town and station sites had already been impacted and lost to archaeology:

> La Bruja, Dcs Hermanos, Palo Horqueta, Palo Matias and Ahorca Lagarto are now under the waters of Lake Gatún and apparently will be further affected by the dredging spoil. Frijoles, also under water, will soon be obscured completely by spoil. . . . The town-and-station site of Tabernilla (in existence at the end of the seventeenth century), will be more completely buried and/or destroyed. (Recent dredging ploughed through part of the town, disgorging artifacts and other remains through the pipes). . . . The part of San Pablo which is under the lake water, is beneath dumps 10 and 11 and will be covered more completely; Bailamonos will probably be obliterated by the spoil of dumps 7–9. The . . . settlements of Gorgona and Matachin, will be either partially buried or removed by the widening of Gamboa Reach. Chagrecito will probably be completely destroyed or buried by the same work. Perhaps the most complete loss to the recent history of Panamá will be Frijoles, which will be completely covered by the dump spoil. (Cooke 1977:19–20)

Cooke also noted some sites above water, such as Gorgona, which he found to be "completely disemboweled by amateur bottle hunters" (Cooke 1977:20). At the time of this writing the Panamá Canal Expansion Program was conducting paleontological and archaeological surveys as part of the cultural resources management program of the project. Although many sites from all periods of Panamanian history (pre-Columbian, colonial, departmental, and republican) have been documented on land within reach of the project, the study does not include underwater heritage except in very specific cases.

The Pacific Mail and the Maritime Landscape of the Panamá Route

The maritime cultural landscape of the Panamá route of the Gold Rush was (and is) more than the shore-side facilities of the steamship companies, the infrastructure of the railroads, or the archaeological evidence of their activities. Part of the cognitive landscape, which is an essential concept for understanding a cultural landscape, is reflected in the place names. Aspinwall, for example, was an attempt to supplant the indigenous name of Colón; town names have been Anglicized on the railroad stops, and the flow of people and goods across the isthmus itself has been significantly reoriented. Another part of the cognitive landscape was the charting of the route, especially on the Pacific coast.

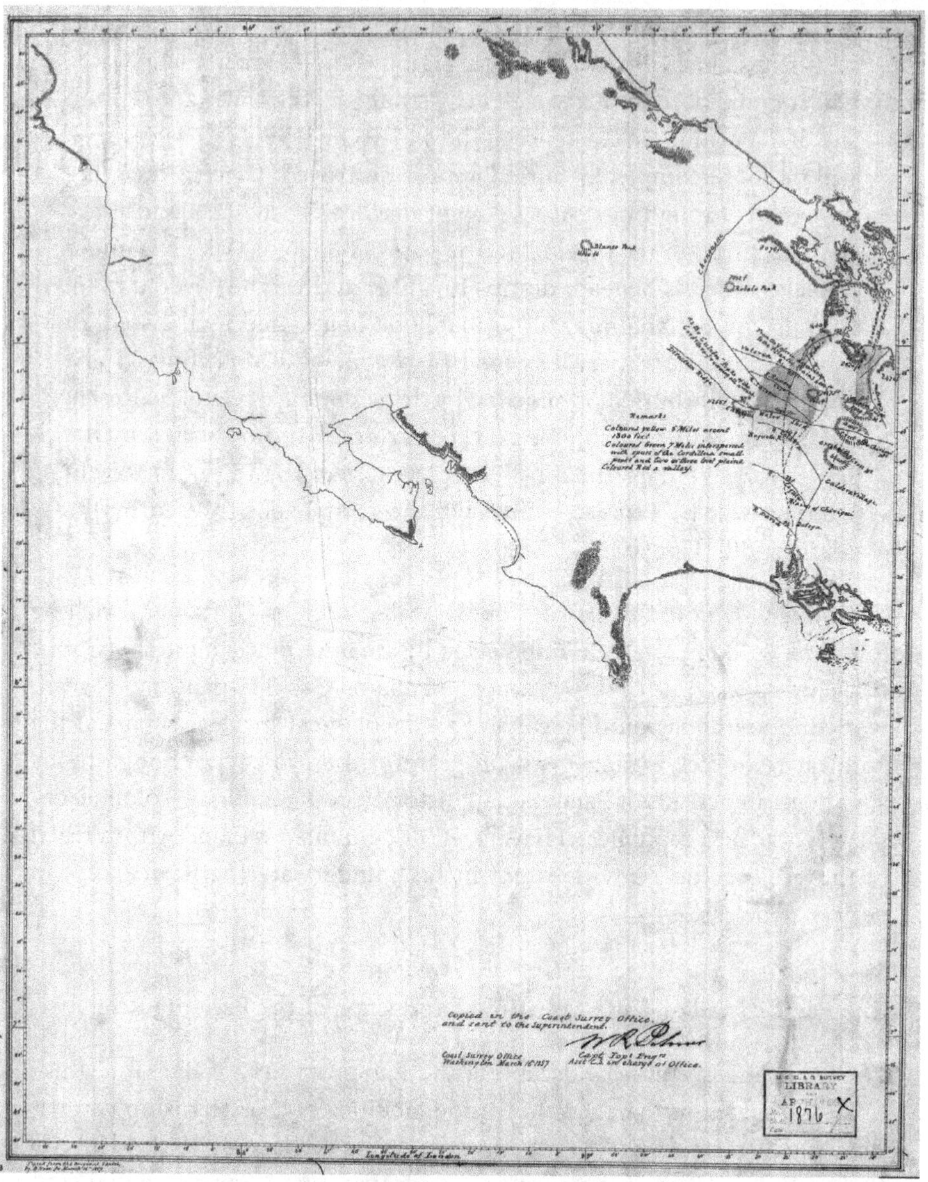

Figure 55. Capturing the maritime cultural landscape at the height of nineteenth-century American interest in the Isthmus of Panamá, this 1859 manuscript topographic sheet by the United States Coast Survey represents more than a nautical chart. Like earlier charts by other powers, it is a symbolic act of possession. U.S. Coast and Geodetic Survey chart, NOAA Central Library (digital file no. 1876-03-1859).

Relying on charts and pilots (published instructions and advice to mariners) on the Caribbean side of the isthmus, the masters of ships plying the route essentially sailed through known waters. The Pacific side was another matter. Although Spanish-speaking mariners were familiar with the coast as a result of preexisting coastal trade from South America up the coast to Mexico (and European explorers had done some charting) no consistent, English-language body of mariner's knowledge existed (see, for instance, Juan and Ulloa 1826). The captains of the ships, especially those in charge of the steamers that began regular service between Panamá and San Francisco, had to learn by experience and build a cognitive landscape of their own. They would then set it down in notations of Spanish or British charts (a number of them used the charts of British explorer George Vancouver at the end of the eighteenth century) or in journals they kept for themselves.

The cumulative knowledge of at least one of the Panamá route steamship masters survives because he published it after the route's heyday. William H. Parker, a former U.S. and Confederate naval officer, joined the Pacific Mail Steamship Company as a captain after the Civil War. Likely drawing on more than his own experience, Parker published his 46-page treatise, *Remarks on the Navigation of the Coasts between San Francisco and Panamá* in 1871. Noting that he had been running steamers on the route for the "last four years," he had decided after conducting his own surveys to write the book in hopes that it would "prove useful to the officers of the P.M.S.S. Co., employed in the same trade, and although much of what I will say is already known to those who have been as long or longer on the coast than myself, yet, as the information has never been collected or put into print, the younger officers of the Company find it difficult to get hold of it" (Parker 1871:3). In the description that follows, Parker moves from the crossing of the bar at San Francisco until reaching Point Puercos, which

> is high and can be passed, say one mile off. The haul up and pass the Frailes, if you can see, but if it should be very thick and rainy, steer so as to give the South Fraile a good berth; then haul up for Cape Mala, and when that is abeam steer N. by E. 1/8 mile E. for Bona Island; pass Bona one mile off, Tobaguilla half a mile, round San Jose Rock, close to, and so on close to Perico Island to the quay at Panamá. (Parker 1871:24)

In such a fashion, the maritime cultural landscape of the Panamá route on the ocean was cognitively captured by the new masters of the American seas. These details were set out on paper, which in time transitioned from a company-published treatise to official U.S. government charts and coastal pilots courtesy of the U.S. Coast Survey, whose first officers crossed the isthmus in 1849 to commence the scientific survey of the Pacific coast. The first coast pilot of the U.S.-controlled (or U.S.-owned) coastline was completed in 1858, but it did not include Panamá, or the rest of Central America and Mexico for that matter. Later editions, such as the fourth *Pacific Coast Pilot* (1889) included portions of Mexico, with the Coast Survey noting that they had relied in some cases on information provided by Panamá route captains. The transfer of knowledge of the Pacific coast of Panamá and the route to and from the two destinations did not take place until the advent of the canal period.[3]

In addition to the concept of the coast and the route as a Gold Rush–driven American maritime cultural landscape, one of the key "acquisitions" of the P.M.S.S.C. was the islands immediately off Panamá City's shores. Perico had been the official port of Panamá since the earliest days of the sixteenth century, and the other islands had also been populated (and to some extent fortified), including Taboga (Castillero 2006:139–150). In 1853 the islands of Naos, Perico, Culebra, and Flamenco were sold to the Panamá Railroad Company and the Pacific Mail Steamship Company for $30,000 (Isthmian Canal Commission 1911:388). In the nineteenth century the Colombian government leased all of the islands to the two steamship companies. An 1865 account noted that the islands of Taboga, Taboguilla, Flamenco, Perico, Islando, and Culebra were

> a beautiful archipelago of ocean gems. The first named, about nine miles from the city, is cultivated in fruits and vegetables for the Panamá market, and having upon it the extensive machine shops of the British Pacific Steam Navigation Company; and the last four, two miles off, belong to the American Pacific Mail Steamship Company, on one of which the shops of this company are erected. The steamers of these two lines lie near their respective islands, the American having an advantage for convenience of loading and discharging in the proximity of its anchorage to the city. (Baxley 1865:41–43)

"Islando" was actually the Isla de Naos, or the "island of the ships." There, the Pacific Mail Steamship Company erected its major industrial facilities.

The Pacific Mail facilities were inventoried in the company's 1904 annual report. Isla de Naos facilities included the company's 884-foot-long seawall and "ways for hauling up launches, 225' long, ways and slides of wood, with iron cross-ties resting on iron frame filled in with stone, with double power

Figure 56. The Pacific Mail Steamship Company maintained their facilities on the island of Naos, which the PMSSC purchased from Colombia in 1852. One aspect of the PMSSC depot there was coaling the PMSSC steamship fleet. The company stored coal in the hulk of the former USS *Warren*, built between 1825 and 1827 as a sloop-of-war and a veteran of Mediterranean, Caribbean, and Pacific service. During the Mexican War and the Gold Rush, *Warren* had served as a U.S. Navy storeship off San Francisco and then at Mare Island. The U.S. Navy sold the worn-out *Warren* to the Pacific Mail Steamship Company on January 1, 1863, who towed it into position for its final duty. In this image taken by Eadweard Muybridge in 1874, *Warren* is aground, surrounded by water deep enough for shallow-draft coal lighters to come alongside and load through a chute that projects out from the side. A walkway connects the coal hulk to the shore and allows access for laborers. Three ocean steamships lie at anchor along with various small craft off the hulk. This is a rare image of a temporary addition to the maritime cultural landscape of Panamá during the pre-canal steamship period. "USS Warren at Naos Island," 1875, Carte de Visite Imperial by Eadweard Muybridge, Vicente Pascual L. Collection. Reproduced courtesy of Vicente Pascual L.

capstan thereon. Landing 150' long, built on iron trestles and planked with wood" (Pacific Mail Steamship Company 1904:16). There were also seven large mushroom anchors to moor ships off the island. On shore, the company had built a two-story frame machine shop, a wood and corrugated iron carpenter shop, a boiler-repair shed, a blacksmith shop, a pipe-fitting shop, a toolshed, a storehouse, laundry facilities, a kitchen, a boathouse, a port captain's residence, a hospital, a doctor's cottage, laborers' and me-

Figure 57. The Pacific Steam Navigation Company, like the American-owned Panamá Railroad and the Pacific Mail Steamship Company, appropriated vast tracts and areas for its use. The island of Taboga was transformed into the PSNC's depot and repair facilities. "Taboga, Bay of Panama," *Illustrated London News*, January 11, 1868, 45. James P. Delgado Collection.

chanics' quarters and mess halls, 100-gallon capacity iron tanks to store fresh water, a fire engine, a steam winch, an iron crane, and a stationary engine with two boilers (United States Hydrographic Office 1904:16).

All of these structures and the facility were deemed eminent domain by the Isthmian Canal Commission of the U.S. government in 1911, and they were removed to make way for fortifications on the islands, which were renamed Fort Grant that same year. The fort was named in honor of General Ulysses S. Grant, who as a young lieutenant spent time on Flamenco Island as the quartermaster in charge of logistics for moving the Fourth Infantry Regiment to California in 1852 (De Mena 1999:105–106). More than 150 of Grant's men sickened and died during a cholera outbreak en route, and some were buried on Flamenco Island; their remains were later removed to Ancon and finally to Corozal cemetery in the Canal Zone (Harp 2001:39–40; Joseph et al. 1996:123). These islands are now a tourist destination, and Isla de Naos is the home of facilities for the Smithsonian Tropical Research Institute (STRI). There are no visible or known traces left of the nineteenth- to early twentieth-century aspects of these islands' maritime cultural landscape.

Traces of the once-extensive maritime infrastructure supporting the Pacific steamship activities on the bay survive on at least one other island, Taboga, and the small islet nearby called El Morro, which became a vital center for ship maintenance during the mid-nineteenth century. There the Pacific Steam Navigation Company built a shipyard, two piers, a coaling station, shops, a hospital, a hotel, offices, and even a cemetery. There were also drinking-water tanks and piping for the bungalows of the yard workers, who also lived in El Morro (Gutierrez 1993:56).

Tomes described the scene:

> There is work there, and Yankee work, too. Large store-houses, built of Maine lumber by Yankee carpenters, crammed full of all kinds of marine stores, and sheds widely extended over countless tons of coal. Cincinnati pork in unnumbered barrels, and American provisions and ship-chandlery in endless variety. Large sea-steamers are leaving there weekly, with the regularity and precision of the Collins line and the Cunarders from Canal Street and Jersey City. (1855a:159)

According to former Canal Zone resident Luis R. Celerier, who visited Taboga in 1974, remains of the old Pacific Steam Navigation Company were visible on the shore. "We ran into the abandoned remains of what had been a shipping company's facility. We saw iron boilers, anchors and other stuff, some of which appeared to have melted into the rocks. With time running out, as the tide was coming in, we had to depart before our route was cut off. Now I know there was a lot more to see, but at the time we did not know what we were looking at, much less what to look for" (Celerier 2011). Celerier also walked to El Morro, the islet attached to Taboga, and encountered a number of graves with eroded and largely unreadable markers. One of these he noted as follows:

> Erected
> To The Memory Of
> CHARLES WILLIAM WALKER,
> sometime commander of the
> Pacific Steam Navigating Company
> mail steamship "Callao"
> who after a short illness
> departed this life on this island
> on the 16th day of August 1859.

Aged 39 years.
This monument was erected by
some of his brother officers . . . [unreadable] . . .
their sincere respect and . . . [unreadable]

The marker for this grave, a stone obelisk, is the most prominent of the funerary complex, and it is still visible alongside other numbered markers such as stone crosses and tablets. Although, as Celerier noted, many grave markers are eroded, there are still some with legible dates, mostly from the 1850s. The concrete evidence of the old depot has all but vanished, but a recent survey (Adrian Mora 2011) documented the remains of not only the cemetery in El Morro but also of the few leftovers of the steamship days: some of the items found included a huge dented wheel (on El Morro), which is now a famous Taboga landmark. There were also ships' anchors, stone-paved trails, and the bases or floors of the old company bungalows.

The broader landscape of the Pacific Mail Steamship Company and the Gold Rush Panamá route is largely confined to place names and unexcavated (perhaps destroyed) archaeological sites in Panamá. And with the destruction by fires and demolition in San Francisco and New York, the company's offices and wharves in its eastern headquarters and California outposts are also gone. What survives above ground (and, to some extent, below ground) from the Panamá route outside the isthmus are the remains of the company's 1850s depot north of San Francisco at Benicia and the wrecks of several steamers previously lost on the coast.

The Historical Archaeology of the Gold Rush in Panamá

The massive influx of gold seekers crossing the isthmus left a profound archaeological stamp on the landscape, largely in the form of discarded goods (including many bottles) on the Chagres, the Camino Real and its attendant settlements and way stations, as well as along the railroad line. It is still unclear how many of these discarded goods have survived years of dredging, canal construction, and collecting. Historical accounts suggest vast amounts of maritime-imported material culture were deposited on the isthmus. But it is only recently that a more scientific record is available via the archaeological work done as mitigation for the recent expansion of the canal. This is in addition to the historical archaeology undertaken in the Casco Viejo in the face of its ongoing remodeling and gentrification (Martín and Mendizábal 2009). This is mainly because the transient gold-seeking population often settled in the city for extended periods, waiting for a ship to take them to San Francisco. The amount of material and commodities required to feed, clothe, medicate, and entertain them was considerable, and it left prominent archaeological traces.

One of the earliest historical archaeological projects in the Casco Viejo took place in 1980, when the former Convento of St. Dominic was excavated (Cooke and Rovira 1980). The excavation revealed structural remains and thousands of artifacts that documented changing social and economic conditions and, in particular, the "demise of peninsular trade monopoly, industrial revolution and the three nation rivalry of Britain, France and the United States" (Cooke and Rovira 1983:52–53). The Gold Rush-era use of the site was well represented in the archaeological record, including its use by W. Rhode, Esq. as a branch of the "American Bread, Pie and Cake Bakery" and as a bathhouse operated by A. G. Monti in 1851 and later owned by a Madame Platet in 1853. In later years, the site was used as a steam bakery by 1874 (Cooke and Rovira 1983:56).

The solid beginnings of historical archaeology in Panamá, which began at Panamá Viejo and other sites in the 1980s, continues with a plethora of restoration projects in the Casco accompanying a swift gentrification process that started in the mid-2000s (Martín and Mendizábal 2009) as discussed in chapter 4. Current legislation not only safeguards the Casco with different categories of protection for the buildings but also obliges restoration projects to carry out archaeological excavations before construction begins. Thus, in the last several years, some 70 or 80 archaeological excavations have taken place in the Casco Antiguo.

As the majority of these projects take place in private residential buildings that are turned into hotels, housing, or other businesses, most of the archaeological contexts being documented are predominantly domestic and have produced copious collections of material culture from the late seventeenth to the early twentieth centuries. Most of the materials found are ceramics, glass, and animal bones (the staples of the Panamanian diet were cows, pigs, and chicken, in that order of frequency). The evidence so far points to a similar ceramic assemblage being used throughout the city, as the excavated samples reveal similar results from house to house: usually 40 percent of the assemblages are formed by Loza de Tierra or *criollo* ware (Linero 2001; Rovira et al. 2006; Schreg 2010; Zárate 2004), another 40 percent by English pearl and white wares from the mid-seventeenth century onward, which replaced the previous majolica wares. The remaining 20 percent is made up of various other ceramic types such as Spanish

Figure 58. Historical archaeology in the Casco Viejo of Panamá has revealed a number of traces of the American occupation during the "fiebre del oro" of 1849–1856, including a wide range of products brought to satisfy a hard-drinking transient population. Stoneware and schnapps or bitters bottles. Photograph by Tomás Mendizábal.

olive jars, red paste containers, stoneware, and porcelain. The English wares and the dark green or black glass bottles found in mid-nineteenth-century contexts attest to the period when British commerce engulfed the isthmus, even when it was being used for the development of the incipient American empire during the Gold Rush period and beyond.

The Panamá Steamer Wrecks

A separate study could be written about the wider global landscape of the Panamá route as evidenced by the sites of the steamships that were wrecked while plying their trade on the route during the Gold Rush years. Only one such site exists in Panamá, and that is the wreck of the steamer *Lafayette*, which was built in 1851 for transatlantic service, diverted to the New York to Chagres run, and lost to a shipboard fire on September 11, 1851, off Chagres (Kemble 1943:233). The wreck was not salvaged, but its remains were subjected to considerable sport-diver collecting during the American occupation of the Canal Zone and the wreck was reportedly used as a bombing target by military forces.

Two Panamá steamers were lost on the Mexican coast during the Gold Rush. The first was *Union*, a small 180-foot-long steamer built in Philadelphia in 1849–1850. This vessel was engaged on the route as an independent steamer operating for owners who were competing with the Pacific Mail; however, *Union* went aground at Punta San Quentin, near Rosario, Baja California, on July 5, 1851 (Kemble 1943:250). The next to be lost was *North America*, a 260-foot long sidewheeler built in New York in 1850. *North America* originally operated on the New York to Chagres run but was sent around Cape Horn in 1851 to operate between Panamá and San Francisco. Shifted to the Nicaragua route at the end of the year, she wrecked 30 miles south of Acapulco on February 27, 1852 (Kemble 1943:236).

Three Panamá steamers were lost on the California coast while in isthmian service during the Gold Rush. The first was *Tennessee*, a 211-foot wooden sidewheeler built in New York in 1848 and diverted from southern coastal service to Panamá in 1849: this was in response to the news of gold and the crowds in Panamá City waiting for passage. *Tennessee* rounded Cape Horn in 1850 and began a long period of service between the isthmus and San Francisco until it ran aground in a thick fog three miles north of the Golden Gate on March 6, 1853, and broke up (Kemble 1943:248). The second was *Winfield Scott*, a solid 225-foot sidewheeler built in New York in 1850 expressly for the Panamá route. After *Winfield Scott*'s arrival to the isthmus in late 1852, it was run by the Independent Line on the Pacific coast. Purchased by the Pacific Mail to replace *Tennessee*, *Winfield Scott* was lost while heading southbound to Panamá. It hit the rocks off Anacapa Island in California's Channel Islands and broke apart on December 2, 1853 (Kemble 1943:252). The third was *Yankee Blade*, a 274-foot wooden sidewheeler built in New York in 1853, placed on the route in opposition service on the run to Chagres through early 1854 and then sent around Cape Horn to Panamá City in early 1854. *Yankee Blade* struck the rocks off Point Arguello in Southern California and broke apart, sustaining a loss of 30 lives and specie bound for Panamá (Kemble 1943:252).

On the Atlantic, two Panamá steamers were hit with tragedy. The first was *San Francisco*, a 281-foot sidewheeler built in New York for the Pacific Mail. The vessel departed New York on her maiden voyage to San Francisco on December 21, 1853, and carried a large contingent of U.S. Army troops and families. Unfortunately, *San Francisco* encountered fierce storms off the Carolina coast and gradually broke apart as it flooded and the boiler fires went out. The exhausted passengers and crew fought to stay afloat from December 23, 1853 to January 5, 1854. Some 200 lives were lost before the survivors were rescued from the sinking hulk (Kemble 1943:245). The second ship, also a victim of a hurricane or gale, was *Central America*, which was formerly *George Law*, a 278-foot sidewheeler built in 1852 for New York to Aspinwall service. After a long term of service on the Atlantic side, the veteran steamer was also damaged by a powerful storm and eventually sunk off the South Carolina coast in deep water on September 12, 1857; *Central America* took with it some 423 passengers and crew and close to $8 million in gold (Kemble 1943:226).

Of these wrecks, the sites of *Lafayette* (as previously noted), *Tennessee*, *Winfield Scott*, *Yankee Blade*, and *Central America* are known. Salvage, collecting, and some archaeological activities have taken place on all of these sites. Although as treasure wrecks, *Yankee Blade* and *Central America* were salvaged by organized commercial recoveries, *Central America* required a highly technical operation, as it was under several thousand feet of water (Herdendorf 1991). Archaeological work on *Tennessee* (Delgado 1983, 1991) and *Winfield Scott* (Delgado 1981) has taken place under the aegis of the National Park Service and the Office of National Marine Sanctuaries in the National Oceanic and Atmospheric Administration. The remains of the structure and machinery of the ships have been studied, as well as some of the material culture reflecting the provisioning of the ships and the effects of passengers on board (Marx 2002).

A separate study could be written on the characteristics, careers, wrecks, and the archaeology of the Panamá steamers. These sites are noted here, as were known wrecks further afield from the isthmus from the colonial period *flotas*. These sites are a reminder that the global importance of Panamá as a major hub of oceanic transit is reflected by a maritime cultural landscape reaching far beyond isthmian shores. However, this concept is not particularly radical. It is, rather, the ultimate expression of how maritime cultural landscapes—especially one associated with something as globally important as the isthmus—can be truly global in its geographical spread.

7

Canal Dreams and Realities, 1861–1902

The American imperialist landscape of the Gold Rush had a profound social and economic effect on Panamá. The "world ushered in by the construction of the railroad was a far cry from the commercial paradise" for instead of "a booming commerce, the railroad brought depression to Panamá City" despite the flow of passengers and gold across the isthmus (McGuiness 2008:80). That was because the commerce and people flowed directly *through* Panamá, which became "increasingly a mere point of transit that goods and people passed over on their way to markets located elsewhere" (McGuiness 2008:80). The proceeds of isthmian transit went to corporations and investors in New York or San Francisco. And the subsidy paid by the railroad went directly to the government in far-off Nueva Granada.

External domination notwithstanding, McGuiness (2008) aptly points to the geography of the isthmus and Panamá in the larger maritime cultural landscape. Unlike San Francisco, New York, Chicago, or other port cities, Panamá was not a confluence. The other cities "sat at the juncture of multiple trade routes, and their urban populations constituted important markets in and of themselves. In contrast, the population of Panamá was relatively small, and the Isthmus primarily served as a junction on a trunk line leading from New York City to San Francisco" (McGuiness 2008:81). In a new age of industrial "progress," entrepreneurs used iron and steam to more effectively utilize the isthmus as a portage. The centuries-old problem of the isthmus as a transit hub was the intervening land mass. The necessity of landing and trans-shipment created a break in the flow of people and goods. Delays meant more than time in the rapidly expanding global economy: delays now cost money, too.

What transpired was a shift away from the river and the emergence of the railroad as a land-based equivalent to a canal. Starting in 1851, as the railroad began to come into prominence, the fortunes of Chagres shifted

Figure 59. "Down by the old sea wall, passengers embarking for an ocean steamer, Panama," H. C. White Company, c. 1907. The waterfront transfer of passengers from the Panamá Railroad to steamers waiting offshore was a six-decades-long tradition until the completion of the canal. Library of Congress, Prints and Photographs Division (LOC catalog no. 98503914).

and thus affected the individual boatmen, merchants, and mule train drivers, small community stores, and inns. The local community was increasingly isolated by this new industrial route. The advent of rail travel in Panamá City in 1855 sealed that city's fate in the same way. Colón, created out of the swamps by the railroad company, became a foreign-dominated enclave, down to its Americanized name of Aspinwall; this helped established a model that American companies would follow for decades to come (McGuiness 2008:82). What arose at Colón would be reproduced in Panamá with the next iteration of the isthmian crossing: the canal. The maritime cultural landscape of the isthmus of the late 1850s, however, also included aspects of resistance and persistence: local boatmen continued to transport some passengers and their baggage to the steamers off the islands when the ferry to Taboga was too full or when wayfarers missed the ferry. The boatmen also transported waterborne fruit and produce vendors who approached the steamers to offer their wares.

What this also underscores is that for most people passing through, their glimpse of Panamá was confined to a few hours. And even as larger numbers passed through the isthmus, this "corresponded with a slippage of Panamá from the consciousness of people in the United States" (McGuiness 2008:83). The only time Panamá captured America's attention was when "incidents" against American lives or property took place: for example, a "riot" in 1856, occasioned by abuse of a local, led to an assault on the railroad station in Panamá City and a loss of American and Panamanian lives. This became known as the "Watermelon Slice" incident. The U.S. government pressed for reparations. Although insisting that the Americans in Pa-

Figure 60. "Three men in a boat transporting bananas to the city market, Panamá," photograph by Frank G. Carpenter, c. 1890–1923. The use of small local craft for transportation remained an essentially unchanged aspect of the maritime cultural landscape of Panamá for centuries. Library of Congress, Prints and Photographs Division, Frank and Frances Carpenter Collection (LOC Call no. LOT 11356-27).

Figure 61. The city of Panamá in 1860 as gold fever subsided. The city's landscape is largely unchanged from the eighteenth century, and the original fortification walls and city gate, later torn down, are intact in this scene. "Vue de Panama—Percement de L'Isthme de Panama," *Le Monde Illustre*, 1860, Vicente Pascual L. Collection. Reproduced courtesy of Vicente Pascual L.

namá had started the riot, the Colombian government eventually acquiesced to pay an indemnity of over $400,000 in 1865.

This was the start of American "gunboat diplomacy." In many ways, it was not dissimilar to the actions of the British against Panamá during the 1739–1740 War of Jenkins' Ear, although in the nineteenth-century version, the American gunboats landed troops and aimed their guns at cities but did not level forts. What followed after 1856 for both the United States and Panamá was a highly political, well-publicized, and emotional use of naval power to reinforce the security of American investment, discourage future "incidents," and protect economic interests at the expense of Colombian (and ultimately Panamanian) sovereignty albeit with the sometimes veiled complicity of the local elites.

In all, American forces landed on the isthmus sixteen times between 1855 and 1903: eight times in Panamá City (1856, 1860, 1865, 1873 [twice], 1885, 1901, 1902); six times at Aspinwall (1868, 1885 [twice], 1901, 1902, 1903); and twice at Bocas del Toro (1895, 1902). The landings were prompted by the threat to American lives and property and the instability of isthmian politics. Theodore Roosevelt justified American fears by noting 53 isthmian revolutions, rebellions, riots, and outbreaks of violence between 1846 and 1903 (Parks 1935:219).

The Decline of the Railroad and the Pacific Mail

The American Civil War also sparked renewed attention to the isthmus, but that attention was focused on the vulnerability of the treasure-carrying steamers to high-seas capture by Confederate raiders. The concern was both highlighted and confirmed when the raider CSS *Alabama* stopped the steamer *Ariel* off the Cuban coast on December 7, 1862, while *Ariel* was running from New York to Aspinwall with the mail, 140 U.S. Marines, and some $1,500 in silver (Kemble 1943:110). The presence of some 700 passengers and crew made it impossible for *Alabama*'s commander, Raphael Semmes, to transfer them to his ship and burn *Ariel*, so he took the money (some $8,000 in U.S. treasury bonds) and the Marines' weapons and then ransomed the ship for $228,000, which was to be paid when the Confederacy was legally recognized at the end of the war (Kemble 1943:111).

Semmes's interception of *Ariel* was a carefully planned and executed maneuver. While his principal goal in entering the Gulf of Mexico with *Alabama* was to interfere with the U.S. Navy's operations against Texas, he entered the gulf with several weeks to prepare for these planned maneuvers: "I resolved to devote this interval to the waylaying of a California treasure-steamer, as a million or so dollars of gold, deposited in Europe, would materially aid me, in my operations on the sea" (Semmes 1869:520). As it turned out, instead, "This was an elephant I had not bargained for, and I was seriously embarrassed to know what to do with it" (Semmes 1869:532). *Ariel*'s captain took no chances on his return voyage from Aspinwall to New York, leaving the regular shipment of specie, totaling about $500,000, behind in Aspinwall in case *Alabama* was waiting to intercept *Ariel* again.

For the second time in the history of isthmian treasure transit, the routing and practices of the treasure ships shifted in response to the threat of high-seas seizure. In addition to a great deal of media consternation, the American response was to dispatch USS *Connecticut* to Aspinwall to collect the specie and order all Panamá steamers to be escorted by a Union warship (Kemble 1943:111). The other impact was the wartime practice, beginning in 1862 and ending in 1865, of splitting the shipments at Aspinwall, placing the majority of the money in Royal Mail Steam Packet Company steamers running to Liverpool. From there the treasure was then trans-shipped to Cunard Line steamers bound for New York. The treasure was safe from Confederate seizure, as it was carried in neutral British ships. Smaller amounts continued to be shipped by the U.S. mail steamers (Kemble 1943:111).

By the end of the war, the Pacific Mail was doing a favorable business. In 1865, 13,150 passengers were carried from New York to San Francisco, and 16,506 crossed in the opposite direction (Kemble 1943:254). Over $35 million in treasure also crossed the isthmus that year, but very little of it was spent there. As a reflection of the end of the Civil War, the numbers of people going to California via the Panamá route the following year nearly doubled to 22,889, while 12,450 took the opposite route (Kemble 1943:254). Not only did passenger numbers increase but so too did the merchandise and freight transported west in the postwar boom: "After 1865, it was usual for westbound steamers to report cargoes of merchandise ranging from 1,000 to 2,000 tons, and generally over 1,500 tons, whereas in the five preceding years cargoes were very seldom over 1,000 and usually about 500 to 600, tons" (Kemble 1943:101).

The Pacific Mail, from 1865 through 1869, underwent a "great expansion," as the company shifted its focus to transpacific operations centered on San Francisco instead of Panamá. This was a result of the soon-to-be-completed transcontinental railroad in the United States, which they realized "would greatly curtail the traffic by way of Panamá" (Kemble 1943:101). The expansion included not only more steamers but also the largest wooden steamships built in the United States. This expansion was for the new line the company was about to open, which would extend from San Francisco to Japan and China. After securing a contract from the U.S. government to carry the mail in 1865—the U.S. government had promised that the Panamá route would be worth pursuing in 1847, but the subsidy for carrying mail via Panamá had diminished in the war years and was soon to end—the Pacific Mail began to bulk up the fleet to meet the anticipated demand for passengers, freight, and mail to and from the Orient when the new service commenced on January 1, 1867.

The major shift for the Pacific Mail and its Panamá steamers after 1869 was not a withdrawal but rather a change in the routing from a more or less direct run to San Francisco to what essentially was a "milk" run, or a round trip facilitating the distribution or collection of freight and products to and from various Central American and Mexican ports. Further, the largest and best ships shifted to the transpacific service, while smaller and older ships stayed on the Panamá route. The company advertised a direct run in 1874, using the steamers *Granada, Colima, Montana,* and *Constitution,* but the passenger numbers were insufficient. *Constitution,* a veteran of the Pacific trade since 1862, was pulled from the route and finally put out of action at San Francisco in 1879. *Montana,* built in 1865, also did not last long in service and was put out of action permanently in 1877. Two new iron-hulled propeller steamers built in 1874, *Colima* and *Granada,* made single voyages across the Pacific in 1875–1876; however, they encountered difficulties during that service and were diverted to the coastal run.

The company also advertised in 1874 its Central American and Mexican Coast Line:

> This way-line to Panamá will consist of the steamers Ancon, Arizona, Costa Rica, Pacific, Winchester and Salvador, with the Honduras at Panamá, which will thence monthly to Central American ports, to assist with the Coast line, enabling them to take more San Francisco and Southern California freight. This will stop, both going and returning, at the following Central American, Mexican, and Southern Californian ports: San Diego, Cape St. Lucas, Mazatlan, San Blas, Manzanillo, Acapulco, Port Angel, Salinas Cruz, Tonalá, San Benito, Champerico, Sesecapa, Tecojate, San José, Acajutla, La Libertad, La Union, Amapala, Corinto, San Juan, and Punta Arenas. (San Francisco *Daily Alta California,* August 6, 1874:1)

This was the new Panamá route. It was still largely unknown, especially to American captains and mates who would be navigating it. This is one reason why in 1871 Captain Parker of the Pacific Mail published advice to help guide inexperienced mariners on this new route and through this unfamiliar landscape (Parker 1871). Charting of the coast and the development of a coast pilot by the U.S. Navy Hydrographic Office, as previously noted (chapter 6, fn. 27), expanded local maritime knowledge as a more global and shared resource after 1889 (United States Hydrographic Office 1893). The railroad did not confine itself merely to serving the U.S. Mail steamers but branched out into shipping, ship chandlery, and tugboat and harbor services. It even launched its own line of ships. These businesses in time overshadowed the actual rail operation. At the urging of its New York–based investors (some of whom were also the controlling figures of the Pacific Mail), it organized a line of sailing ships from Aspinwall to New York and Liverpool to carry its supplies and goods and then created the Central American Steamship Line. This proved profitable and soon became one of the railroad's principal income streams, bringing in fifteen times the revenues that the New York to California business did by 1860 (*Panamá Canal*, August 13, 1939:42).

Connections to a variety of ports notwithstanding, the new northern run of the steamers of the Pacific Mail and the railroad did not equal the glory days of the Gold Rush. In 1878 James Douglas Jr. spoke to the American Geographical Society in New York about his recent journey along the west coast of South America by steamer from Panamá to Valparaíso. Douglas reported that the isthmus was relatively quiet and its formerly active maritime trade at an ebb. The "death-blow was given to Panamá by two causes, working almost contemporaneously," he noted (Douglas 1878:201). The first "death blow" was the completion of the transcontinental railroad in the United States when the Central and Union Pacific railroads met in 1869, "which withdrew from Panamá much of the trade of China and Japan, and the Californian traffic" (Douglas 1878:201).

The second was the establishment of direct steamship service from west coast ports to Liverpool by Britain's Pacific Steam Navigation Company. After a "disagreement with the Panamá Railroad over freights," the P.S.N.C. experimented with steamers running from Callao and Valparaíso directly to England (Douglas 1878:201). The experiment "succeeded, and thenceforward most of the transit trade, which they formerly brought to Panamá, has been diverted" (Douglas 1878:201). Douglas reported that the P.S.N.C. "almost monopolizes the freight and passenger traffic of the west coast of South America," with small steamers serving "every inlet and roadstead" and larger vessels connecting Callao, Arica, Iquique, Valparaíso, and Concepción (Douglas 1878:202).

With the railroad's future looking bleak, a renegotiation of its concession with Colombia took place in 1867, when a financially strapped Bogotá secured a new contract: while this granted the railroad a 99-year license, it had cost a million dollars plus a $250,000 annuity. The railroad was clearly struggling and so dropped its interests in the shipping companies. When the French arrived to dig a canal in 1880, the railroad negotiated with them, and in 1883 the Panamá Railroad ceased to be an independent operation and became a subsidiary of the French canal company. That did not end the railroad's difficulties. The partnership with the Pacific Mail became strained, and in 1896 the Pacific Mail ended its steamship service between New York and Colón. This was another damaging blow to the railroad (Kemble 1950:20).

Panamá Route Steamer Wrecks of the Post–Gold Rush Period

As was the case with the previously mentioned Spanish *flota* and Gold Rush–era steamer wrecks, the more expansive maritime cultural landscape of the Panamá route includes wrecks on the Pacific side of the isthmus. Post–Gold Rush losses began with the small, wooden-hulled, 460-ton propeller steamer *Columbus*. Built in 1847 for service between Philadelphia and Charleston, *Columbus* was swept up in Gold Rush fever and sent around Cape Horn to San Francisco, arriving in June 1850. Sold to the Pacific Mail in 1851, it ran on the Panamá route through 1854. Briefly chartered to the U.S. Navy, it was then sold to the Panamá Railroad Company but was later lost after hitting the reef off Punta Remedios at Acajutla, El Salvador, on December 9, 1861 (Kemble 1943:221). The wreck, partially salvaged at the time of its loss and subsequently subjected to contemporary looting and salvage, nonetheless remains in place off Acajutla: it retains its original engine and a substantial part of the hull remains. Studied by archaeologist Roberto Gallardo, this wreck is a highly significant historical archaeological site in El Salvador.

The worst Panamá route post–Gold Rush disaster was the destruction by fire of the massive 2,067-ton wooden sidewheeler *Golden Gate*. Built in New York in 1850 by famed shipbuilder William H. Webb for the Pacific Mail, *Golden Gate* entered service as the "queen steamer of the Pacific" (according to contemporary accounts) after its launch in early 1851, departing for San Francisco in the fall and arriving in November of the same year (Delgado 1991:63). Accommodating 800 passengers, *Golden Gate* was one of a new series of Gold Rush arrivals introduced to counter overcrowding and to speed up the transit time from Panamá to San Francisco. After a long period of service in which the steamer set records for speed and was heralded for its accommodations and service, it was tragically lost after departing San Francisco on July 21, 1862 (Kemble 1943:145,228; Goss 1953). While running three to four miles off the coast of Manzanillo, Mexico, fire broke out in the galley and quickly spread on July 26 (San Francisco *Daily Alta California*, August 7, 1862). Passengers and crew panicked, and as the steamer raced for the beach, flames fanned by the wind spread rapidly (Chavanne 1940).

All told, 223 people died (175 of them passengers) before the ship ran aground 300 yards offshore and burned to the waterline (San Francisco *Daily Alta California*, August 7, 1862): "What was not burned of the steamer was broken up; the bow and stern came ashore, and in the morning there was nothing left but the bedplate, wheels and attachments. The beach was strewn with various portions of the wreck" (San Francisco *Daily Alta California*, August 7, 1862). Bodies were washed ashore and buried nearby; the U.S. consul reported that he had led a party to the wreck site and buried 26 victims (San Francisco *Daily Alta California*, August 17, 1862).

Lost with the steamer was $1,400,747.24 in treasure that had been bound for New York and London and sent by 19 separate consignees (San Francisco *Bulletin*, July 21, 1862). As the gold was insured, Lloyds' San Francisco–based insurance agent headed to Manzanillo, as did other underwriters and salvagers such as Thomas J. Smiley and a man named Irelan. Smiley and Irelan recovered some $100,000 between them, ultimately paying Lloyds $40,000 after litigation in Admiralty Court.[1] An 1878 salvage by Sidney Cook reportedly recovered $1,298,000-worth more of the gold. Additional treasure said to be on the steamer was not recovered, and that inspired new salvage attempts in 1908, when a long pier was built some 300 feet offshore to reach the wreck in the surf (it was destroyed by storms). Another expedition was supposedly undertaken in 1931–1932. A salvage expedition in 1986 involved building a cofferdam around the wreck, but the project ended when the expedition leader was murdered. Known as the Playa de Oro, the site reportedly (some say apocryphally) yields gold coins, which are occasionally spotted on the beach.[2]

The site of the wreck, 18 miles north of Manzanillo, is between 150 to 300 feet offshore in relatively shallow water and covered with sand. The captain of *Golden Gate* noted in his report on the loss that the wreck lay on a "shelving beach and heavy surf" (San Francisco *Daily Alta California*, August 7, 1862). The conditions have made access to the wreck difficult for every salvager in the century that followed, and three persons were killed on the site during the 1908 salvage. Mexico's avocational group CEDAM (Club de Exploraciones y Deportes Acuaticos de Mexico) conducted some dives and recovered artifacts, including some of the salvage gear from the 1903 expedition. There has been no archaeological work done on the wreck. The steamer's bell, recovered during one of the early salvage projects, was returned to San Francisco and is now in the collection of the San Francisco Public Library in its San Francisco History Room. CEDAM has a display dedicated to the lost steamer in their museum in Puerto Aventuras, Mexico, and has published a book on the wreck (Torres 2003).

The next wreck was SS *Golden City*, another of the large wooden steamers of the Pacific Mail. Built by William H. Webb in New York, the 3,589-ton

Golden City was said to accommodate 2,000 passengers (*New York Times*, August 14, 1863). Launched in August 1863, *Golden City* was sent to California to commence operations on the Panamá route in November of the same year (Kemble 1943:228). The steamer's career was short. After departing San Francisco for Panamá with passengers and specie, the steamer ran aground on the evening of February 22, 1870, in thick fog off Baja California's Isla Magdalena. *Golden City* got stranded and broke apart on the shoals of Cabo San Lázaro, but the passengers, baggage, and the treasure were saved (*New York Times*, March 2, 1870). No archaeological work has been done here, but a recent boating guide noted that "a few of the *hundido*'s [shipwreck's] weathered keel bones are still visible in the shallow water SW of Boca de Soledad, and the nearby beach yields bits of corroded silverware and crockery shards" (Rains 2006:59).

Another of the large wooden sidewheelers built by William Webb in New York for the Pacific Mail would be the next to wreck. SS *Sacramento*, a 2,682-ton, 304-foot-long steamer launched in May 1863 ran a regular service between San Francisco and Panamá for nine years before it was lost. Departing Panamá on November 22, 1872, with 80 passengers, 288 tons of general merchandise, and $337,000 in silver bullion and specie, *Sacramento* called at Acapulco, Manzanillo, San Blas, Mazatlán, and Cabo San Lucas without incident (San Francisco *Daily Alta California*, December 13, 1872). On the evening of December 5, 190 miles south of San Diego, *Sacramento* hit an uncharted reef near Isla San Jerónimo on the Baja California coast and was stranded. The passengers, their baggage, and the treasure were safely landed on the island (some seven miles away), while a small boat with an officer and crew sailed to San Diego for help (San Francisco *Daily Alta California*, December 18, 1872). *Sacramento* flooded and eventually disintegrated, leaving only the main shaft of the engine's walking beam exposed above the waves. "Sacramento Reef," as it would subsequently be called, is now on the charts and avoided by mariners (Rains 2006:39). There has been no reported diving or archaeological work on the site.

The next Pacific Mail steamer to be lost and left in the maritime cultural landscape was the 1871-built SS *Honduras*. Built in Liverpool, the iron-hulled, 1,816-ton propeller steamer came into the Pacific via Cape Horn in 1872 and joined the P.M.S.S.C. fleet. After a 14-year career on the coast, running to the various ports "as far up as Acapulco and sometimes down the South American coast" (*New York Times*, April 27, 1886) in which "she was engaged principally in the coffee trade between Panamá and Champerico and way ports" (San Francisco *Daily Evening Bulletin*, April 27, 1886), *Hon-*

duras was lost on the bar of the Río Lempa off Jiquilisco Bay, El Triunfo, El Salvador, on April 25, 1886. The passengers and crew were saved, but the steamer was a total loss. The wreck was not salvaged, and as of this writing Salvadorian archaeologist Roberto Gallardo is searching for it in order to conduct an archaeological survey.

The Pacific Mail then suffered the loss of the iron-hulled steamer *Starbuck* off Nicaragua in 1899. Built in 1881 in Sunderland as the steamer *Olivetto* and registered in Shields, the steamer had a checkered career. Going ashore at Moriches on Long Island on December 23, 1884, *Olivetto* remained stuck on the beach for months before being pulled free. Purchased by G. Starbuck and towed to New York, the steamer was repaired and improved in Greenpoint, New York, in the spring and summer of 1885 (*New York Times*, April 2, 1885; *Newtown* [Long Island] *Register*, February 26, 1885; San Francisco *Daily Alta California*, July 21, 1886). The Pacific Mail bought the steamer, (renamed by Starbuck after himself) to replace their wrecked transpacific liner *City of Tokio*, which wrecked at the entrance to Tokyo Bay in June 1885 (*New York Times*, March 24, 1886).

The "new" steamer, about half the size of *City of Tokio* at 2,157 tons gross and 266 feet in length, departed New York for China via the Suez Canal on May 5, 1886; it finally arrived in San Francisco via Hong Kong in July (San Francisco *Daily Alta California*, July 21, 1886). Considered "a slow steamer" with a maximum speed of nine knots, *Starbuck* was soon pulled from the transpacific run and sent to the Panamá route, exemplifying the decline of the route's importance (Tate 1986:32).

Starbuck was wrecked on the night of February 28, 1899, after leaving Panamá, having just come in from Champerico on January 29 to load passengers and cargo. *Starbuck* struck a shoal seven miles southeast of Cosequina Point and a mile and a half from the beach on the coast of Nicaragua while bound for the Honduran port of Amapala (San Francisco *Chronicle*, March 1, 1899, San Francisco *Call*, March 1, 1899; United States Hydrographic Office 1904:297). The passengers were saved, but the steamer was lost (San Francisco *Call*, March 4, 1899). There is no known report on the remains of the wreck or of any investigation of the site.

The next vessel on the Panamá route to be hit with misfortune was *Granada*, which was one of the first iron steamers built for the Pacific coast and the Pacific Mail. Built in Wilmington, Delaware, by John Roach in 1873, the 280-foot-long, 2,572-ton screw-propelled steamer was first used in the transpacific service, but was too small (Tate 1986:28,31). After being used on the run between San Francisco, the South Pacific, New Zealand,

and Australia, *Granada* ended up on the Panamá route. *Granada* struck a reef and grounded near Punta Tejupan, between Acapulco and Manzanillo, on June 22, 1889. The official explanation was that a strong inshore current swept her off course. The vessel was a total loss and was sold by the underwriters for $9,000 (Los Angeles *Herald*, October 26, 1889). A wreck that is likely *Granada* is marked on the charts and is dived, but it has not been surveyed or archaeologically studied (Rains 2006:221).

The same stretch of coast also claimed the 2,905-ton Pacific Mail steamer *Colima*, *Granada*'s onetime transpacific running mate, which foundered off Manzanillo while en route from San Francisco to Panamá on May 27, 1895. When the ship was 50 miles from Manzanillo, a strong current (it was claimed) took the steamer off course, and *Colima* struck a reef: "From all sources of information thus far received it is positive that the accident was not due to the carelessness of the officers and crew nor to any mistake on their part. A strong veering wind caught the vessel and drove her upon the reef and stove a hole in her bottom, causing her to sink inside of ten minutes" (Berkeley *Gazette*, May 31, 1895). The remains of the vessel reportedly sank deep, and there are no accounts of its rediscovery or of any salvage.

There are two other wrecks from the post–Gold Rush, precanal Panamá route. The steamer *San Blas*, another Roach-built iron-hulled steamer, was lost off Acajutla, El Salvador, when it struck a reef on December 17, 1901 (San Francisco *Call*, December 19, 1901). Built by John Roach at Chester, Pennsylvania, in 1882 for the Pacific Mail Steamship Company, the 2,180-ton *San Blas* was intended for the Panamá run and worked the route for nearly two decades. The wreck was salvaged at the time of its loss, and since then it has been periodically mined for scrap iron over the last century. An archaeological survey of the site in 2011 by Roberto Gallardo delineated the wreck's scatter and more intact remains within a 150- to 200-meter by 100-meter area from shallow water up to the beach itself; a number of artifacts remain on the site, but some have also been recovered (Gallardo 2013).

Gallardo has also documented the partially scrapped shallow-water remains of the former Pacific Mail (later Panamá Railroad) steamer *Colón*, which wrecked off Acajutla on April 11, 1904 (Gallardo 2013a). Built by Roach and launched in November 1872, the iron-hulled screw steamer had a long and famed history on the route: first on the Atlantic/Caribbean run to Aspinwall and then on the Pacific, where it was from 1893 to 1904. On its final voyage, *Colón* struck the reef at Punta Remedios and ran aground. The remains of the steamer are visible on the beach at Acajutla, a more exposed but still distant element of the maritime cultural landscape of the Panamá route beyond the immediate area of the isthmus itself.

The Pacific Pearl Company

The pearl beds in the Bay of Panamá were important assets of the pre-Columbian and colonial eras on the isthmus. The landscape is dominated by an archipelago of some 43 islands and hundreds of exposed rocks: these are visible remnants of a coast submerged by a rise in sea level after the Last Glacial Maximum. The shallows around the islands became an ideal habitat for the Pacific pearl oyster, *Pinctada mazatlanica*, which thrives on rocky substrates in waters ranging from wading depth to 36 meters. In Panamá, the islands' first inhabitants harvested the oysters for food, not only from the shallows but also from deeper waters as breath-holding divers began working this area some 9,000 years ago. Pearls and pearl-shell ornaments are found in burials as well as drilled pearl necklaces and jewelry (Linné 1929:68,70). As seen in chapter 1, the importance of marine resources in the pre-Columbian world even permeated the symbolic sphere, when around the mid-first millennium AD, found artifacts from the thorny shells of *Spondylus princeps* became important signifiers (along with gold) of rank and status for the societies that ringed the Gulf of Panamá.

The first Spanish explorers and conquistadors to reach the isthmus searched for pearls (Castillero 2004i:449; Jaén Suárez 1998:245–248). Balboa was the first not only to reach the Pacific but also the Pearl Islands, which he had heard about from native sources: "I believe that there are many islands in that sea. They say that there are many large pearls, and that the caciques have baskets of them. . . . It is a most astonishing thing and without equal, that our Lord has made the lord of this land" (letter from Vasco Nuñez de Balboa to the King on January 1513, qtd. in Altolaguirre y Duvale 1914:19; Richman 1919:73–74). Following Balboa's 1513 sighting and exploration of the Pacific shore and of the islands and their pearl beds, the Spanish conquered the indigenous people and enslaved them as pearl divers, which helped secure a monopoly controlled by Seville. They renamed the islands the Archipiélago de las Perlas (or the "archipelago of the pearls"). The high mortality rates of the natives due to disease and overwork led to demand for slaves from Africa to replace the native divers. Concurrently, at least on one occasion in the 1570s, overexploitation led to the exhaustion of the rich pearl beds (Castillero 2004i:450). After their replenishment a decade later they continued to be harvested; however, the supply was exhausted again in the 1750s. But the beds continued to replenish themselves until the 1860s and 1870s when the beds were permanently depleted in the Gulf of Panamá. This prompted a move to pearl beds on the coast of Veragus and Chiriquí provinces in the west of Panamá: this continued until the 1930s to 1940s, when the business was definitively abandoned (Camargo 1983:33). Today, the Pearl Islands are populated by the descendants of African slaves (MacKenzie 1999:58–65; Mellado 2010).

The maritime cultural landscape of the islands is one not only of submerged pearl beds but also of isolated villages, which were (and still are, in some cases) pearl fishers' settlements. Another prominent landmark is the eighteenth-century cathedral in the Casco Viejo. Its twin spires are decorated with mother-of-pearl, the gift to the church of grateful pearl merchants who lived a separate and more opulent life in the city. The oldest surviving home in the Casco Viejo is the Casa Góngora, built in 1756 by pearl merchant Pablo Góngora de Cáceres (Castillero 2004i:452). This is another seemingly land-bound maritime element in the maritime cultural landscape of Panamá. Among the decorative elements of the home are giant scalloped pearl shell-shaped elements above the doors, which can be seen as a not-so-subtle hint as to what financed the house.

During the first half of the nineteenth century the pearl-diving business continued with rich returns. In 1836 a figure of 60,000 pesos in revenue was reported (Jaén Suárez 1998:247). The Gold Rush period saw a decline in the activity in the fisheries, although this activity resumed again in the 1860s (Camargo 1983:48). The possibility of a revival, one that would replace labor with industrial technology, appealed to Americans and Britons passing through Panamá in the early nineteenth century. With the effort of divers who aligned themselves with urban entrepreneurs, a small trade revived. The entrepreneurs may not have enslaved the divers but likely exploited them or paid them in species—that is, with pearls. A July 1852 article in the San Francisco *Daily Alta California*, quoting from the *Panamá Herald*, noted, "There are, at this time, from twelve to fifteen hundred persons engaged in the pearl fisheries of these islands" (*Daily Alta California*, July 19, 1852).

The pearl divers recovered between $80,000 and $150,000 in pearls each year and from 900 to 1,000 tons of pearl shells with an average value of $40,000: "These shells were formerly esteemed as worthless, but recently they have become the chief article of export from this country, being worth from thirty to forty dollars per ton" (*Daily Alta California*, July 19, 1852). Brief experiments with diving bells and sub-marine armor (forced-air div-

Figure 62. "Panama Bay, Pearl fishers," c. 1883. The pearl fishery, a dominant element of the isthmian maritime cultural landscape from precontact times, was extensively exploited by the conquering Spanish. The indigenous population was eradicated by massacre, slavery, and disease. The fishery persisted with the use of African slaves through the early nineteenth century. The pearl fishery was largely overfished, and by the last decades of the nineteenth century it was no longer in use. That did not stop American entrepreneurs from adopting "modern" technology to "revive" the fishery. They failed, and the fishery returned to a small-scale, nonindustrial effort. Here tourists visit a pearl-fishing schooner as the fishermen search oysters recovered by breath-holding divers. Library of Congress, Prints and Photographs Division (LOC call no. LC-F8-4659-B).

ing helmets and suits) were tried with little success, and the fishery continued to languish (*Scientific American*, August 2, 1862).

The end of the Civil War in 1865 brought a new crop of entrepreneurs from the United States with more "know-how" and enterprise: and thus came the advent of the iron submersible. The goal was to harvest not only pearls but pearl-shell (mother-of-pearl), which was in demand for ornamentation on a variety of items ranging from pearl buttons on clothing to knife handles. Organized in New York City as the Pacific Pearl Company (Pacific Pearl Company 1866), the new enterprise focused on the late war-built, 36-foot *Sub Marine Explorer*, a sophisticated mobile diving bell and submarine built in Brooklyn by engineer Julius H. Kroehl and retired shipbuilder Ariel Patterson (Delgado 2009). After failing to sell their craft to the U.S. Navy in 1865, the company partially dismantled the sub and shipped it to Panamá with Kroehl.

Crossing the isthmus on the railroad with his craft packed piecemeal in crates in September 1866, Kroehl reassembled it on the bay front next to the railroad depot, taking advantage of their machine shop and pier (*Panamá Star and Herald*, September 12, 1867). After successful test dives in the bay off Isla Flamenco, Kroehl died of malaria, and the sub sat idle on the beach at Flamenco until 1869, when engineer Henry Dingee arrived from New York and took it to the Pearl Islands to harvest pearls.

The *Panamá Mercantile Chronicle* reported on the "experimental expedition of the Pacific Pearl Company to the island of St. Elmo, in the Bay of Panamá" in August:

> The *Explorer* is 36 feet long, 12 feet high, and 13 feet broad, its bottom is perfectly flat, and has two hatches 4 ½ feet and 6 feet long respectively. These hatches, as the machine approaches the bottom, are opened for the purpose of gathering the oysters, the water being kept at bay during the submersion by the by the air contained within the machine. Through these apertures, when the machine rests on or near the bottom, the oysters are collected and stowed away by the men within. The shape of the machine resembles somewhat the upper segment of a short, thick cigar, with a turret in the middle of the top part for the entrance of the men who descend in it. The machine, when under water, is moved over the bottom in search of oysters by means of a small propeller, three feet in diameter, worked by hand by the men inside. (*Panamá Mercantile Chronicle*, August 13, 1869)

The use of a pressurized air tank allowed the operator to match the ambient water pressure at depth. This also allowed the craft to become the equivalent of a modern "lock-out" bell as the crew gathered as many oysters as the craft could carry. After blowing out seawater ballast with more compressed air, the pearls would then be brought to the surface (Delgado 2009).

In an August 1869 story, the *New York Times* reported on the brief commercial use of *Sub Marine Explorer*:

Inflated with forty-six pounds of compressed air, then partially filled with water, it went down at 11 A.M., remaining under water four hours, when it rose to the surface with 1,800 oysters, or about seven-eighths of a ton of shell. The machine afterward made one downward trip each day for eleven days, at the end of which all the men were again down with fever; and it being impossible to continue working with the same men for some time, it was decided, the experiment having proved a complete success, to lay the machine up in an adjacent cove and to convey to the Company the gratifying intelligence. We understand Mr. DINGEE proceeded to New York on the 31st ult. with the proceeds of the experimental trial—some 10 ½ tons of pearl shells and pearls to the value of $2,000, more or less. (*New York Times*, August 29, 1869)

The account went on to note that "the engineer of the 'Pacific Pearl Company' by whom this success was achieved, is now in this city, and his submarine iron diver is safely moored at St. Elmo" (*New York Times*, August 29, 1869). It never left the island: the Pacific Pearl Company proved to be

Figure 63. Wreck of *Sub Marine Explorer* exposed by low tide on the beach at Isla San Telmo. Photograph by James P. Delgado.

an economic failure and disbanded, abandoning the *Explorer* at its job site where the sub would become a permanent element of the maritime cultural landscape of the islands (Delgado 2012).

Partially stripped, blasted open, and left to the elements, the *Sub Marine Explorer* still lies in the intertidal zone of Isla San Telmo. Misidentified as a World War II Japanese midget submarine (or as a boiler) the craft's relative isolation and its infamous repute among the pearl divers in neighboring villages (they thought it was a "craft of death") meant little to no exploration or serious inquiry. In 2001 author James Delgado was shown the craft while passing through the islands and, after identifying it in 2003, commenced a several-year project to document it:

> To that end, it was also very clear at the beginning of the project to document and assess *Sub Marine Explorer* that it not only needed to be assessed within its cultural, historical and technological contexts, it also needed to be assessed as part of a larger environment, namely the cove, the pearl beds, Isla San Telmo, and even the *Archipiélago de las Perlas*. This required the integration into the team of oceanographers and marine biologists, and, significantly, the local population of fishermen and pearl divers who continued to work the waters as their ancestors had for centuries past. . . . In the 2008 field season, as will be seen, we merged local diver knowledge with breath-holding inhabitants of the neighboring village of La Esmeralda along with remote sensing data from a state-of-the-art REMUS autonomous underwater vehicle to better assess where *Explorer* had and had not worked in 1869. Where the REMUS went, into deeper waters, *Explorer* had once gone according to the available written record. These were areas with few oysters and pearls. Where the divers went, while clearly reflecting the effects of centuries of over-fishing, was where the oysters thrived—and where *Explorer* did not go. Local knowledge clearly demonstrated a major factor in the failure of the Pacific Pearl Company, namely failure to obtain local knowledge and thus understand the physical and maritime cultural landscape into which the Pacific Pearl Company "dropped" *Sub Marine Explorer*. Simply stated, Isla San Telmo was not at the heart of the pearl diving area in the archipelago, and the submarine not only worked off a less than rich island, it did so in depths where resources were scarce. Thus the submarine on a beach, when examined in a larger context, is another material example of a timeless lesson, that of assumption and faulty

> research, and inadequate planning. The submarine was built in an atmosphere of expansion, speculation and risk, all married to a sense that technology and a can-do attitude would win the day. They did not. (Delgado 2012:157–158)

The study of *Explorer* also concluded that it represents another nineteenth-century effort to employ technology for resource exploitation. However, that technology was deployed in typical nineteenth-century fashion: blindly and without any concern for habitat, fisheries management, or sustainability. In 1889 Dr. Wolfred Nelson, a former resident of Panamá, opined that the pearl fisheries, although "at one time of inestimable value," had been "destroyed by the reckless methods employed. Men in diving armor ruined them by taking up too many oysters, and for many years no fishing was allowed" (Nelson 1889:74; see also Camargo 1983:49).

Another resident of Panamá, Tracy Robinson, noted that "from 1860 to 1870 pearls and pearl shells from the fisheries in Panamá Bay figured to a considerable extent; but the oyster beds were overworked, and gave out, so that shipments almost entirely ceased" (Robinson 1907:198). The submarine is also another maritime artifact of an American effort to use technology to capitalize on the resources of the isthmus to again make Panamá "into a nexus of the world economy" (McGuiness 2008:7).

With the seeming end of the Isthmus of Panamá as a valuable global transit hub, the Pacific Pearl Company focused on exploiting another maritime aspect of the isthmus by integrating its pearls, a natural resource of Panamá, into the expanding global market and as part of dreams of an ever-expanding American empire in the Pacific. The Panamá Railroad and the steamers that connected to Panamá on other side of the isthmus were already less-than-successful aspects of the use of American technology to incorporate Panamá into a U.S.-dominated market system, It was therefore assumed that the submarine would be another aspect of this strategy and part of their larger agenda to industrialize and consolidate control and profits from the rich natural and mineral resources of the West and the Pacific as a whole.

The French Canal

The "revival" of Panamá envisioned by many as the advent of the canal, long the dream of entrepreneurs but always thwarted by the terrain and the technology of the times. American interest, strongest at the time of the

Figure 64. The timeless waterfront landscape of Panamá City as depicted during the French era in 1881. The shallow harbor in front of the city, with its extreme tidal range, serves as the moorage for shallow-draft bongos and *canoas*. From Armand Reclus, *Panamá et Darien Voyages d'Exploration* (Paris: Librairie Hachette, 1881).

Gold Rush, ebbed in the aftermath of the Fiebre del Oro, but not before one last concerted search for a route for a canal following the Civil War. The U.S. Navy, as well as agents of the French and British empires (Cullen 1853), had surveyed possible routes on more than one occasion. The first was a disastrous jungle trek led by Lt. Isaac Strain of USS *Cyane* in 1854 across the Darién. The next was led by Commander Thomas Oliver Selfridge, U.S.N. in 1870, on the instructions of Secretary of the Navy George Robeson, who noted "no matter how many surveys have been made, or how accurate they may have been, the people of this country will never be satisfied until every point of the isthmus is surveyed" (qtd. in Selfridge 1874:3).

Departing New York on January 22, 1870, with a survey party (including five civilian scientists from the U.S. Coast Survey) and equipment in the steamer USS *Nipsic* and the storeship USS *Guard*, Selfridge's expedition landed on February 21 where Strain's had: Caledonia Bay, the site of the ill-fated Scottish colony. The expedition exhaustively surveyed the Darién, the Gulf of San Blas, and various rivers over the next months, finding no easy route, only meandering trails, mighty rivers, and mountains reaching some 1,000 feet in elevation. To build a canal would require tunnels, blasting, and a route extending farther than the distance of a straight line spanning the isthmus, but nonetheless Selfridge ended his report by noting,

> It is a satisfaction to know that the Isthmus of Darién is no longer a doubtful land, and that as far as its adaptability as a ship-canal is in question it has been thoroughly explored. The United States has now, through the various expeditions fitted out for the purpose, the whole data to decide upon the feasibility of a project that has been the dream of centuries, and the best location for an enterprise the greatest and most important the world has yet seen. (Selfridge 1874:92)

Other expeditions on the isthmus continued to probe and document the area, but it was not the United States that took the next step of actually digging a canal. The expeditions led by Lucien Napoleon Bonaparte Wyse in 1876, 1877, and 1878 suggested that the French would finally undertake the enormous task after a series of exhaustive surveys (Reclus 1997).

The success of the Suez Canal in 1869 inspired its creator, Ferdinand de Lesseps, to tackle the isthmus. *La Société Internationale du Canal Interocéanique*, established in 1876, gained a concession from Colombia along similar terms to those of the railroad. The *Société* brought in de Lesseps to be the public face of the project, raising money for a sea-level canal that was to be dug straight across and through the mountains (McCullough 1977; de Banville 2012). The canal's dimensions were to be 22 m (72.2 ft) wide at the bottom, sloping up to a bank 27.5 m (90.2 ft), with an average depth of 9 m. The decision to excavate the canal at sea level, widespread corporate corruption, and the persistent problem of tropical diseases such as malaria and yellow fever—all of these factors were not only fatal to the project but also proved deadly to tens of thousands of workers.

Colonel William C. Gorgas, chief medical officer of the Isthmian Canal Commission, estimated that at least 22,000 died during the French canal project (Abbot 1914:309–310), and some of the major elements in the maritime cultural landscape of the isthmus are the "French cemeteries" now at the bottom of Lake Gatún. There were cemeteries dotted around the Panamá Canal area, the largest ones being those at Mount Hope (originally set aside as a burial ground for railroad workers in the 1850s), Ancon (later used for those who died during the U.S. canal project), and Paraiso, with its iron crosses and monument inscribed "A La Memoire de Francais Morts Lors de la Construction du Canal de Panamá." Other cemeteries existed at town and construction sites that are now under water. One noted by canal workers (and visible until 2015) was the eroded graveyard at the old site of Gorgona, where Tomás Mendizábal recently surveyed and excavated three tomb shafts—with no trace of human remains.[3] Other cemeteries such as

Figure 65. Eroded by fluctuating water levels in the canal, graves of canal workers from the French period at the often-inundated site of Gorgona are empty outlines in the mud in 2010. The site has since been completely washed away. Photography by Frederick Hanselmann.

those at Gatún, Bohio Soldado, Empire, and Matachin were documented, but no human remains were found there either. These cemeteries, while known to be "French," are so designated because of their association with that canal project, as the majority of those interred were from the labor force of Jamaicans, Barbadians, and other West Indians from the Caribbean islands. However, the former mortuary officer of the U.S. Army in Panamá, Erik Nicolaisen, stated that during the American era of the canal, some articles in those cemeteries were reutilized, including the characteristic white-painted iron crosses, although it is not known who is buried in these graves. The canal maintained these burial grounds until the 1960s, and then in the 1970s their complete removal was ordered, and the crosses were sold for scrap iron (Erik Nicolaisen, personal communication 2014). The most surprising fact gathered from research on the cemeteries is precisely the surprising lack of records and information about their use by the French. Although there is plenty of documentation on French companies and the American canal construction at the National Archives in Washington D.C. (McCullough 1977:620) there is still a paucity of information on the burial grounds.

The World Monuments Fund aptly terms these "burial landscapes" and notes that they

> are an important reminder of the lives lost to one of the most significant and iconic water passages in the world, and of the racial, social and economic exclusion many suffered in its construction.[4]

Furthermore, no documentation has been found as to who was buried at these cemeteries. While the French kept track of the deceased workers, only French deaths at company hospitals were recorded, while the rest of the workforce, who perished in the field or in their homes from accidents or illness, were not accounted for. In this manner 5,618 French deaths were recorded at the hospitals between 1881 and 1889, but it is still uncertain whether they were actually buried there or repatriated to France (Abbot 1914:309–310). There were even rumors that the Afro-Antillean workers were simply thrown in the fills and buried in the earth-moving works (McCullough 1977:173). The dearth of information may be attributed to an effort by the Société Internationale du Canal Interocéanique to keep a lid on the scale of the mortality rates in Panamá and to deny the existence of epidemics there, as they did with their financial troubles or reports of delays and problems with the construction of the canal. This was most likely done to keep their stock value from falling (McCullough 1977:138–140,161). For this they even bribed the French press so only good news would be reported (De Banville 2012:97).

The French canal project commenced in January 1881 and continued until 1889. The physical obstacles to the sea-level canal led to its abandonment in 1887 and the adoption of a canal with locks that would allow ships to "climb" over the isthmus. However, the exorbitant human and financial costs, as well as ongoing engineering challenges, led to the collapse of the effort and its end on May 15, 1889. The value of their market stock crashed in early 1889, and on February 4 the company was officially dissolved. This collapse led to national scandal followed by investigations and trials as evidence of bribes to politicians, excessive cost overruns, and other corruption began to mount. De Lesseps and his son Charles (who had supervised much of the work) were convicted, and the younger de Lesseps was imprisoned. Even the famous engineer of the Eiffel Tower, Gustave Eiffel, was indicted and sentenced to two years in prison, although he was later acquitted. The older de Lesseps was not as complicit in the crimes as he was simply naïve, but the entire political class of France was shaken up by what proved to be the worst scandal of the nineteenth century borne from the worst financial disaster of the era: 1,200 million francs ($240 million) were lost by the shareholders, which constituted practically every family in the country (for a thorough analysis, see De Banville 2012:108–122.)

After this interregnum, work on the canal resumed under the auspices of the Compagnie Nouvelle du Canal du Panamá in 1894. Although excavation continued, the work did not progress much because the company focused on maintenance of its equipment and enough work to satisfy the terms of its arrangement with the Colombian government. By the time all work stopped in 1903, the French efforts had moved 59,747,638 cubic meters (78,146,690 cubic yards) of dirt and rock from the canal and had blasted a route through the summit at Culebra. The Culebra Cut, as it is still known, accounted for nearly 25 percent of the excavated material, and that only leveled the summit by 5 m (17 ft.).

American interest in the canal was rekindled at the end of the nineteenth century, although it was suspected at the time that they wanted the French company to fail so they could build the canal themselves (De Banville 2012:99–102). The war with Spain and the need to rapidly move U.S. Navy ships from one coast to another had been highlighted by the need to bring battleships into the Caribbean from the Pacific to counter the Spanish fleet in Cuba in 1898. The formation of the U.S. Isthmian Canal Commission in 1899 and the subsequent presidency of Theodore Roosevelt (a strong proponent of an American canal in Panamá) fed the hope that the canal could be sold for the French asking price of $109 million. When the U.S. offer did come, it was for $40 million, and the Compagnie Nouvelle du Canal du Panamá took the money. In the meantime, with American support, Panamá had separated from Colombia on November 3 1903, becoming an independent republic, and soon the United States "negotiated" for a new canal treaty. The United States received, it was estimated, about $25 million in cost savings for the work done by the French, even though the Americans used a different approach. The remaining French equipment and infrastructure (including 2,148 buildings) was valued at $17.4 million. The end of the French canal era came officially on May 4, 1904, and the American era began. The isthmus was about to undergo its most dramatic change—one that would forever alter the landscape and the nature of Panamá.

Traces of the French

The last visible trace of the French ship canal is a small section that starts on the shores of Límon Bay close to the Gatún locks. Other once-visible traces were absorbed into the American canal at Balboa and the Gaillard Cut (Austin 1971). In addition to the ship canal, the French also excavated two other major works: the diversions. These were two channels, one that drained water west of the Chagres and another that drained water east into Manzanillo Bay. Portions of the diversions remain visible as of 2014. The former offices of the French company have been restored and now serve as the Panamá Canal Museum on the Plaza Catedral in the Casco Viejo.[5] Also in the Casco, the Plaza de Francia overlooks the bay. Designed by Leonardo Villanueva Meyer in 1923, the monument incorporates the old city wall, with an obelisk in the center (crowned with a French rooster) and with marble plaques and busts commemorating the principal figures of the French effort, including de Lesseps. Appropriately, the French Embassy faces the square and the monument.

More extensive remains of the French period are abandoned in the jungles in and around the former Canal Zone, and in some cases there are still finds of submerged French equipment and town sites. This included unused equipment as well as equipment used during the American effort and then left at mostly inaccessible sites that were to be inundated with the completion of the canal between 1911 and 1914. A 1989 proposal for dives to document (and in some cases recover) these artifacts for museum display, "History under the Canal," succinctly noted that "literally tons of the original French plant and the channels that they dig still exist at their original locations, in what once was the valley of the Chagres and is now Gatún Lake," including steam engines and "Gigantic excavators, like extinct dinosaurs, buckets poised to take the next bite" (Wiskowski 1988:1).

Among the sites and equipment noted were an intact Franco-Belge 0-6-0 tank-type locomotive at Peña Blanca with two rows of 56 four-cubic-meter dump cars, a line of some 40 standard dump cars, disassembled dump cars, a crane, a shop yard with three disassembled excavators, locomotives, rock drills, boilers, steam engines, and rail and spare parts at Bohio. The proposal noted that this was a submerged site that, despite damage and destruction from subsequent dredging and dumping in 1985, "offers a view of the workings and layout of an important French Canal era work camp," as well as the site for locks and a dam (Wiskowski 1988:15). As a "pristine example of an 1880s Canal construction site," Bohio included "the

Figure 66. Different elements in the maritime cultural landscape converge at the tip of the Casco Viejo: the seawall and battery, now capped by the Plaza de Francia's monument to the French canal builders, the islands in the Bay of Panamá, and the causeway linking the islands to the mainland and protecting the Pacific entrance to the canal. Photograph by James P. Delgado.

original track line, down to the rails, ties, spikes, coral ballast, brick foundations, and equipment neatly stacked as it was left" (Wiskowski 1988:16). Another submerged site, Tabernilla, includes a now-silted channel dug by the French through the plain of Tabernilla and five of seven reportedly abandoned excavators, including two 250-foot-long, 200-ton Le Brun excavators documented in 1989 (Wiskowski 1988:21). Nearby, the site of Chagresito, used as a storehouse and workshop site, was documented as holding abandoned equipment and foundations, but it was reported damaged by dredging in the 1980s (Wiskowski 1988:21). More recent reports by divers note that Tabernilla remains a site visited for its bottles and relics and that it retains much of its original topography, including, in one area, a set of concrete steps depicted in a historic photograph that the divers followed down on their dive. Other popular dive sites include the town site of Gorgona, which is partially exposed at low tide.

While the Panamá Canal Authority's ongoing dredging and the modern expansion of the canal have damaged or destroyed submerged sites in Gatún Lake, they have recovered and conserved some artifacts, including a French locomotive and dump cars from 14 m (45 ft.) depths in 2000. A graveyard of old dredges and barges at Diablo, however, visible at low tide, was removed in 2007. In 2011, as part of the Canal Authority's CRM program, one of the coauthors of this book, Tomás Mendizábal, witnessed the underwater recovery of French industrial machinery near the ancient town of Bohio Soldado. Among the items found were boilers, wagons, axles, and track—all taken from a now-submerged terrace of the Chagres where sonar images showed a field thick with abandoned equipment. But many other remnants of the French effort remain strewn across the jungles surrounding the canal.

Figures 67a–c. Other archaeological finds during the recent expansion of the canal included large numbers of bottles and ceramics left in dumps associated with railroad and canal construction. The profusion of alcoholic beverage bottles points not only to a predominately male population of laborers but also to the ready supply of goods thanks to Panamá's role as a maritime link in global trade. All of these bottles came from the site of Gorgona, now submerged under Lake Gatún. Photographs by Tomás Mendizábal/Autoridad del Canal de Panamá (ACP), 2015. Reproduced courtesy of ACP.

Figures 68a–d. Archaeological mitigation during the recent expansion of the canal documented the recovered remains of French canal equipment and machinery abandoned after the collapse of the French effort and subsequently inundated by the American canal. A 1910 ACP image shows abandoned French ladder dredges. Also shown are a Decauville dump cart, railcars, and a steam engine raised from the site of Bohio Soldado in 2011. Decauville Materiel de Chemins de Fer of Paris was founded by Paul Decauville in 1875, an early pioneer of industrial railways and railway equipment. Photographs by Tomás Mendizábal/Autoridad del Canal de Panamá (ACP), 2011. Reproduced courtesy of ACP.

8

Fortification and Control, 1903–2015

The twentieth century brought the most profound changes to the Isthmus of Panamá since the arrival of the Spanish. The American-imposed landscape of the Gold Rush and the changes wrought by the French from the 1870s through the end of the nineteenth century paled in comparison to a new and successful American-led initiative to build the Panamá Canal. As was the case with the railroad, the canal firmly cemented the fact that the isthmus was now possibly the most critical maritime transit hub in the world; however, the commerce that flowed through it wasn't very beneficial, economically or otherwise, to the inhabitants of the isthmus. As had been the case with the *trajín* of the sixteenth and seventeenth centuries and the Gold Rush later on, the profits flowed to investors in foreign lands and to a well-connected and select local elite. The creation of the canal (or more properly, the creation of the Canal Zone) made Panamá a de facto colony of the United States despite its ostensible independence from Colombia.

In 1913 Willis J. Abbot observed that most Panamanians viewed the United States and its citizens with "hardly concealed contempt." The Panamanian "on the street," noted Abbot, was less than pleased with the canal and the "American invasion" because "he got none of the ten million dollars, or of the $250,000 annual payment. . . . The influx of the Americans brought him no particular prosperity, unless he drove a hack" (Abbot 1913:233). Resentment, perhaps not of the canal but of the Canal Zone and its circumstances, led to Panamanian efforts to rally their national identity in a project to reclaim it and also the maritime landscape it encompassed. Those efforts were ultimately successful at the end of the twentieth century. The twenty-first century ushered in a new era and renewed investment, which would expand the canal's capacity. What hangs in the balance, at least for Panamanians, is how to equitably distribute the wealth generated by the canal so that it reaches the average Panameño. This would also help redefine what it means to be Panamanian in light of the departure of the colonial enclave and the return of total sovereignty over the territory.

The Americans "Return"

The American "return" to the canal came after decades of discussion, negotiation, planning, and surveying for a canal across the isthmus at Nicaragua. An 1884 treaty with Nicaragua for a canal never made it to the Senate for ratification. And probably in deference to British views and a long-standing agreement between the United States and Great Britain, the Clayton-Bulwer Treaty of 1850 made any canal a neutral passage under international guarantee (Williams 1916:286). Requests for American financial backing of the faltering French canal in Panamá in the 1890s also led to considerable communication between Washington and London. But after 1898 a growing entente between the United States and Great Britain led to renegotiation of the Clayton-Bulwer Treaty that was signed in 1900, allowing the United States the right to construct an isthmian canal under the general principle that it would be a neutral waterway with right of passage for all nations (Williams 1916:302–303). Disagreement in the Senate and changes unacceptable to Britain led to more negotiation. Ultimately a final agreement, the Hay-Pauncefote Treaty, was signed in November 1901. In this treaty, Great Britain acquiesced to the United States' view that "the right to protect and control the canal was only a reasonable demand, considering the whole cost of construction was to be borne by the American nation" (Williams 1916:309).

American interest in the canal had been heightened by failed French effort and a strong belief that with American enterprise, ingenuity, and capital the task could be done but by an emerging strategic need.[1] That need came at the end of the nineteenth century as the United States embarked on colonial expansion as a result of its war with Spain in 1898. The United States was not only becoming a colonial power but was also assuming a stronger role in the global economy and as a military power, particularly during the presidency of Theodore Roosevelt. During the war with Spain, the lengthy 68-day, 14,000-nautical-mile voyage of Pacific-based battleship USS *Oregon* to the Caribbean, sent to try and thwart a feared Spanish naval attack had demonstrated the need for a quicker "maritime highway" across the isthmus. That and the acquisition of new American possessions in the Pacific—Guam and the Philippines, soon followed by Hawaii—necessitated a means for more expedient travel between the seas. A canal, whether

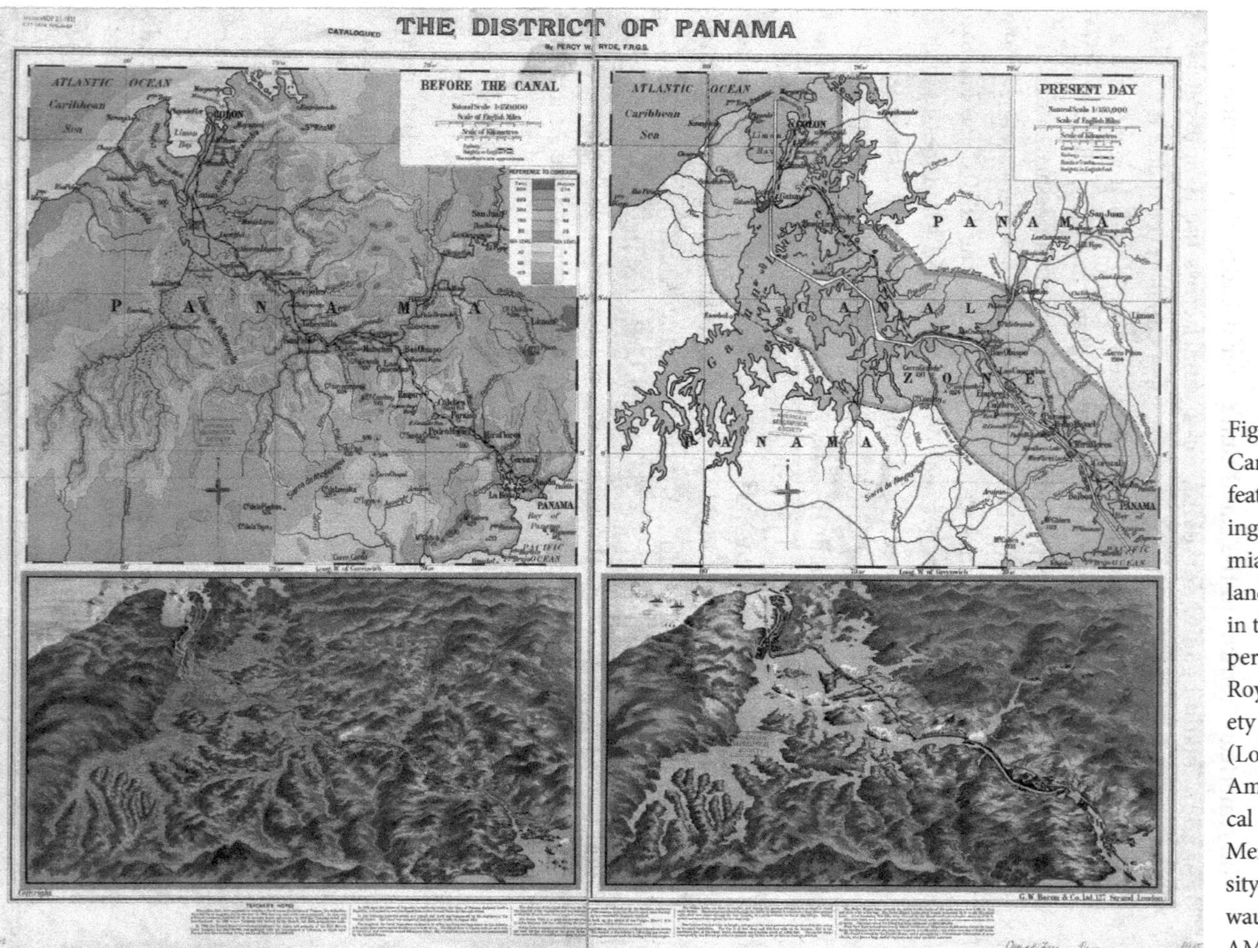

Figure 69. The Panamá Canal and its various features in the evolving, changing isthmian maritime cultural landscape are depicted in this amazing two-perspective 1915 map by Royal Geographic Society fellow Percy W. Ryde (London: G. W. Bacon). American Geographical Society Collection, Meier Library, University of Wisconsin–Milwaukee (digital file no. AM001208).

in Nicaragua or Panamá, was "essential for the United States to coordinate its transcontinental bases of commerce and project its naval might in both the Atlantic and the Pacific" (Adas 2006:193).

The site for the American canal was decided by adroit political maneuvering in Washington, the forced "fire sale" of the French assets, and a Washington-backed "revolution" supported by U.S. warships anchored off the isthmus that led to an independent Panamá ceding the rights for a transisthmian canal in the Hay-Bunau-Varilla Treaty. This treaty was signed in November 1903 and ratified by the Senate in February 1904 in which the new republic also ceded its sovereignty to an 80-kilometer-long, 16-kilometer wide strip of land, designated as the new "Canal Zone," in exchange for a one-time payment of 10 million dollars and an annual stipend of $250,000 to start in 1912. Additionally, the treaty ceded to the U.S. control of Panamanian waters from each oceanic terminal to the limit of nation's sea border, three nautical miles offshore (the story has been documented extensively, see among others Abbot 1913, 1914; Bennett 1915; De Banville 2012; McCullough 1977; Major 1993; Parker 2008).

The Canal Zone: A Dominant Feature of the American Maritime Cultural Landscape

The Canal Zone (or the "C.Z." as it was quickly designated) became more than a political or social division: it also became and remains a prominent feature of the twentieth- and twenty-first-century maritime cultural landscape. The zone had and retains profound significance for both Americans and Panamanians, reflecting a cultural divide between both. As Frenkel (2002) notes,

> Canal Zone towns were designed to remove white American residents from an array of "Others," specifically an "Other" natural landscape (the Panamanian "jungle"), an "Other" cultural landscape (Panamanian Cities), and an «Other» people (the West Indian Panamá Canal labour force and Spanish-speaking Panamanians). The negative nature of these representations undergirded American perceptions of the Canal Zone. Importantly, the manner in which Americans understood Panamá bolstered the imperial practice of rationalizing discrimination against tropical people, the need for segregated housing, and the creation of an Americanized landscape. In doing so, American representations of Panamá as "Other" engendered an American sense of superiority. (Frenkel 2002:85)

Within the borders of the Canal Zone, in addition to the towns and other infrastructure, is a watershed within a vast tropical rainforest with a mean annual rainfall of 2842 mm. This rainfall feeds the Río Chagres, the heart of the canal, and other major waterways such as the Río Grande and Río Cocolí as well as smaller streams—all of which now drain into the artificial lakes (Larson and Albertin 1984). This represents a major restructuring of the landscape, with the riparian resources sublimated to the needs of the canal and protected as a source to feed the canal and keep it open through consistent flooding of Gatún and the Alajuela lakes region (Carse 2012). This vast artificial lake, Alajuela, was formed by damming and flooding the old Chagres river valley. It comprises 32 k (20 mi) of the canal; when at its optimal level of 26 m (85 ft) above sea level, its 425 sq k (164 sq mi) area holds 5.2 cubic km (183,000,000,000 cu ft) of fresh water (Larson and Albertin 1984). This keeps the canal operational and serves as Panamá City's water supply. In terms of the maritime cultural landscapes representing not only human responses to the environment but also human-induced changes to the environment, the canal and its lake are probably the world's largest artificial maritime cultural landscape elements.[2] It is also a landscape that now-retired British ambassador to the United States, Viscount Bryce, in 1913 famously noted was "the greatest liberty Man has ever taken with nature" (Bryce 1913:36).

As noted, in addition to the regulated control of the Canal Zone environment, the zone became a fenced enclave supporting the canal and housing the American citizens who worked on the canal and their families as well as the troops sent to protect the canal. The "Zone" was so separate and such an artificial construct that, in many ways as historian Andrew Missal argues, it was an "American utopia" that was neither part of the United States nor a part of Panamá (Missal 2008:122).[3] The creation of the new zone led to the displacement of older settlements, some of which dated back centuries, such as Miraflores, Gorgona, or Gatún. A large number were simply dismantled, and most flooded and then "vanished" from the landscape beneath the lakes. The example of Chagres is particularly relevant.

In 1911 Chagres was described as a "sleepy settlement of a few hundred people, containing a modern church and a public school" (Anderson 1911:8). The following year, *The Panamá Guide* noted that tourists who wished to visit Fort San Lorenzo could only reach it by water, either by sea from Colón, or down the river from Gatún: "The little village of Chagres, at the foot of the castled hill, is the seat of an alcaldia, the capital of the district about. It has neither industries nor commerce, except for local purposes."

(Collins 1912:198). Around the same time, visiting journalist Willis J. Abbott paid a visit to Chagres, which he described as fronting "a bay perhaps a quarter of a mile wide" and as "a native village of about fifty huts with an iron-roofed church in the center" (Abbott 1913:79).

By that time, the United States had established Fort Sherman, which stood several miles away on the shores of Limón Bay to help guard the approaches to the Panamá Canal that were then under construction. In May 1915, "The Canal Zone government bluntly informed Panamá that certain uncultivated public lands about the mouth of the Chagres River were being taken over . . . for the defense of the Canal Zone," and in December, the area of expropriation was extended to a "triangular space bounded by the Chagres, the Caribbean Sea, and the Canal Zone." (McCain 1937:147) The government of Panamá responded on December 21, 1915, saying that although defense of the mouth of the river was necessary, the United States could hopefully "work out a plan that would not require the occupation of the village of Chagres." (McCain 1937:148). The United States demanded control of the site of Chagres, and so the government of Panamá acceded to American demands. Soon a new village site, Nuevo Chagres, was created. By the onset of World War I, Chagres had been abandoned, ending the occupation of a site inhabited for at several centuries. Subsequently, the site of Chagres and river mouth, occupied by the U.S. Army, remained an active and occasionally fortified military reservation until 1999. Following the U.S. withdrawal, the area and the waters around it became a protected zone: once again it was a feature in a Panamanian cultural landscape that was no longer dominated by American interests and needs.

Altering the Environment

Adapting the environment of the isthmus to suit the needs of the new canal involved more than the management of the natural environment in the zone. It also involved the tackling of a major environmental concern: disease. Malaria and yellow fever had wreaked havoc on the labor forces of both the railroad and the French-occupied canal. By the early twentieth century, the role of the mosquito (*Anopheles*) as the transmitter of the *plasmodium* that causes malaria was known, based on the pioneering work of French doctor Charles Laveran, Cuban doctor Carlos Finlay, American doctor Walter Reed, and British doctors Patrick Manson and Ronald Ross. Under the supervision of Dr. William C. Gorgas, a U.S. Army colonel and the chief sanitary officer of the Isthmian Canal Commission, another major shift in the landscape took place (Gorgas and Hendrick 1924; Gibson 1950). As they were mosquito breeding grounds, swamps and ponds were drained of standing water, and water wells in the cities were closed. New public water systems were built, and the paving of streets in Colón, Panamá City, and other locales took place. There was also widespread fumigation: nondrained water areas were covered with a sheen of oil to stop mosquito infestation, and there was the compulsory use of mosquito netting.

Public water systems were also built to rid the region of open sewers and rain barrels and to provide fresh drinking water. Large hospitals were built, malaria and fever victims were quarantined, and by 1906 malaria and fever had practically been eradicated from the Canal Zone. All in the Canal Zone, the drainage canals and the still-standing hospital buildings in Colón and Panamá City were the "modern" face of the cities. Although these were not elements traditionally associated with a maritime landscape, they were and remain prominent features of the maritime cultural landscape of Panamá.

Shaping the Landscape: The Canal

The first work to commence under American control was steam-shovel work at the Culebra Cut on November 11, 1904. Six months after the formal turnover of the project to the United States in May, the Americans picked up where the French had left off, and the decision of whether to continue a sea-level canal or pursue a lock-based canal remained up in the air until 1905. The decision to build locks increased the amount of earth to be removed, which of course meant more time and cost, but it proved successful. After three years of design and meetings, work toward the final goal commenced in earnest in 1908. Three divisions—Atlantic, Central, and Pacific—were formed to undertake the work at each entrance and in the heart of the isthmus at the continental divide. Under the supervision of the assistant chief engineer of the project, six subdivisions were organized to tackle the major physical elements:[4]

1. Masonry and locks (including valves for flooding and draining)
2. Lock gates
3. Operating machinery and electrical installations
4. Emergency dams
5. Spillways
6. Aids to navigation

Figure 70a–b. *Top*: "Culebra Cut, deepest section" during construction of the Canal, c. 1905–1914. *Bottom*: "The Culebra Cut, looking south" after excavation and flooding of the canal, with the steamer *Jutlandia* passing dredges, c. 1910–1920. Library of Congress Prints and Photographs Division, Detroit Publishing Company Photograph Collection (LOC call nos. LC-D4-73157 and LC-D4-73303).

In addition, while the new owners inherited a considerable number of French buildings and equipment, not all of it was in good condition. Repair and demolition followed, and significant effort was put into building employee infrastructure. This infrastructure included roads, housing, commissaries, cafeterias, recreational facilities, and schools as well as sewers and water supply systems, warehouses, workshops and repair facilities, docks, and wharves. Large amounts of American-manufactured equipment was also shipped to the isthmus, including steam shovels, rolling stock, pneumatic drills and jack hammers, cement mixers, and dredges. Another major effort was the improvement of the railroad and ultimately its relocation in the face of the impending flooding of sections of the old route for the new canal. To facilitate the relocation, the engineers used large amounts of excavated soil and rock from the Culebra Cut to fill swamps and create a more solid rail bed.

The decision by the United States to focus on health and proper infrastructure eventually paid off: the canal was completed with some 5,609 deaths—a marked decrease from the railroad and French canal loss figures. Investment in recreational facilities and entertainment and the encouragement of families also played a key role in retaining employees and experience through the multiyear project. Another successful decision to have the project undertaken by U.S. Army engineers was led by Colonel George Washington Goethals, who took control of the project in 1907. The U.S. Army was not in charge, however. It was a situation where military men were working for the civilian-led Isthmian Canal Commission, which had total control over the project.

As a result of the concerted work undertaken between 1907 and 1914, the United States spent $375 million, employed more than 75,000 people, and removed 182,610,550 cubic meters (238,845,582 cubic yards) of earth. Adding what the French had accomplished in their excavations, digging the canal during three decades of work removed 387,510,055 cubic meters (506,845,558 cubic yards) of dirt, mud, and rock from the isthmus to facilitate the link to the oceans. Much of the excavation came from the 312-foot-high summit at Culebra, an 8.75-mile cut where on average 267 feet had to be taken out to reach a uniform elevation of approximately 45 feet above sea level; this would join the Río Grande to the Pacific and the Río Obispo, which fed into the Chagres and then the Caribbean Sea. The work was sped by methodically chipping, drilling, blasting, and digging. In all, some 60 million pounds of dynamite were used in the blasting (Snapp 2000:105). Landslides constantly plagued the work: in fact, a total of 26 landslides stalled progress and required the removal of an additional 25 million cubic yards of soil that had obstructed the excavation.

As it was excavated, the rock and soil fed thousands of dump cars that rolled on double-reinforced steel rails to form large breakwaters at each entrance, or as noted earlier, carried fill for the relocated railroad as well as dikes to keep the lakes from overflowing. Other excavated spoil was deposited at lowland sites that, once flooded, would not pose a threat to navigation. The Pacific breakwater formed a massive causeway that still links the canal entrance to the offshore islands of Flamenco, Naos, and Perico. A great deal of the soil and rock removed from the canal also went into the massive earth dam on the Chagres at the site of the village of Gatún. In addition to blocking the river and diverting it to create Lake Gatún, the dam and its spillway feed a power station for lock operations.

Three sets of locks serve as the means of lifting ships up from sea level on the Caribbean and, after the transit, locking them down to sea level on the Pacific, and vice versa. The locks—Gatún, Pedro Miguel, and Miraflores—are massive double-chambered concrete structures. The Gatún locks alone required 2 million cubic yards of concrete (Snapp 2000:97). The locks are more than the sum total of the concrete that forms their massive walls and floors as they try and augment the terrain that allows ships to ascend or de-

Figure 71. Gatún Dam spillway under construction. The damming of the Chagres made the American canal possible, eliminating the need for extensive digging of a sea-level canal. "Gatun Lake spillway, Panama Canal," 1914, Library of Congress Prints and Photographs Division, Detroit Publishing Company Photograph Collection (LOC reproduction no. LC-USZ62-117349).

Figure 72. "Approaches to Gatún Locks," drawing by Joseph Pennell, 1912. The massive concrete locks of the canal's Caribbean and Pacific entrances provided a series of staged "lifts" to raise vessels to the elevation of Gatún Lake. The locks remain one of the largest and most complex engineering feats of the American canal. Library of Congress Prints and Photographs Division (LOC reproduction no. LC-USZ62-138620).

Figure 73. The Gatún locks, c. 1913, facing the Atlantic (Caribbean) entrance, with tugs, dredges, and barges ready for the first lockage up into Lake Gatún. The massive maritime infrastructure of the canal included a fleet of working vessels to maintain the system and to assist vessels transiting. Library of Congress Prints and Photographs Division (LOC reproduction no. LC-USZ62-117347).

scend from the artificial lake. The locks make up part of a complex system, fed by water tunnels 18 feet in diameter, that channel 52 million gallons of water through all six of the locks every time a ship transits (Snapp 2000:75). Massive steel gates, weighing ten tons each, are situated in the tunnels and swivel to control the water: "When filling the double locks, the lower chamber valves are closed and the upper chamber valves open and gravity does the rest. To drain water from the lock, the opposite is done. A total of 114 rising stem valves and 120 cylindrical valves are used in operating all six locks" (Snapp 2000:75). It took four years to complete the locks.

Closed at first by temporary dams, each lock was later rigged with mitre-lock steel gates built by a Pittsburgh steel bridge company. The gates were made in sections as 92 individual leaves 65 feet wide, 7 feet thick, and from 47 to 82 feet high. The tallest leaves on the Pacific side at Miraflores weighed 662 tons each but were framed structures with a steel shell formed of inner-and-outer-laid strakes riveted into place like a ship's hull. In all, 6 million rivets were driven to build the lock gates. Each leaf is neutrally buoyant and as a floating structure, requires less power to open and close them. Two sets of gates on each face provided a redundant safety feature (Snapp 2000:91,95).

Gatún's locks form the northern (Caribbean) entrance to the canal, while Pedro Miguel's locks bring ships from Lake Gatún into Lake Miraflores, formed from the waters of the Río Grande and the Río Cocolí by yet another dam. The final locks, seven miles from the Bay of Panamá, are Miraflores. From there, ships follow the flooded Río Grande Valley and a channel dredged (and blasted) to the Pacific. A fleet of dredges, starting with older ones inherited from the French, worked in tandem with drill barges to create the channel into the bay.

The canal's landscape as designed and maintained includes aids to navigation in the form of both day markers and lighthouses. In all, 35 range lights were built to help guide ships through the canal, and they join other lighthouses on the coast built to guide ships safely to the canal. These include the 1894 steel skeletal tower, the French-built lighthouse at Isla Grande (and its sister at Toro Point), Farallón Sucio, and the Limón Bay breakwater lights. Also included are the concrete historic range lights at Gatún, Peña Blanca, Buena Vista, Tabernilla, Gamboa, San Pablo, Miraflores, Balboa, Flamenco, the Atlantic and Pacific entrance ranges, the coastal lights on the Pacific at Peñon Limoncillo, Isla Boná, Isla Iguana, Punta Mala, Frailes del Sur, Morro de Puercos, and Isla Jicarita.[5] Two historic lighthouses no longer exist: the Gatún Northbound Front range light and the iron skeleton light erected on the Colón breakwater by the Panamá Railroad Company in 1852, which was apparently taken down in 1914.

Although ships usually operate under their own power and under the control of a canal pilot, in the locks they are towed by massive electric towing locomotives that run on tracks on each side of the lock. The first 40 of these 42-ton "mules" were built by General Electric. Capable of pulling 25,000 pounds each with their 75-horsepower tractor motor, they remained in operation until 1965, when they were replaced by 55-ton, Mitsubishi-built locomotives. These mules had 170-horsepower engines and pulled 70,000 pounds. More recent models from Mitsubishi have 290-horsepower motors (Snapp 2000:140).

From the beginning of the project, it was clear that facilities and infrastructure for its ongoing maintenance and operation were required to replace temporary camps and facilities. The canal ship repair facilities at Cristóbal were one important element involved in maintaining the floating stock of dredges, barges, floating cranes, tugs, launches, and other vessels in the working fleet of the Panamá Canal Commission and the railroad. A

Figure 74a–b. Lighthouses are a recurring element in the maritime cultural landscape of the Panamá Canal, including one of the best-known—a 90-foot-high (27.5 m) steel skeleton tower built by the French in 1893. It stands at Toro Point on the shore-side end of the West Breakwater at the west side of the entrance to Limón Bay from the Caribbean. Another is the concrete, American-built Gatún Northbound Rear Range Light of 1914. It stands next to the locks, and is the most prominent lighthouse on the canal. Fig. 74a: Photograph by James P. Delgado. Fig. 74b: U.S. Navy photograph by Chief Mass Communication Specialist Holly Boynton.

more extensive shipyard with three dry docks was built at Balboa on the Pacific side. In 1914 the canal fleet stood at 189 vessels; a year later, after the canal opened, the number of registered vessels in that fleet stood at 31 railroad vessels and 173 vessels in the canal fleet (Bureau of Navigation, United States Department of Commerce 1915:467–471).

The shipyard remains part of the modern maritime cultural landscape; among its features is an original 1916 steam crane, now converted to diesel, which remains in use (Snapp 2000:155). Gamboa on the canal was selected as the site for the Canal Maintenance (Dredging) Division. Developed into a small community in the early 1930s, Gamboa remains as a prominent element in the maritime cultural landscape of the canal with dredges and other vessels at its docks (when not working) and two gigantic cranes, *Hercules* and *Titan*. The original steam cranes for handling the gates of the canal were *Hercules* and *Ajax*, built in 1912 with 250-ton lifting capacity. *Hercules* remains moored at Gamboa, along with *Titan*, a German crane built between 1938 and 1942 and brought to the canal in 1946 as a war prize (Snapp 2000:154).

The landscape of the canal also includes extensive facilities at both entrances that handle cargo, fuel, and provisioning, with docks, wharves, piers, and container-handling facilities. The hope and ambitions of those who desired a canal were realized through the steady growth of canal traffic through the twentieth century as well as by the critical role the canal played in World War II.

The maritime cultural landscape of the canal comprises more than the canal (or the Canal Zone) and its primary infrastructure. The maritime cultural landscape that evolved from 1907 to 1914 did not culminate with the first passage of a ship through the canal in August 1914 but continued and evolved over the next several decades.[6] The construction of the Madden Dam and the flooding of Madden Lake (now Lago Alajuela) in the 1930s was the largest single modification of the canal in the twentieth century. The canal continues to evolve at the centennial of its initial completion with an expansion program to accommodate larger ships. Because of that, as part of a unique international agreement between the United States and Panamá ICOMOS (International Commission on Monuments and Sites) Committees, the Canal Authority (ACP), and the U.S. National Park Service's Historic American Building Survey/Historic American Engineering Record/Historic American Landscapes Survey Division, the Panamá Canal Documentation Project was inaugurated in March 2001. It archived significant construction drawings, generated new documentation (both drawings and photographs), and created a detailed preservation record of the canal's structures and technology as well as of "singular buildings within the Canal Zone, like the Administration Building at Balboa, the house of the Administrator of the Canal, the Hospitals at Colón and Panamá City, the lock control houses, the lighthouses, the railroad terminals, etc." (Patiño and Cliver 2003). The project focused on more than just these aspects. As the authors noted,

> The five U.S. community sites, the six forts, two air force bases and the facilities of a single naval station that were turned over to the Panamanian government on December 31, 1999, with the property transfer and as part of the privatization process, typical changes in the urban and architectural character of the Canal are occurring, necessitating the need for documentation of these early twentieth century landscapes as part of the Historic American Landscapes Survey ~ HALS. (Patiño and Cliver 2003)

The project generated a considerable corpus of documentation, and the U.S. copies are archived in the Library of Congress and available online.

The Landscape of Strategic Vulnerability: Fortifying the Canal

The strategic benefits of the canal and its vulnerabilities were apparent to any student of isthmian history, which is why American efforts to build the canal had focused on nullifying the nonfortification clause on the Clayton-Bulwer Treaty of 1850. The Hay-Pauncefote Treaty, while allowing the United States to diplomatically proceed with constructing the canal, did not nullify either international or domestic opposition. As one of the treaty's authors argued, "we are legally and morally bound to abstain from fortifying" and because "the advantages . . . are more than offset by their disadvantages . . . it is bad public policy and strategy to fortify" (Davis 1909:354). That view was not upheld by either politicians, notably President Theodore Roosevelt, or by military leaders and thinkers. Alfred Thayer Mahan was one skeptic who wrote that

> primarily, and above all, it will be the most important link in the line of communications between our Atlantic and Pacific coasts. There is throughout the whole length and extension of our seacoast . . . no single position or reach of water comparable to Panamá.(Mahan 1911:333)

As Mahan was penning his argument, Congress was already debating what would become a $12 million bill to fortify the Canal Zone and its approaches. Even the Spooner Act of 1902 foresaw the construction of defenses for the canal, but it was not until November 1909 that the Panamá Fortifications Board was created, which was an official joint army-navy board of senior officers directed to devise a defense plan for times of war and peace. The U.S. Army Corps of Engineers was to draft fortification plans to be submitted to the board: this was done to protect the maritime entrances and approaches to the canal and other sensitive installations such as the locks, dams, bridges and tunnels; build permanent garrisons for personnel during peacetime; and scout additional defense sites outside the Canal Zone proper (McGovern 1999:9).

Construction of land and sea fortifications began around 1911, and by the time many of them were completed in 1916, the cost had gone up to over $15 million (McGovern 1999:11–12). The decades that followed introduced additional fortifications and improvements as tactics and weapons evolved (Hoffmann 2009). This left behind an important defensive infrastructure in the isthmian maritime cultural landscape that was unparalleled in its 500-year span of modern history (Conn et al. 2000; De Mena 1999; Enscore et al. 2000; Gardner and Carpenter 1965; Johnson 1994a, 1994b; Morris 2013; Small 1983).

Ultimately the defensive structures built on the isthmus consisted of several forts, encompassing not only fortifications but also barracks and a variety of structures to support infantry, artillery, seacoast mines, and aerial operations. There were even naval support bases. The fortification of the canal was only one part of the equation, as troops were needed to patrol the zone and repel enemies who landed and engaged in jungle warfare or attempted to sabotage the canal.[7] The forts included bases at the Caribbean and Pacific entrances and also along the canal: Forts Sherman, Clayton, de Lesseps, Randolph, Amador, Grant, Davis, Gulick, and Kobbe. There was also a U.S. Navy submarine base at Coco Solo, the navy sector of Fort Amador, and three airfields (four if one counts a temporary field at the parade ground of Fort Sherman): France Field, Albrook Field, and Howard Field. All of these were built and in place before World War II and most by the time World War I commenced. The airfields took shape between 1918 and 1931.[8]

The defensive landscape of the canal took shape primarily at the entrances. Between 1912 and 1917 a series of reinforced concrete seacoast artillery batteries were constructed on both coasts: the Pacific batteries on

Figures 75a–c. The U.S. Army's major contribution to the maritime cultural landscape was extensive fortifications and forts built in the early twentieth century to protect the Panamá Canal. Battery Baird was a reinforced concrete fortification set into earthworks. It served as the emplacement for four 12-inch seacoast mortars that would provide plunging fire into the decks of attacking enemy warships. The battery included open mortar pits and subsurface corridors that connected them to underground magazines and quarters. Photographs by James P. Delgado.

Flamenco, Perico, and Naos islands on the bay, now linked by a seawall/causeway created from excavated spoil for the canal and designated as the "Fortified Islands" (McGovern 1999:17–23). More fill, dumped into a mangrove swamp on the bayshore near Balboa, became the site of newly built Fort Amador (Johnson 1994a:7). Initially under the aegis of the Isthmian Canal Commission, after 1916 construction of the defenses of the canal was assumed by the U.S. Army Corps of Engineers, overseen by Lt. Col. Eben E. Winslow, who was "the Army's leading expert on fortifications" (Smith 1993:34). As early as 1914, the news that the canal was fortified was heralded publicly (Maigne 1914).

Guarding the canal was also a new priority for the U.S. Navy, which established a naval radio station at Balboa in 1918, a submarine base at Coco Solo (on the Caribbean side) in 1919, and nearby, in conjunction with the Panamá Canal Commission, a radio compass station on Galeta Island. These facilities grew through the years; in 1920, Coco Solo gained a new designation when a naval air station with seaplanes opened there. Additional facilities added in the 1930s and up through World War II included Rodman Naval Station on the Pacific, which included tank farms for naval fuel and provided provisions and support, including repair for the Pacific fleet

Rodman was substantially built up in 1943. A naval ammunition depot was opened at Balboa in 1935, and with the beginning of the war, Rodman became a major U.S. Marines barracks and headquarters. Rousseau Naval Hospital arose on the Pacific side in World War II, and after the war it was converted to housing. The navy sector at Fort Amador, formerly the Balboa Naval Radio Station, served as the major U.S. Navy headquarters on the isthmus through 1993 while other facilities—including the redesignated Galeta as a U.S. Naval Security Group Activity (naval communications)—served with Coco Solo (which ceased being a submarine base in 1944) through the Cold War, Vietnam, and into the 1990s.

The batteries, the epitome of American seacoast defense at the beginning of World War I, covered the approaches with a variety of seacoast ordnance consisting of both rifles and, more importantly, mortars: this way, there was the option of lobbing shells onto the unarmored decks of attacking ships (see McGovern 1998 for a thorough discussion). They are generally massive, thickly walled, reinforced concrete structures hidden in the jungles of the Canal Zone near the coastlines; these are now a permanent part of the maritime cultural landscape.

The range of gun emplacements included 6-inch (barrel diameter) rifles mounted on disappearing carriages that could be elevated on counter-weighted arms to fire and then dropped behind their protective battery walls on the recoil to then be reloaded. There were also 12- and 14-inch rifles on disappearing carriages as well as barbette-mounted guns. On a barbette, a gun could rotate up to 360 degrees, while a disappearing gun generally had a 170-degree arc (Hoffman 2009; Johnson 1994a and 1994b). The ranges of these weapons were impressive; the 6-inch guns had a range of 15,000 yards (8.5 mi/13.71 k) while the 14-inch guns had a range of 24,000 yards (13.6 mi/21.94 k), and the 12-inch mortars could lob a shell 17,900 yards (10.17 mi/16.36 k).

The significance of the canal and its defense was further illustrated not only by the well-built (hence expensive) and commanding locales of the initial batteries but also by extensive seacoast mine facilities and two styles of unique guns. The first were 14-inch guns mounted on railroad carriages. These guns, officially Model 1910, Mk. II 14-inch rifles, were introduced in 1928. Capable of rolling on 5-inch rails, the guns were located at each entrance of the canal; however, as portable weapons they could be moved into position across the isthmus. Battery #1, located on the northeast tip of Isla Margarita on the Caribbean entrance, had two positions built to accommodate the guns, while Battery #8, on Culebra Island on the Pacific, also had two positions. Heralded in a 1934 *Popular Mechanics* article, these "rolling forts" or "gun-trains" were said to be able to cross the isthmus in just two hours (*Popular Mechanics*, December 1934, 62(6):844–845; see also Small 1983).

The ultimate seacoast guns, 16-inch naval guns, mounted on both barbettes and a disappearing carriage, were also installed at Panamá. Two batteries, Haan and Murray, were built at the Bruja Point Military reservation (later Fort Kobbe) on the Pacific, and a third 16-inch gun was on a disappearing carriage and mounted atop Isla Perico at an elevation of 230 feet above sea level. With its 170-degree arc, these 16-inch guns could cover a wide area and had a range of 48,000 yards (27.27 mi/43.89 k); this meant that they could literally fire a shell weighing more than a ton over the horizon. To protect some of the batteries after the lesson of aerial reconnaissance and bombardment had been hammered home during World War I, some of the Panamá batteries were covered by protective concrete and earth casemates (McGovern 1999:43–53).

Further, beginning in the late 1910s as airstrips were being built on the isthmus, the various forts also added antiaircraft batteries, most of them housing 75mm AA guns (McGovern 1999:113–114). Not all the AA guns were emplaced; some AA batteries were positions for mobile 75mm guns. AA guns were also emplaced on temporary mounts at the mouth of the Río Chagres to stop any attempt by a low-flying torpedo bomber to run up the Chagres and attack the Gatún dam. Around the beginning of World War II—and especially after the United States joined the war—the 75mm gun positions were complemented by 105mm guns as well as by 90mm AAA batteries (Brooks 2013:191–192) and myriad other mobile antiaircraft defenses that included batteries for radar, searchlights, machine guns (.50-caliber), barrage balloons, and smokescreens (Brooks 2013:182–183).

The seacoast defenses of the canal remained in place throughout World War II, though by then some of the guns were obsolete and overexposed, like the 12-inch mortars, all of which had been removed from their batteries and scrapped by 1943. The other batteries retained their guns until the 1946–1948 period, when they were destroyed much like the guns emplaced in New York and San Francisco. The old batteries, too difficult and expensive to break down, remained and were adapted for other uses. Battery Kilpatrick at Fort Sherman, for example, was used for the U.S. Army's Jungle Warfare School and also housed a zoo in order to familiarize trainees with crocodiles and other jungle life. As with many other antiaircraft gun batteries, Battery Warren, at the summit of Isla Flamenco, became a HAWK (Homing-All-the-Way-Killer) missile battery after these surface-to-air weapons became operational in 1959 (Berhow 2005; see also McGovern 1999:26).[9]

World War II brought astounding changes to the military landscape of the isthmus. Especially since it had broken out on both oceans, the war made Panamá a major strategic point. And it was the most important strategic junction for the United States. Concern over the vulnerability of Panamá in the face of an impending global war was evident as early as 1939, when, at the start of the European war in September, new security provisions were put into effect at the canal, including the installation of detection equipment for hidden bombs. Measures introduced in short order included restricting commercial traffic to one side of the dual locks, the inspection of all ships passing through the canal, no photography, and ultimately, mining the canal entrances, placing low altitude barrage balloons over the locks, and placing antisubmarine/antitorpedo nets at each entrance. Radar installations were also emplaced to alert the military to approaching ships and planes. After 1941, troop levels at the canal jumped to 47,000 just prior to the Pearl Harbor attack, and after that, by late 1942, the figure was 67,000 troops. Those numbers were cut in half by 1944, when the threat of invasion or major attack had passed (Brooks 2013:203–204).

Physical changes to accommodate the troops and augment defense include 9 new airbases, 10 new ground-force posts, 30 aircraft warning stations, 634 searchlights and AA gun emplacements, and 134 sites outside of the Canal Zone, including military installations in the Pearl Islands. The entire isthmus became a heavily fortified armed camp as well as a major route for warships—battleships, aircraft carriers, destroyers, and submarines coming from East Coast shipyards to enter the Pacific War—transiting between the seas. Repair facilities as well as hospitals also served a vital need (Johnson 1994a; Brooks 2003; Hoffman 2009). Furthermore, the fueling facilities were greatly augmented with additional storage tanks and a welded steel fuel pipeline completed in 1943 that traversed the isthmus. It was augmented with new lines in 1944; when completed, the $20 million Trans-Isthmian Pipeline handled a daily flow of 265,000 barrels of fuel oil, 47,000 barrels of diesel, and 60,000 barrels of gasoline.

Following the war, the United States abandoned or turned over 98 of the external sites, sought to retain 36, but agreed not to remain in the face of Panamanian opposition. The military had departed from all of the sites by January 1948, except those areas within the Canal Zone. Regardless of which branch of service, each of these sites—including those abandoned and "returned to the jungle"—remain as elements of the isthmian maritime cultural landscape. Other bases and forts began to revert to Panamá after the 1977 Carter-Torrijos Treaty, which formally ended the Canal Zone and brought about a gradual obsolescence of the canal and its facilities as it was no longer of use to the nation in which it was situated. Some bases closed and were relocated as early as 1979; others were moved twenty years later at the end of the American era.[10] The now-closed (and in some cases deteriorating or converted former forts and bases) are all powerful and tangible reminders that Panamá is probably the world's largest, most diverse, and most crowded maritime cultural landscape.

The war left another submerged element in the maritime cultural landscape. Following the Pearl Harbor attack, submarines from Coco Solo were sent through the canal and from Balboa to guard the approaches on the Pacific against possible Japanese assault. While on a patrol on January 24, 1942, operating in darkness with three other subs and an escorting sub chaser, USS *Sturdy* (PC-460), S-26 was accidently rammed and sunk by *Sturdy* 14 miles west of San José Light off the Pearl Islands in the Gulf of Panamá. The submarine sank quickly, and only three men survived. Coming to rest in 300 feet of water, S-26 was not salvaged and to this day remains on the seabed with 46 of its crew (Roscoe 1949:91).[11]

Panamá in America: The P.P.I.E., the P.C.E. and Other Continental Reflections

In addition to the scattered shipwrecks of vessels engaged in isthmian activities in past centuries, the maritime cultural landscape of Panamá includes yet another distant element. To celebrate the opening of the canal, the world's fair known as the Panamá-Pacific International Exposition opened in San Francisco despite the war raging in Europe. The exposition's official poster, the result of a prize competition, featured a painting by San Francisco artist Perham Wilhelm Nahl entitled "The Thirteenth Labor of Hercules."[12] It depicted the demigod as a giant nude figure dividing the land and pushing it apart with his legs, arms, and back while, in the distance, the fair's buildings loomed on the horizon. The meaning implicit in the poster was not only the near-mythic alteration of the isthmian landscape to create the canal but also the rebirth of San Francisco, a city intimately tied to Panamá since the days of the Gold Rush and the destination of many a Pacific Mail steamship. San Francisco had been devastated by the earthquake and fire of April 22, 1906, just eight years earlier.

The P.P.I.E. commenced on February 20, 1915, and remained open through December, hosting 18,876,438 visitors. Located on the city's north shore, facing the Golden Gate and Marin County across the bay, the P.P.I.E. was built over a former marsh (now landfill) on a 630-acre (250 ha) site covered with landscaped paths, fountains, gardens, and a series of ornate and exquisite architectural landmarks modeled from plaster and burlap that housed displays of various industries, products, and arts as well as state and national pavilions. All of this was centered on a 43-story tower covered in cut glass (the "Tower of Jewels") that was electrically illuminated at night (Moore 2013). Following the closing of the exposition, nearly all of its buildings were demolished, and most of the grounds became the setting for residences built in what is today the Marina District. The major "survivor," the Bernard Maybeck–designed Palace of Fine Arts, lasted until the 1960s, when its decaying form was replicated in cast concrete thanks to philanthropist Walter Johnson. The redone palace ultimately served as the setting for the Exploratorium, San Francisco's science center, until it relocated to the central waterfront in 2013. The Palace of Fine Arts survives as

Figure 76. The opening of the canal was celebrated in the United States with two major expositions in California, one in San Diego and the other in San Francisco, as shown in this lithograph, "Aeroplane view, main group of exhibit palaces, Panamá Pacific International Exposition" (San Francisco: Pacific Novelty, c. 1914), Library of Congress Prints and Photographs Division (LOC reproduction no. LC-USZCN4-8).

a 1966 replica and a beautiful oasis of architecture, greenery, and reflecting pools. It stands as the most distant major element of the maritime cultural landscape of the Panamá Canal.

In 1909 civic leaders in San Diego, California, commenced planning and lobbying for another fair: the Panamá California Exposition. San Diego business leaders were keen to tout their city as the first American port ships transiting the new canal would reach. After launching a bid for federal and state funding (which did not come), the organizers raised private capital and built the exposition's buildings and gardens in San Diego's City Park, which had been renamed Balboa Park in 1910 as part of the drive to create the exposition. The buildings were designed by architects Bertram Goodhue and Carleton Winslow in the Spanish Colonial style and were a visual masterpiece on the 640-acre (260 ha) fairgrounds, which were landscaped and decorated with sculptures. A prominent display was a 250-foot (76m) long replica of the Panamá Canal. The exposition opened on January 1, 1915, and remained open through January 1, 1917. In all, some 3.7 million people visited the exposition.

A hundred years later, the Panamá California Exposition has made Balboa Park a significant and prominent landmark in the cultural landscape of San Diego as well as being part of the broader maritime cultural landscape of Panamá. Balboa Park, listed on the National Register of Historic Places and a National Historic Landmark, survives both as a legacy of civic planning and pride and a historical reminder of the exposition. Several structures designed and built to be permanent features are landmarks in the park. They include the California State building and the Fine Arts building, both of which are now home to the San Diego Museum of Man, as well as the Chapel of St. Francis of Assisi, the California Bell Tower, the Cabrillo Bridge, the Botanical Building, and the Spreckels Organ Pavilion (Christman 1985; Amero 2015).

Other monuments and memorials in the United States exist as distant reminders of the canal past: from the graves of the canal builders like David Gaillard and William Gorgas at Arlington or George Washington Goethals's grave at West Point. There are other reminders, like the Goethals Bridge of New York, connecting Elizabeth City, New Jersey, with Staten Island. There are also relics that were brought to the United States from Panamá, ranging from an original railroad car now displayed outside the Paterson Museum in Paterson, New Jersey, or the more extensive Panamá Canal Museum, formerly in Seminole, Florida; however, as of 2012 it became part of the University of Florida's Latin America Collection. The myriad small reminders, as well as the human stories and memories of the tens of thousands of former "Zonians" (some of whom remain in Panamá), speak powerfully to the fact that the isthmus and its canal remains possibly the single greatest maritime achievement in the history of the world.

Post-Panamax

As the end of the twentieth century was at hand, the United States relinquished its final control of the canal under the terms of the 1977 Carter-Torrijos Treaty, and the isthmus was finally united under a single governing entity: the Republic of Panamá. Thus ended decades of Panamanian struggle that had occasionally flared into violence, the root causes of which were not understood by most Americans, many of whom had no real geographical concept of where the Panamá Canal actually was (LaFeber 1978:viii). During the whole of the republic's existence, itself an artifact of American canal ambition, it had never exercised full sovereignty over all of its land. Now it gained the Canal Zone, which was the most prominent element of the national landscape (other than the canal itself) and all that the zone contained. It also inherited more than the maintenance of the canal and its attendant royalties. Panamá inherited the need to deal with the increasing demand for the canal and to address its inadequacies.

After it opened, the canal's traffic was light: this was primarily due to the war diverting most shipping to Europe. But by the 1920s some 5,000 ships were transiting the canal each year, including some of the world's largest.

Figure 77. The increasing size of ships meant that the locks would eventually be too small for ships to transit the canal, leading to U.S. plans for an expansion that would have dealt with the issue. Here, prior to World War II, USS *Nevada* (BB36) dwarfs the lock at Pedro Miguel. "Aerial view of the Pedro Miguel locks of the Panama Canal," Department of Defense, Department of the Navy, National Archives, National Archives Identifier: 6415255; Local Identifier: 330-CFD-DF-ST-87-12760.jpeg).

The 888-foot-long, 106-foot-wide aircraft carriers USS *Saratoga* and USS *Lexington* squeezed through the canal in March 1928, knocking down the locks' lampposts. By the time World War II began, canal traffic was up to more than 7,000 ships a year, and that figure doubled after the war (McCullough 1977:611–612). The need to address the inadequacies of the canal first came into focus in the 1930s, and a study presented to Congress in February 1939 suggested that, in addition to new fortifications, a new set of locks be excavated alongside the existing ones. These new locks could accommodate larger warships.

Congress authorized the "Third Locks" project in August 1939, and on July 1, 1940, excavation of lock pits began at Miraflores, followed by the commencement of excavation at Gatún on February 19, 1941. The project was to be completed by early 1946, but it was cancelled in May 1942 due to the war effort. At the same time, the need for additional water for the canal had led to the aforementioned construction of the Madden Dam and the subsequent formation of Lake Alajuela. Plans to dig a sea-level canal across the isthmus were revived in the mid-1960s as part of Project Plowshare. The excavation would be done by a number of nuclear weapons buried far underground, the detonation of which would create a deep channel (Kaufman 2013). The project was seriously debated while tests with weapons to determine how well they would work as excavation tools took place in the Nevada desert. However, Plowshare and its nuclear transisthmian canal were cancelled at the end of 1969 in the face of fears over environmental and diplomatic concerns and doubts over its feasibility (Kaufman 2013:193).

The traditionally but partially excavated "third locks" remained a part of the historic maritime cultural landscape. These two huge trenches later became lakes near both entrances to the canal. In 2007, following a national referendum, Panamá revived the "Third Locks" project. The issue was more than volume of traffic but also about the fact that the original locks, with their dimensions of 305 m (1000 ft) long by 33.5 m (110 ft) wide, limit transits to "Panamax" vessels no greater than 965 ft long (294.1 m) by 106 ft in breadth (32.3 m). And there are now hundreds of thousands of vessels around the world that are post-Panamax. The landscape of the canal is again changing; seven years since the project began and at the time of writing, the centennial of the canal's opening was being celebrated. Vast new locks are rising at Gatún and Miraflores with a new water recycling system. New and deeper channels have been dredged, sharp "turns" in the landscape have been restructured, entire hills have disappeared, the navigation channel has been widened, and the level of Lake Gatún will be raised by 45 cm. As the work continues, and as this book has demonstrated, evidence from every period of human history in Panamá has come to light. This has happened both through an archaeological project dedicated to recovery and mitigation and through the occasional accidental discovery.

It is a powerful reminder of the ongoing dream of an isthmian passage between the seas. But it is also a reminder that, in this twenty-first-century maritime cultural landscape, thousands of years of human activity in this environment are rediscovered or lost on a massive scale, seen previously in works like the Aswan High Dam or the Three Gorges Dam. In such cases, necessity and profit drive the agenda as they have since the earliest civilization. The difference now is that we have the ability as a species to not only react to but also to reshape our environment. And the canal itself, in its century of operation, powerfully illustrates this idea in the form of the vast and dynamic maritime cultural landscape that is the Isthmus of Panamá.

Conclusion

The maritime cultural landscape of the isthmus in its first decades of Spanish exploration, conquest, and assimilation into a colonial empire reflected the first sporadic efforts both to understand and dominate the landscape. This included symbolic acts of possession, such as Anglicizing the names of indigenous landmarks and sites, but also the establishment of initial internal trade routes and settlements, often at preexisting native sites such as Santa María la Antigua del Darién, Panamá City, and Acla. In all three cases the precontact sites were sustainable for their original inhabitants and their use of the land. This was largely because the indigenous inhabitants had relied on open access to the marine environment for sustenance. The conquering Spanish utilized the same sites and found them insufficient for use as sheltered and accessible ports for larger vessels. Obviously just because an element of the landscape proves useful for one particular group of people does not always guarantee that other groups will have the same uses for it.

Santa María la Antigua del Darién and Nombre de Dios were eventually abandoned in favor of other settlements. This was because they were not ideally tied to locales that provided a closer and more defensible node in the Spanish push to link isthmian ports to their wider and growing empire (and later to transport the mineral wealth of the new colonies to Spain). At this point in the early sixteenth century, the maritime cultural landscape that survived for thousands of years was practically wiped out with the death of many of the indigenous peoples of eastern Panamá who suffered the brunt of the initial Spanish invasion. The invasion left only small and isolated enclaves hidden in the jungles of Daríen (Romoli 1987).

In the western half of the country, indigenous peoples were able to put up more effective resistance and for a while retained the use of the maritime cultural landscape. In time, however, they had to relocate farther up the mountains to avoid the invaders. Thanks to their navigational technology, the Europeans became the undisputed rulers of the isthmian seas and their shores. The shift to Spanish patterns of settlement reflected the beginnings of human efforts to adapt the maritime cultural landscape of the isthmus for use as a key route in global trade as Spain built its overseas empire.

A century after the initial exploration, invasion, and settlement of the isthmus, Panamá went from a land whose people were ruthlessly exploited to a major transit hub and a critical node in the Spanish overseas empire. This made it a key element in the emerging global economy. That foreshadowed the even greater role the isthmus assumed in the centuries that followed and that continues to the present day. The landscape of the colonial period included the infrastructure developed by Spain to utilize the isthmus' narrow breadth as a point of transit, having ports on both coasts. It also comprised the imperfect land- and water-based transit routes across it, including both the royal roads and the Chagres.

The archaeological work in Portobelo and Panamá Viejo reflects the rise of the isthmus as a regular mode of transit. Among these important archaeological finds were the shipwrecks found off the Panamanian coast: these were the remains of ships that transported the treasure and cargoes that crossed the isthmus. Whether identification of the wreck of what appears to be the *Nuestra Señora de la Encarnación* is correct (though it likely is), that site represents a significant aspect of the isthmus' maritime cultural landscape: it is the only shipwreck from the period to be archaeologically studied. It also sadly reflects another aspect of the landscape: namely, the incessant problem of looting, souvenir collecting, and treasure hunting, all of which have specifically targeted the archaeological heritage of Panamá. Had a different archaeological approach been available for this and other sites, identification of this site might be easier, and a more diverse archaeological record from this and other sites would be available for study, museum display, and cultural tourism. Furthermore, the landscape elements noted in this chapter could have been discussed in greater depth. The concept of plundering Panamá is, sadly enough, an ongoing theme reflected in the landscape, especially historically, as this book has explained. We did not set out to write a history of plundered sites and opportunities lost to archaeology, but the record speaks for itself.

The later years of the colonial era were seen as a period of waning Spanish authority as well as exceptional challenges faced by the Panamanians. The seventeenth-century assaults of the buccaneers, privateers, and pirates culminated in the sack and destruction of Panamá Viejo and relocation of the capital city. It also led to a massive program of fortification for a link that, ironically, global trade was beginning to bypass. The landscape contains the new city, forts, and an archaeologically rich collection of elements, surviving place names (Puerto Escoces, for example), and the persistence of the indigenous people who remain part of the landscape, the Guna and the people of Bocas del Toro. The landscape also incorporates Spanish elements, as in the short-lived Daríen colony and the Spanish siege camp there.

The wrecks of Morgan's ships, including *Satisfaction*, are clearly extant but have probably been archaeologically compromised by looting. The wreck of the Scottish colony's *Olive Branch* is another example of underwater cultural heritage that reflects foreign incursion on the isthmus.

The fate of the Morgan wreck site, as was the case with the previously mentioned Playa Damas wreck or the *Chaperon* of 1681 (see chapter 3), was an ignominious one. And the challenges to the architectural and archaeological integrity of Casco Viejo, Portobelo, and San Lorenzo—along with the possible loss of their World Heritage status or inclusion in the endangered sites list—again reflect a troubling aspect of how the nation's cultural patrimony has been treated.

Christopher Ward (1993), the leading English-language scholar of isthmian commercial trade, notes that after 1740, "All commercial activity in Panamá . . . did not stop." The isthmus remained significant in regional commerce and was still "the principal entry point for English goods shipped through Jamaica to Peru," while shipments of royal silver continued to cross it (Ward 1993:155). Although trade had declined, Ward notes that the isthmus "was still acknowledged by strategists in Europe," as a passage between the seas (Ward 1993:156). The Caribbean became the focus of intense international competition and trade in the eighteenth century, and after 1770 commercial activity increased, even in Panamá (Ward 1993:157; Castillero 2004j:457). As the nineteenth century dawned, war in Europe not only spilled over into the Caribbean but also helped spur independence movements in the Spanish colonies as Spain fell to Napoleon.

Within the first two decades of the nineteenth century, Panamá was finally free from Spanish control. Spain left a lasting legacy, both tangible and intangible, on the isthmus. Yet by the mid-nineteenth century the Isthmus of Panamá had changed very little from the Spanish colonial era. It was marked with centuries of physical evidence left by human responses to the isthmus, from fishing villages to ports, forts, and shipwrecks. All of that changed dramatically in the century that followed. An industrialized world arrived at the isthmus and began to shape it with renewed purpose as an even more facile and powerful gateway from the Caribbean to the Pacific. Those industrial and colonial powers then began to mold that gateway to the needs of an increasingly complex and encompassing global economy.

What reawakened interest in Panamá was the California Gold Rush. Gold provided the capital needed to begin the industrial transformation of the isthmus. Unlike the earlier dramatic changes brought about by the Spanish conquest—centuries of development of the Camino Real, the Chagres as a river route, and the settlements and forts—these changes were propelled by the influx of capital, the Industrial Revolution and an emerging global economy, and the aggressive energy of the young United States. The impacts on Panamá were profound in many ways, reflected by a major new city, Colón (Aspinwall); a railroad that bridged a gap previously thought impassable except by foot and mule train; and an influx of foreign capital and ambition evident in place names, infrastructure, and discarded material culture brought in ships and deposited on jungle trails, in the river, or in the urban centers.

The events surrounding the Gold Rush, while dramatic, were harbingers of even greater change and a major physical restructuring of the isthmus. They resulted in the conception and construction of one of the major maritime cultural landscapes in the world: the Panamá Canal. The decades following the Gold Rush would witness a decline in American interest and investment, but others eager to reap the benefits of the isthmus would rally—only to falter before the final and successful physical "parting" of the isthmus in the twentieth century.

The isthmus began to be physically transformed in the late nineteenth century as colonial, entrepreneurial, and industrial forces increased efforts not to respond to the landscape and environment but rather to shape it. This process had begun during the Gold Rush era. And after the rush subsided and interest in the isthmus declined, Panamá could have once again returned to a quiescent state, as it had after 1740. However, the growing strength of the world system and the global economy refocused attention on Panamá after 1865. The maritime cultural landscape of the period reflects that; however, the landscape also reflects its global nature through the distant and yet linked Panamá route steamers whose wrecks are also landscape elements even if they were thousands of miles from Panamá.

While Panamá at the end of the nineteenth century saw massive industrial efforts to adapt the environment, the remaining sites ironically (but powerfully) reflect how that environment ultimately prevailed as represented by the abandoned *Sub Marine Explorer* and the submerged cultural landscape of the French canal as well as the French graveyards.

The late nineteenth-century, however, saw a renewed effort by the United States to shape the landscape of the isthmus. The United States completed the canal and assumed control of it while ostensibly "creating" a new nation: the Republic of Panamá. The isthmus of that time embodied the centuries old dream of the "land divided, the world united." The twentieth century witnessed not only the construction of the canal's massive locks and dams but also the creation of a politically separate, controlled "Canal Zone" as a country within a country. Known as a "fifth frontier" to Panamanians, it was a buffer zone and watershed used for defensive purposes. Extensive fortifications, a relocated railroad, new ports, and infrastructure that included administrative, industrial, and residential compounds—set aside for the vast number of Americans who worked the canal—created a separate but unequal Panamá. The Canal Zone essentially excluded Panamá's inhabitants from a landscape they had inhabited for centuries. This extraordinary example of American imperialism would set the tone for the rest of the twentieth century, while unknowingly focusing the creation of Panamanian identity around a single project: the struggle for the recovery of the canal.

As we now mark a century since the completion of the canal, the maritime story of the Isthmus of Panamá within the context of its landscape is vast, diverse, and complex. This overview is by no means comprehensive. The level of historical detail varies according to what investigative work has been done on the elements of the landscape (as can be seen in more complete discussions of the mouth of the Chagres, Puerto Escoces, Panamá Viejo, the Casco Antiguo, and within the canal itself). Details about a number of "elements," not only shipwrecks but also terrestrial (but nonetheless maritime-related) sites, both from the pre-Columbian and the historic period of the last 500 years, are also forgotten and in some cases have been destroyed by subsequent development and more than a century's looting, treasure hunting, and souvenir collecting. The ongoing issue of looting offers an ironic reflection on the fact that for five centuries one of the most persistent aspects of maritime culture in this landscape has been the plundering of its resources. Sites such as the Playa Damas wreck, the other shipwrecks of Nombre de Dios and Portobelo, and more recently the *San José* wreck all speak to individual and often private nonscientific recovery and salvage work, which for scholars has become an unfortunate part of dealing with isthmian cultural patrimony.

In the twenty-first century, Panamá's maritime culture persists in a variety of forms. The canal is still Panamá's single greatest economic asset and is the greatest physical manifestation of maritime activity on the isthmus. This maritime culture is also evident in the various ports and harbors not tied to transisthmian traffic between the seas but in coastal activities, including trade, tourism, and commercial fishing. The role of the maritime world is also characterized by ongoing illicit activity. This is reminiscent of the centuries-old activities of the privateers, buccaneers, and pirates who utilized the intricacies of the coastal islands and islets and the remote jungles of parts of the isthmus. Except now, these places are being used by drug traffickers and other smugglers. This unfortunate fact makes Panamá, again, an obligatory route on the way to the richest market in the world: the United States.

The maritime cultural landscape also includes traditional pearl diving in the Islas de las Perlas. Here, in remote villages and settlements, the descendants of black slaves occupy a landscape and fishery once the home of the now-extinct indigenous population. Killed off by disease and overwork, the natives of the islands were replaced by slaves from Africa who brought aspects of their own culture to the isthmus. The pearl fishery is in decline due to centuries of overfishing and the collapse of the market for natural pearls as the result of the development and domination of farmed pearls. Yet the people of villages like La Esmeralda on Isla del Rey continue to venture out to sea, holding their breath as they dive beneath the waves and going many meters underwater to wrench oysters from their firm grip on the seabed. Just as their ancestors did, these pearl divers pry open the shell in hopes of finding their prize, always anxious that it may be one of the fabled great pearls that bring riches to the finder. More often than not, what emerges is a small, misshapen product of the bivalve that is kept and sold to transient tourists on the occasional fishing or yachting trip. Regardless, this seemingly timeless aspect of maritime culture persists in the Islas de las Perlas.

Our discussion of the maritime cultural landscape of Panamá ends, as it began, with the indigenous population. In Guna Yala (the archipelago of San Blas), some 30,000 Guna reside on some 41 of the nearly 400 islands, islets, and cays in the semiautonomous region of the Comarca Guna Yala. This 232-mile area of the Caribbean coast is revered as an eco- and cultural-tourism destination, self-governed by a people who have persevered for centuries in the face of colonial ambition, war, disease, and the forces of cultural assimilation—not to mention the extinction many of their neighbors faced in the wake of the Spanish conquest. For the better part of 300

Figure 78a–b. Pearl diver with his gear and pearl diver's traditional boat, village of La Esmeralda, Isla Del Rey, in the Pearl Islands. Photographs by James P. Delgado.

years, the Guna struggled for independence against the Spanish amidst culturally and politically diverse groups that included oppressive Spanish colonial administrators, priests, and missionaries, African mulattos, and privateers and pirates from various nations (Castillero 1995).

Upon Balboa's arrival and the Spanish conquistadors in 1510, the Guna populated most of the Caribbean coast of the Darién along the Gulf of Urabá. Balboa spared most of the local population, despite the fact that they were cruelly overworked. Under Pedrarias Dávila and his brutal quest for gold, most Guna within the region were wiped out or fled west (Castillero 1995). When Spanish attempts at pacification through the establishment of a Dominican mission failed in 1651, troops were stationed in the region, which caused the Guna to revolt and eventually drive out the foreign soldiers and colonists (Castillero 1995; Severino 1956; Stier 1979; Howe 1998).

Due to the strategic advantages of the northern shore of the Darién, pirates and privateers often used the coast of San Blas to acquire provisions, as sea turtles and manatees were abundant, the islands and coves were good for hiding and careening ships, and the natives could serve as guides (Galvin 1998). This created yet another worry for the Spanish: Indians in league with pirates. Even so, this proved tumultuous for the Guna. They even found themselves pitted against one another, specifically during Henry Morgan's attack on Panamá in which Indians fought for both sides: the "mission" Guna fought alongside the Spanish, and the "unpacified" Indians fought alongside Morgan (Exquemelin 1969; Howe 1998). Throughout the late seventeenth century, the Guna continued to aid privateers and pirates (Dampier 1699; Wafer 1729).

By 1681 the Guna were living along the rivers on the coast of the isthmus (Wafer 1729). Surgeon and privateer Lionel Wafer's account, which described the people and their customs (as he understood them) as well as the geography of the region, attracted non-Spanish attention to the area. The archipelago offered both tactical and strategic benefits. Isolated and approachable in many cases only by small boat, for centuries it offered a setting in which an enemy force could neither approach nor land in force, keeping only to some islands, bays, and channels with larger vessels. In this way, the Guna were protected. They resisted Spanish attempts to assimilate and enslave them, allying themselves with the privateers and buccaneers. They were unlike their indigenous brethren who held out in Bocas del Toro and fought against all Europeans. The Guna also allied themselves with the Scottish colonists who came to the Darién between 1698 and 1700, and accounts note that some 80 Guna warriors joined the Scots in their last stand against the Spanish at Fort St. Andrew in 1700.

A tacit admission of the Guna ability to evade Spain's grasp is even present in the final surrender negotiations of the Scots in 1700. As part of the terms of the surrender, the Scots requested amnesty for their Guna compatriots and fellow warriors. The Spanish commander, Don Juan Pimienta, demurred:

> An indemnity for the friendly Indians was refused, as the general said they were the King of Spain's subjects, and as such he knew how to deal with them; but he intimated that he would not trouble them if they did not trouble him. (Parlane 1888:38–39)

Pimienta's face-saving actions notwithstanding, returning to the maritime landscape of Guna Yala ensured their freedom from harm.

Guna raiding parties attacked Spanish gold mines in the eastern Darién at Cana in 1684, 1702, 1712, 1724, and 1734 (Castillero 1995; Severino 1956; Ward 1993; Howe 1998). Around this time, Spain's grip on the New World weakened severely, with its imperial system of silver fleets and trade fairs collapsing. Spain nonetheless continued to recolonize and exercise control of the Darién because of the region's importance as an interoceanic crossing. Yet in 1728, another massive revolt occurred, and the Guna resistance continued with British assistance in the form of weapons, letters of alliance, and even military advisors (Howe 1998; Rojas y Arrieta 1929). This back-and-forth action continued until 1785, when Spain attempted to defeat the Guna in a final push, building four small forts along the San Blas coast and three more in the southern Darién in an attempt to cut them off from their allies.

Despite fierce attacks from the Guna and the diseases associated with life in the tropics, the garrisons withstood these onslaughts. After being abandoned by the British, the Guna then signed a peace treaty. Two years later, however, the new colonial administration found their efforts to be unsustainable, and by 1792 the forts had been abandoned (Howe 1998; Castillero 1995; Rojas y Arrieta 1929; Severino 1956; Stier 1979). The Guna had at last achieved peace in the region. It is estimated that nearly half of the Guna population perished from war and epidemics in the late eighteenth century alone (Howe 1998). By the mid-nineteenth century the Guna had begun moving down the coast from sites near river mouths and then onto inshore islands: this was a process that continued for more than 80 years (Howe 1998). This new environment provided greater access to trade as

Figure 79. Two Guna women in traditional garb navigate the waters of Guna Yala in a traditional watercraft. Photograph by Alfredo Maiquez, reproduced by permission.

well as relief from mosquitos, snakes, disease, and exposure to other epidemics (Howe 1998).

As a September 2012 blog by David Dudenhoefer, "Native Strength," notes, the Guna left southern, isthmian Colombia and their Darién homeland in the rainforest for the sanctuary of the islands. There they adapted to the maritime landscape and modified aspects of their culture to

> become exemplary seafarers, traveling between their islands, fishing grounds and coastal farms in dugout canoes powered by lateen sails or outboard motors. They fish for food and income, shipping lobster and other commercial species to Panamá City. They also grow coconuts on the uninhabited islands and coastal lowlands, which they sell to the Colombian traders who ply their territorial waters in large boats. (Dudenhoefer 2012)

The freedom of the Guna continued until the early twentieth century and the creation of the new República de Panamá in 1903. Panamanian authorities moved into Guna Yala, as did foreigners intent on developing banana and coconut plantations and harvesting and extracting sea turtles, rubber, gold, and fish—an ongoing aspect of the saga of isthmian history. Panamanian police stations were built in the islands and enforced a government policy of assimilation and a government directive to make the people "modern" and "nonprimitive"—and hence less of a burden on the state by becoming part of the system (Sánchez Laws 2011:18).

For nearly two decades the Guna endured abuse and the loss of autonomy. Finally, on February 25, 1925, open revolution broke out, led by a famous chief and medicine man, Nele Kantule. Police stations were seized, hostages were taken, and the Guna created the independent Republic of Tule. Facing a lack of military support and pressure from the United States, Panamá negotiated. In this instance, the United States showed surprising restraint but nonetheless could not accept another independent state in the region. Therefore, the United States mediated the conflict. In exchange for the Guna's acceptance of government schools, Panamá allowed Guna Yala the authority to govern themselves without a colonial police presence, and the Guna returned to being part of the República de Panamá. In the years that followed, various Panamanian constitutions and laws (in 1938, 1945, 1953, 2000, and 2001) saw the semiautonomous region of Guna Yala ultimately emerge as a triumph of indigenous persistence and survival (Tice 1995:39–44; Howe 1998; Howe 2002:19–21). This was no mean feat in the face of almost half a millennium of intense pressure from the forces of empire to channel the resources of once "peripheral" states into a growing global economy.

In the twenty-first century, however, Guna Yala now faces another onslaught from those same forces. And this may eventually cause the loss of the landscape that nurtured and protected the Guna until now. Pressures from the national government to allow the clearing of forests to develop cattle ranches would lead to erosion and the siltation of the shores, burying spawning grounds and habitat and impacting fishing, which is the primary source of sustenance for the Guna. Increased pressure from foreign fishing boats and crocodile poachers, overharvesting of shellfish for restaurants, and the migration of some Guna to "foreign" places like Panamá City to make a living also have had an impact (Hinrichsen 1998:xxiii).

But there is a greater threat. Residing on 41 islands mere feet above sea level, the Guna are now, like other indigenous, island-dwelling and coastal people, facing the impact of climate change and sea-level rise. Models for sea-level rise vary, but even moderate levels pose a problem with greater impact from storms and wave surges. The existing maritime cultural land-

Figure 80. Traditional Guna mola depicting the culture's continual connection to the sea and its resources. Here, working from a canoe, breath-holding divers harvest their food. Photograph by Frederick Hanselmann, Hanselmann Family Collection.

scape is marked by seawalls that were built by the Guna from stones and coral harvested from the sea. The seawalls were erected to keep waves from washing into their homes, but the sea is becoming increasingly aggressive. Atencio López, president of the Institute for Research and Development—an office of the Guna General Congress—notes that removing coral heads from nearby reefs to build those seawalls has actually exacerbated the problem, since coral reefs serve as natural barriers, causing waves to break before they reach the shore. "Climate change is going to cause the sea level to rise and

> that our territory is one of the most vulnerable regions. Few of our people believe this, because until now we have lived from the sea and nature has never hit us with hurricanes or other disasters, so it seems inconceivable, but the international experts tell us that our islands are going to disappear," López says. (Dudenhoefer 2012)

The challenges of sea-level rise and resultant migrations of the humans who inhabit the shores are one of the early and persistent aspects of the maritime cultural landscape. For the Guna, the people of Bocas del Toro, and for all other coastal inhabitants, the next century will be marked by this inevitable and major next phase of adaptation to the maritime landscape and its resultant cultural reflections.

Ultimately (and appropriately) we conclude with a focus on the original inhabitants of the isthmus. We see not only the persistence of culture but also, through the indigenous perspective, the strongest and most elemental and enduring aspect of human adaptation to the marine environment—one that will continue to shape humanity in significant ways.

Figure 81. The seemingly timeless maritime cultural landscape of Panamá with its numerous islands faces major changes in the next century due to climate change and sea-level rise. For the people of Guna Yala living in the San Blas archipelago, the rising waters will bring dislocation and cultural change. Photograph by Juan Sisto, reproduced by permission.

NOTES

Chapter 2. The Isthmus Encountered and Conquered, 1501–1540

1. The Caribbean Gulf Coast was finally charted in 1519–1520 by the voyage of Alonso Álvarez de Piñeda along today's Texas coast (Weddle 1992). This ended the quest for a passage through the western Caribbean to a more distant sea.

2. In a radio interview for Radio Programs of Peru, RPP. See http://www.rpp.com.pe/2013-07-06-arqueologos-descubren-mas-vestigios-de-ciudad-hispana-mas-antigua-noticia_610855.html.

Chapter 3. The Isthmus Challenged and Fortified, 1540–1738

1. Not to be confused with (1) Venta de Cruces, a town located farther down on the Chagres but connecting the Camino de Cruces with Panamá City and the river or (2) the town of Chagres, which stood next to San Lorenzo Fortress at the mouth of the Chagres River.

2. In 2011 the media reported on the discovery of two circa sixteenth-century wrecks off Portobelo being investigated by underwater explorers, not archaeologists. It was suggested the wrecks were associated with Sir Francis Drake's 1596 attack. No evidence of this identification was available then, nor has it become available, and there has not been any report on or documentation of the sites. See http://beforeitsnews.com/alternative/2011/11/ship-remains-off-panama-coast-could-be-those-of-sir-francis-drake-1352640.html.

3. According to a website listing of Panamá's shipwrecks at http://www.angelfire.com/pa2/Panama2Hot/shpwrk.html.

4. IMDI maintains a website that allows purchasers to "authenticate my artifact" from the wreck at http://sanjose1631.com/. In response to archaeological concerns, UNESCO sent a scientific delegation to investigate the matter. See http://www.unesco.org/new/en/media-services/single-view/news/unesco_sends_mission_to_panama_to_examine_the_wreck_of_17th_century_spanish_galleon_san_jose/#.VcEeSPNViko.

5. In a 2002 press interview, the then Panamanian minister of culture claimed that research showed some 59 "galleons" had been lost off the isthmus. See http://www.rense.com/general29/spapn.htm.

Chapter 4. Buccaneers, Pirates, the Morgan Attack, and the Scottish at Darién

1. A recent archaeological research project carried out by Universitat de Barcelona and Patronato Panamá Viejo (in which Mendizábal participated) has located the remains of the first of such settlements, la Villa de Santiago del Príncipe, on the outskirts of Nombre de Dios (Mendizábal and De Gracia 2014).

2. A 2011 expedition was the latest announced effort to find the coffin. See http://www.cnn.com/2011/11/08/world/europe/pirate-passion/.

3. Salvage Concession Contract No. 231 of July 25, 2003, between the Economy and Finance Ministry and IMDI, S.A. This contract was amended and extended on March 19, 2010, and IMDI S.A. continues operations as of this writing.

4. Post deconcretion, one gun is now known to measure exactly 1.1 m in length, with a 16 cm breech diameter, a 12.7 cm muzzle diameter, and a weight of 131 lbs.

5. There exists an extensive corpus of literature on the subject, such as Cundall 1926, Russell Hart 1929, Higgins 1986, Storrs 1999, Prebble 2002, Gallup-Díaz 2004, Watt 2007, and Horton 1980, 2009.

6. A French merchantman, sometimes incorrectly referred to as *Maurepas*, it was armed with 42 guns, described as "very leaky," and had been involved in the raid on Cartagena, from whence she fled, laden with bullion, to the protection of the Scots. While leaving the Scottish harbor on Christmas Eve 1698, she was cast upon an "iron shore" and sank with the loss of 24 of the ship's company (Horton 1979:2).

7. Chasse (2005) suggests close to 2,000 deaths and the loss of 10 ships (2).

8. All metallic artifacts of the 2003 expedition are under storage and curation at the conservation laboratory of Patronato Panamá Viejo.

9. In the Report of the joint WHC-ICOMOS Reactive Monitoring Mission of the World Heritage property "Archaeological Site of Panamá Viejo and Historic District of Panamá," Panamá, 25–28 November 2013, (http://whc.unesco.org/en/documents/128501), the mission has given Panamá three options to avoid delisting of the property, in view of the fact that Cinta Costera III was a fait accompli: (1) based on the original extension dossier of 2002, submission of a significant boundary change to focus the site only on Panamá Viejo and to also include the new buffer zone by law 91/2007 and review the statement of Outstanding Universal Value; (2) submission of option I with an addition of a reduced area in the Historic District where the attributes that convey the contribution of this component to the Outstanding Universal Value of the serial property are present; (3) submission of a (phased) approach by 1 February 2015 in which an overall new vision is included regarding components of the property as parts of a broader territorial system related to interoceanic and intercontinental commerce over five centuries.

Chapter 6. The Isthmus during and after the "Fiebre del Oro," 1849–1861

1. There is no truly accurate means of calculating the value of dollars at that time to modern figures, but as a general rule of thumb, it is estimated that one dollar in the period would be equal to four dollars in 2014. See http://mykindred.com/cloud/TX/Documents/dollar/. This means that the amount shipped across the isthmus was worth approximately 2.84 billion dollars in today's money.

2. Colombia balked at the name; it was presumptuous on the part of the Americans, to be sure. Bogotá named the new town "Colón" after Christopher Columbus. It existed

as a port with two names: Colón to locals and Aspinwall to visitors. But in 1890 Colombia stopped delivering mail marked "Aspinwall." It has been known as Colón ever since (Tejeira 2011:47).

3. When done, these pilots for Mexico and Central America were completed by the U.S. Navy Hydrographic Office, drawing on surveys done by U.S. Navy ships from 1873 to 1901. A work in progress, the first pilot was published in 1887, followed by a second revised edition in 1893 and the third edition in 1904 (United States Navy Hydrographic Office 1904:v).

Chapter 7. Canal Dreams and Realities, 1861–1902

1. An extensive and excellent website created and maintained by Andrew Czernek documents the ship's sinking and its salvages. It also offers a number of contemporary sources, including transcripts of newspaper accounts and the correspondence of the Lloyds' agent, Francis W. Lodge, which were provided to him by descendants. http://freepages.misc.rootsweb.ancestry.com/~ssgoldengate/.

2. The online forum TreasureNet.com has archived a 2009 discussion on the various salvage projects. See http://www.treasurenet.com/forums/shipwrecks/118423-looking-info-ss-golden-gate.html.

3. The survey took place as part of the archaeological cultural resource management for the Canal Expansion Programme, which included the widening of the canal at Gorgona. Also, an excellent online article by Luis R. Celerier, "The Mystery of the French Cemeteries" in *Bits & Pieces—History of Panama*, documents the known and probable cemetery sites on the isthmus. See http://www.panamahistorybits.com/article.asp?id=2012-04-26b (accessed June 18, 2014). See also U.S. House 1978 and Joseph et al. 1996.

4. See "Mount Hope Cemetary" on the World Monuments Fund website, http://www.wmf.org/project/mount-hope-cemetery.

5. The structure later housed the U.S. Isthmian Canal Commission offices, and after 1912, the Main Post Office. The museum is currently open Tuesdays through Sundays from 9:30 a.m. to 5:00 p.m. The museum's website is http://museodelcanal.com/.

Chapter 8. Fortification and Control, 1903–2015

1. Michael Adas summarizes it as "unbounded energy, inventiveness, adaptability and faith in technological solutions" that resulted in the successful U.S. canal project, all part of a concerted American effort to utilize its resources, people, and drive to become a respected global power and to make the twentieth an "American century" (Adas 2006:188–190).

2. Carse (2012) offers a fascinating and brilliant perspective in discussing the Canal Zone watershed within the context of "nature as infrastructure," noting that "the water that facilitates interoceanic transportation and global connection falls as rain across the watershed surrounding the canal and is managed by an extensive system of locks, dams, and hydrographic stations. These technologies—which correspond with the popular understanding of infrastructure as hardware—were largely constructed during the early twentieth century. Since the late 1970s, however, administrators and other concerned actors have responded to actual and potential water scarcity within the canal system by developing a managerial approach that integrates engineered technologies and new techniques of land-use planning and environmental regulation across the watershed. Through this process,

techno-politics and environmental politics have become increasingly inextricable in the transit zone. Whereas canal administrators previously emphasized the control of water in its liquid state, watershed management emerged as an attempt to manipulate water flows through the legal protection of forests and restriction of agriculture. As forested landscapes have been assigned new infrastructural functions (water storage and regulation), *campesino* farmers have been charged with a new responsibility (forest conservation) often at odds with their established agricultural practices" (Carse 2012:539; see also Carse 2014).

3. Also see Knapp and Knapp (1984) for a utopian view of the "Zone" and "Zonians."

4. Every imaginable detail of canal construction was documented in the *Canal Record*— the magazine produced by the Isthmian Canal Commission (ICC)—as well as in its yearly reports and, from 1915 on, in reports of the Canal Zone governor to the U.S. government. These documents are an invaluable source of information for all aspects related to the first two decades of the canal.

5. The website *Lighthouses of Northern Panama* (https://www.unc.edu/~rowlett/lighthouse/pan.htm) does an exceptional job cataloguing and documenting the lighthouses of Panamá.

6. S.S. *Ancon*, on August 15, 1914, made the transit in nine and a half hours.

7. Forts Clayton and Davis were specifically built for the infantry in 1920–1921.

8. Concerns over aerial attacks were publicly announced even before the canal's official opening. In the April 1914 issue of *Sunset*, a popular U.S. magazine, author Riley E. Scott argued that the canal was vulnerable, especially its locks (Scott 1914). Scott, a 1904 West Point graduate commissioned as a second lieutenant, served briefly in the coast artillery as a first lieutenant before resigning in 1908. His patent for dropping aerial bombs was filed in May 1910 and published in 1911. Scott wrote about his patent in the October 1911 *Scientific American*. The Riley bomb site was successfully tested by him at College Park, Maryland, in 1911, just nine months after the first aerial bombs were successfully dropped from a plane. His bombs all hit within 10 feet of a 4 × 5-foot target from a 400-foot altitude. The former lieutenant warned readers about the vulnerability of the new canal.

9. The MIM23A HAWK was a 16-foot-long weapon that could reach speeds of MACH 2.5 and had a 22-mile range (Berhow 2005). It carried a 54 kg (119 lb) fragmentation warhead and was designed to take down attacking aircraft.

10. Fort Grant reverted to Panamá in 1979. Its facilities on Naos were used by the Panamanian military until 1989 while Flamenco became a prison. It is now a Panamanian Coast Guard base. Culebra is home to a yacht club and a research facility for the Smithsonian Tropical Research Institute, as is Naos Island. The causeway joining the island with the mainland (as well as with the islands) is part of an eclectic twenty-first-century mix of new developments, including restaurants and yacht harbors.

11. According to the Submarine Force Museum and Library's excellent website on wartime submarine losses ((http://ussnautilus.org/blog/the-loss-of-uss-s-26-ss-131/), "Water gushed into the boat through the huge hole in her side and the open bridge hatch. In less than a minute she sank, bow first. The next morning divers attempted a rescue of any Sailors who might still be alive—they noted that at least one crewmember had survived long enough to close the bridge hatch, which stubbornly resisted the divers' attempts to reopen it. After 25 unsuccessful trips to the bottom the effort was called off. None of the divers reported hearing tapping from inside the hull, so it is doubtful that anyone was left

alive. To this day S-26, a protected war grave, lies upright and intact in 300 feet of water. She and the 46 men who went down with her remain on eternal patrol."

12. Nahl (1869–1935) was from a German family that had immigrated to California during the Gold Rush via the Panamá route, arriving in San Francisco in 1851. His father Hugo Wilhelm (1833–1889) and his uncle Charles Christian Nahl (1818–1878) are remembered today as some of the greatest artists to depict the California Gold Rush with portraits, city and camp life views, and some of the great iconic scenes of the Panamá route: the oil paintings *Chagres River Scene (Crossing the Chagres)*, *Boaters Rowing to Shore at Chagres*, and *Incident on the Chagres*, though romantic and exaggerated, are based on their experiences crossing the isthmus (Driesbach, Jones and Holland 1998:56–58).

REFERENCES

Abbot, Willis J.

1913 *Panama and the Canal: In Picture and Prose*. Syndicate, London.

1914 *Panama and the Canal. The Story of its Achievement, Its Problems and its Prospects*. Dodd, Mead, New York.

Adas, Michael

2006 *Dominance by Design: Technological Imperatives and America's Civilizing Mission*. Belknap Press of Harvard University Press, Cambridge, Massachusetts.

Alba, Almyr, and Manuel Trute

2003 *Portobelo–San Lorenzo: Una aproximación a la conservación integrada de recursos culturales y naturales en peligro*. World Monuments Fund, New York.

Altolaguirre y Duvale, Angel

1914 *Vasco Nuñez de Balboa*. Real Academia de la Historia, Madrid.

Alzate Gallego, Adriana

2011 La Arqueología Colonial Como Herramienta Para Contrastar La Historia Escrita. *ArqueoWeb* 13:4–14.

Amero, Richard

2013 *Balboa Park and the 1915 Exposition*. History Press, Charleston.

Anderson, Charles L. G.

1911 *Old Panamá and Castilla Del Oro*. North River Press, New York.

Arango, Julieta De, Félix Durán, Juan Guillermo Martín, and Silvia Arroyo (editors)

2007 *Panamá Viejo: De la aldea a la urbe*. Patronato Panamá Viejo, Panamá.

Arcila Vélez, Graciliano

1986 *Santa María de la Antigua del Darién: La Primera Ciudad de la América Continental y la Primera Sede Episcopal de América*. Presidencia de Colombia, Secretaría de Información y Prensa, Medellin.

Aritio, Luis Blas

2012 *Vasco Núñez de Balboa y los Cronistas de Indias*. Comisión Nacional para la Conmemoración del Quinto Centenario del Descubrimiento del Océano Pacífico, Panamá.

Arnold, J. Barto, and Robert S. Weddle
1978 *The Nautical Archaeology of Padre Island: The Spanish Shipwrecks of 1554*. Academic Press, New York.

Arroyo, Silvia
2010 El Plan Maestro del Conjunto Monumental de Panamá Viejo: 10 años después. *Canto Rodado* 5:185–212.

Autenrieth, Dr. E. L.
1851 *A Topographical Map of the Isthmus of Panama, Together with a Separate and Enlarged Map of the City of Panama, With a Few Accompanying Remarks for the Use of Travellers*. J. H. Colton, New York.

Bancroft, Hubert H.
1886 *History of Central America*. 3 vols. History Company, San Francisco.

Baxley, Dr. H. Willis
1865 *What I Saw on the West Coast of South and North America, and at the Hawaiian Islands*. D. Appleton, New York.

Belcher, Captain Sir Edward
1843 *Narrative of a Voyage Round the World, Performed in Her Majesty's Ship Sulphur, During the Years 1836–1842, including Details of the Naval Operations in China, from Dec. 1840, to Nov. 1841*. Henry Colburn, London.

Belecki, Hanna
2007 Spanish Inheritance and Cultural Adaption: Small Finds from Panamá La Vieja. Master's thesis, Tübingen University, Germany.

Bennett, Ira E.
1915 *History of the Panama Canal: Its Construction and Builders*. Historical Publishing, Washington, D.C.

Berhow, Mark A.
2005 *U.S. Strategic and Defensive Missile Systems, 1950–2004*. Osprey, Botley, Oxford, UK.

Biese, Leo. P.
1964 The Prehistory of Panamá Viejo. Smithsonian Institution Bureau of American Ethnology Bulletin 191, *Anthropological Papers* 68:1–75.

Bigelow, Poultney
1906 An American Panama: Some Personal Notes on Tropical Colonizations Affected by Geological and Political Conditions. *Bulletin of the American Geographical Society* 38(8):489–494.

Blashford-Snell, John
1981 *Operation Drake*. W. H. Allen, London.

Blunt, Edmund M.
1854 *The American Coast Pilot; Containing Directions for the Principle Harbors, Capes and Headlands on the Coasts of North and South America*. 17th ed. Edmund and George W. Blunt, New York.
1857 *The American Coast Pilot; Containing Directions for the Principle Harbors, Capes and Headlands on the Coasts of North and South America*. 18th ed. Edmund and George W. Blunt, New York.

Bohn, Bartholomew, and Luz G. Joly
1978 Patrones de Construcción del Camino de Cruces y el Camino Real y su Relación Histórica. In *Actas del V Simposium Nacional de Antropología, Arqueología y Etnohistoria de Panamá*, edited by the Instituto Nacional de Cultura, pp. 323–356. Universidad de Panamá, Panamá.

Bonnycastle, Richard Henry
1818 *Spanish America: Or a Descriptive, Historical and Geographical Account of the Dominions of Spain in the Western Hemisphere.* Vol. 1. Longman, Hurst, Rees, Orme, and Brown, London.

Borthwick, John David
1948 *Three Years in California*. Biobooks, Oakland.

Brady, Scott
1999 A Historical Geography of the Earliest Colonial Routes across the American Isthmus. *Revista Geográfica* 126:121–143.

Branton, Nicole
2009 Landscape Approaches in Historical Archaeology: The Archaeology of Places. In *International Handbook of Historical Archaeology*, edited by T. Majewski and D. Gaimster, pp. 51-65. Springer, New York.

Brinkbäumer, Klaus, and Clemens Höges
2007 *The Voyage of the Vizcaína: The Mystery of Columbus*. Harcourt, New York.

Brizuela, Alvaro
1996a Informe Final de Excavación en El Cabildo, San José, Hospital de San Juan de Dios, Calle Obispo. Unpublished report for Patronato Panamá Viejo, Panama.
1996b Arqueología Historíca en las Ruinas de la Antigua Ciudad de Panamá. Paper presented at a conference at the University of Xalapa, Mexico.

Brooks, Charles M.
2003 *Guarding the Crossroads: Security and Defense of the Panama Canal.* R&P Group, Panama.

Bryan, G. S.
1941 Geography and the Defence of the Caribbean and the Panamá Canal. *Annals of the Association of American Geographers* 31(2):83–94.

Bryce, James
1913 *South America: Observations and Impressions*. Macmillan, New York.

Bureau of Navigation, United States Department of Commerce
1915 *Forty-Seventh Annual List of Merchant Vessels of the United States.* Government Printing Office, Washington, D.C.

Camargo, Marcela
1983 Las pesquerías de perlas y conchas madreperla en Panamá. *Revista Lotería* 326–327(May–June):32–76.

Campbell, R. J.
1976 Crossing the Isthmus: An Anonymous 1846 Account. *Americas* 28(5):14–16.

Campos Carrasco, Juan M., and Félix Durán Ardila
2006 La traza urbana colonial de Panamá Viejo: Su recuperación. *Canto Rodado* 1:41–64.

Carrington, John W.

1849 *The Passage of the Isthmus, Or, Practical Hints to Persons about to Cross the Isthmus of Panama.* Jennings and Harrison, New York.

Carse, Ashley

2014 *Beyond the Big Ditch: Politics, Ecology, and Infrastructure at the Panama Canal.* MIT Press, Cambridge, Massachusetts.

2012 Nature as Infrastructure: Making and Managing the Panama Canal Watershed. *Social Studies of Science* 42(4):539–563.

Castillero, Alfredo

1994 *Arquitectura, Urbanismo y Sociedad. La Vivienda Colonial en Panamá: Historia de un sueño.* Fondo de Promoción Cultural Shell, Panamá.

1995 *Conquista, Evangelización y Resistencia: ¿Triunfo o fracaso de la política indigenista?* Instituto Nacional de Cultura, Dirección Nacional de Extensión Cultural, Panamá.

1999 *La Ciudad Imaginada: El Casco Viejo de Panamá.* Ministerio de la Presidencia, Panamá.

2004a Los primeros europeos. El Descubrimiento del Istmo: De Bastidas a Balboa. In *Historia General de Panamá,* Vol. 1, Tome 1, edited by Alfredo Castillero, pp. 79–103.

2004b Las Ferias del Trópico. In *Historia General de Panamá,* Vol. 1, Tome 1, edited by Alfredo Castillero, pp. 331–355.

2004c El transporte transístmico y las comunicaciones regionales. In *Historia General de Panamá,* Vol. 1, Tome 1, edited by Alfredo Castillero, pp. 355–398.

2004d La trata de esclavos. In *Historia General de Panamá,* Vol. 1, Tome 1, edited by Alfredo Castillero, pp. 454–490.

2004e Conflictos Sociales, guerra y Pax Hispana. In *Historia General de Panamá,* Vol. 1, Tome 1, edited by Alfredo Castillero, pp. 491–513.

2004f Las fortificaciones. In *Historia General de Panamá,* Vol. 1, Tome 1, edited by Alfredo Castillero, pp. 27–51.

2004g Destrucción de Panamá La Vieja y fundación de la Nueva Panamá. In *Historia General de Panamá,* Vol. 1, Tome 1, edited by Alfredo Castillero, pp. 334–357.

2004h Los Edificios Religiosos en la Nueva Panamá. In *Historia General de Panamá,* Vol. 1, Tome 2, edited by Alfredo Castillero, pp. 375–398.

2004i El oro y las perlas en la economía colonial. In *Historia General de Panamá,* Vol. 1, Tome 2, edited by Alfredo Castillero, pp. 431–456.

2004j Decadencia de las ferias, crisis comercial y nuevos soportes económicos. In *Historia General de Panamá,* Vol. 1, Tome 2, edited by Alfredo Castillero, pp. 457–489.

2004k La economía hasta mediados del siglo XIX. In *Historia General de Panamá,* Vol. 2, edited by Alfredo Castillero, pp. 46–62.

2006 *Sociedad, Economía y Cultura Material. Historia Urbana de Panamá la Vieja.* Patronato Panamá Viejo, Panamá.

2008 *Los Metales Preciosos y la Primera Globalización.* Banco Nacional de Panamá.

2010 *Cultura Alimentaria y Globalización: Panamá, siglos XVI al XXI.* Nikos Café, Panamá.

2013 *El Descubrimiento del Pacífico y los orígenes de la globalización.* Comisión Nacional para la Conmemoración del Quinto Centenario del Descubrimiento del Océano Pacífico, Panamá.

2014 *La Ciudad Imaginada. Historia Social y Urbana del Casco Viejo de Panamá.* Odebrecht, Panamá.

Castillero, Alfredo (editor)

2004 *Historia General de Panamá.* 3 vols. Comité Nacional del Centenario de la República de Panamá, Ciudad de Panamá.

Castillero Reyes, Ernesto

1932 *El Ferrocarril de Panamá y su Historia.* Imprenta Nacional, Panamá.

1962 *La Isla que se Transformó en Ciudad. Historia de un Siglo de la Ciudad de Colón.* Imprenta Nacional, Panamá.

Castro, Filipe, and Carlos Fitzgerald

2006 The Playa Damas Shipwreck: An Early Sixteenth-Century Shipwreck in Panama. In *Underwater Cultural Heritage at Risk: Managing Natural and Human Impacts,* edited by Robert Grenier, David Nutley, and Ian Cochran, pp. 38–40. UNESCO, Paris.

Castro, Guillermo

2001 On Cattle and Ships: Culture, History and Sustainable Development in Panama. *Environment and History* 7:201–217.

2004 El Istmo en el Mundo: Elementos para una historia ambiental de Panamá. In *Historia General de Panamá,* Vol. 2, edited by Alfredo Castillero, pp. 121–140.

Caughey, John Walton (editor)

1951 *Seeing the Elephant: Letters of R. R. Taylor, Forty-Niner.* Ward Ritchie, Pasadena.

Cedeño Censi, Diógenes

1996 *El Cuarto Viaje de Cristóbal Colón: Por la ruta de las tormentas.* Editorial Universitaria, Panamá.

Chartrand, René

2006 *The Spanish Main, 1492–1800.* Osprey, Botley, Oxford, UK.

Chassé, Patrick

2005 Hereticks for Believing the Antipodes: Scottish Colonial Identities in the Darién, 1698–1700. Unpublished Master's thesis, University of Victoria, British Columbia, Canada.

Chatters, James C., Douglas J. Kennett, Yamane Asmerom, Brian M. Kemp, Victor Polyak, Alberto Nava Blank, Patricia A. Beddows, Eduard Reinhardt, Joaquin Arroyo-Cabrales, Deborah A. Bolnick, et al.

2014 Late Pleistocene Human Skeleton and mtDNA Link Paleoamericans and Modern Native Americans. *Science* 344:750–754.

Chavanne, Andre

1940 The Burning of the *Golden Gate* in July 1862: The Impressions of a Survivor. Edited and translated by Desiré Fricot. *California Historical Society Quarterly* 19(1):27–42.

Christman, Florence
1985 *The Romance of Balboa Park*. 4th ed. San Diego Historical Society.
Church, Col. George E.
1903 The Republic of Panama. *Geographical Journal* 22(1):676–685.
Churchill, Charles William
1977 *Fortunes Are for the Few: Letters of a Forty-Niner*. Edited by Duane A. Smith and David J. Weber. San Diego Historical Society.
Cipriani, Roberto, Hector M. Guzman, and Melina Lopez
2008 Harvest History and Current Densities of the Pearl Oyster *Pinctada Mazatlanica* (Bivalvia: Pteriidae) in Las Perlas and Coiba Archipelagos, Panama. *Journal of Shellfish Research* 27(4):691–700.
Coates, Anthony G. (editor)
1997 *Central America: A Natural and Cultural History*. Yale University Press, New Haven, Connecticut.
Collins, John Owen
1912 *The Panama Guide*. Quartermaster's Department, ICC Press, Mount Hope, Canal Zone.
Conn, Stetson, Rose C. Engelman, and Byron Fairchild
2000 *Guarding the United States and its Outposts: The Western Hemisphere*. United States Army in World War II. Center of Military History, U.S. Army, Washington, D.C.
Cooke, Richard G.
1988 Some Ecological and Technological Correlates of Coastal Fishing in Formative Pacific Panama. In *Diet and Subsistence: Current Archaelogical Perspectives, Proceedings of the Nineteenth Annual Conference of the Archaeological Association of the University of Calgary*, edited by Brenda V. Kennedy and Genevieve M. LeMoine, pp. 127–140. University of Calgary Archaeology Association, Calgary.
1992 Prehistoric Nearshore and Littoral Fishing in the Eastern Tropical Pacific: An Ichthyological Evaluation. *Journal of World Prehistory* 6(1):1–49.
2005 Prehistory of Native Americans on the Central American Land-Bridge: Colonization, Dispersal and Divergence. *Journal of Archaeological Research* 13(2):129–187.
Cooke, Richard, Ilean Isaza, John Griggs, Benoit Desjardins, and Luis Sánchez
2003a Who Crafted, Exchanged, and Displayed Gold in Pre-Columbian Panama? In *Gold and Power in Ancient Costa Rica, Panamá, and Colombia: A Symposium at Dumbarton Oaks, 9 and 10 October 1999*, edited by J. Quilter and J. W. Hoopes, pp. 91–158. Dumbarton Oaks Research Library and Collection, Washington, D.C.
Cooke, Richard G., Máximo Jiménez, and Anthony J. Ranere
2008 Archaeozoology, Art, Documents, and the Life Assemblage. In *Case Studies in Environmental Archaeology*, edited by E. J. Reitz, C. M. Scarry, and S. J. Scudder, pp. 95–121. Springer, New York.
Cooke, Richard G., and Anthony Ranere
1999 Precolumbian Fishing on the Pacific Coast of Panama. In *Pacific Latin America*

in *Prehistory: The Evolution of Archaic and Formative Cultures*, edited by Michael Blake, pp. 103–121. Washington State University Press, Pullman.

Cooke, Richard G., Anthony Ranere, Georges Pearson, and Ruth Dickau

2013 Radiocarbon Chronology of Early Human Settlement on the Isthmus of Panama (13,000–7000 BP) with Comments on Cultural Affinities, Environments, Subsistence, and Technological Change. *Quaternary International* 301(July 8). http://dx.doi.org/10.1016/j.quaint.2013.02.032. Accessed March 14, 2015.

Cooke, Richard G., and Beatriz E. Rovira

1983 Historical Archaeology in Panama City. *Historical Archaeology* 36(2):51–57.

Cooke, Richard G., Luis Sánchez, and Koichi Udagawa

2000 Contextualized Goldwork from "Gran Coclé," Panama: An Update Based on Recent Excavations and New Radiocarbon Dates for Associated Pottery Styles. In *Precolumbian Gold: Technology, Style and Iconography*, edited by C. McEwan, pp. 154–176. British Museum Press, London.

Cooke, Richard G., and Luis Sánchez

2001 El Papel del Mar y de las Costas en el Panamá Pre-Hispánico y del Período del Contacto: Redes Locales y Relaciones Externas. *Revista de Historia* 43:15–60.

2004 Panamá prehispánico. In *Historia General de Panamá*, Vol. 1 Tome 1, edited by Alfredo Castillero, pp. 3–46. Comité Nacional del Centenario de la República, Panamá.

Cooke, Richard G., and Gonzalo Tapia Rodriguez

1994 Stationary Intertidal Fish Traps in Estuarine Inlets on the Pacific Coast of Panama: Descriptions, Evaluations of Early Dry Season Catches and Relevance to the Interpretation of Dietary Archaeofaunas. *Proceedings of the Sixth Meeting of the Fish Working Group of the International Council for Zooarchaeology, Offa* 51:287–298. Schleswig.

Cramer, Katie L.

2013 History of Human Occupation and Environmental Change in Western and Central Caribbean Panama. *Bulletin of Marine Science* 89(0):1–28.

Cruxent, José M.

1959 *Informe sobre un reconocimiento arqueológico en el Darién, Panamá*. Publicaciones de la revista Lotería No. 9. La Academia, Panamá.

Cullen, John

1853 *Isthmus of Darien Ship Canal*. 2nd ed. Efingham Wilson, London.

Cundall, Frank

1926 *The Darien Venture*. Hispanic Notes and Monographs Series Vol. 11. Trustees of the University of California, Berkeley.

Curtis, William Eleroy

1900 *Between the Andes and the Ocean: An Account of an Interesting Journey Down the West Coast of South America from the Isthmus of Panama to the Straits of Magellan*. Herbert S. Stone, Chicago.

Dampier, William.

1699 *A New Voyage Round the World*. James Knapton, London.

Davis, George W.

1909 Fortification at Panama. *American Journal of International Law* 3(4):885–908.

De Banville, Marc
2012 *Canal Francés. La Aventura de los Franceses en Panamá*. 2nd ed. Ediciones Canal Valley, Panamá.
De Mena, Dolores
1999 *The Era of U.S. Army Installations in Panama*. Updated reprint. History Office, U.S. Army South Headquarters, Fort Clayton, Panamá.
Deagan, Kathleen
1987 *Artifacts of the Spanish Colonies of Florida and the Caribbean, 1500–1800*. Vol 1. Smithsonian Institution, Washington, D.C.
1993 *Observations and Recommendations for an Archaeological Plan of Action for Portobelo and San Lorenzo de Chagres, Republica de Panamá*. University of Florida and the Florida Museum of Natural History, Gainesville.
Delgado, James P.
1981 Watersoaked and Covered with Barnacles: The Wreck of the S.S. *Winfield Scott*. *Pacific Historian* 27(2):5–21.
1983 Underwater Archaeological Investigation of Gold Rush Steamships on the California Coast. *Proceedings of the First Biennial Conference on Research in California's National Parks*:17–23. University of California Davis Press.
1985 Great Leviathan of the Pacific: The Saga of the Gold Rush Steamship Tennessee. Unpublished Master's thesis, Program in Maritime History and Underwater Research, East Carolina University, Greenville.
1990 *To California by Sea: A Maritime History of the Gold Rush*. University of South Carolina Press, Columbia.
2009 *Gold Rush Port: The Maritime Archaeology of San Francisco's Waterfront*. University of California Press, Berkeley.
2012 *Misadventures of a Civil War Submarine: Iron, Guns, and Pearls*. Texas A&M University Press, College Station.
Delgado, James P., Frederick H. Hanselmann, and Dominique Rissolo
2009 A Submerged Cultural Resource Reconnaissance: Mouth of the Río Chagres and Approaches in the República de Panamá. *INA Annual*. Institute of Nautical Archaeology, College Station, Texas.
2011 The "Richest River in the World": The Maritime Cultural Landscape of the Mouth of the Río Chagres, República de Panamá. In *The Archaeology of Maritime Landscapes*, edited by Ben Ford, pp. 233–245. Springer, Dordrecht, Netherlands.
Delgado, James P., Allen G. Pastron, and Rhonda K. Robichaud
2007 *This Fine and Commodious Vessel: Archaeological Investigations of the Gold Rush Storeship General Harrison*. Archeo-Tec, Oakland.
Díaz López, Laurentino
2001 *Nombre de Dios: La ciudad de la altiva cerviz*. Editorial La Antigua, Panamá.
Dillehay, Tom D., Mario Pino, E. M. Davis, S. Valastro, A. G. Varela, and R. Casamiquela
1982 Monte Verde: Radiocarbon Dates from an Early-Man Site in South-Central Chile. *Journal of Field Archaeology* 9:547–550.
Douglas, James Jr.
1878 Journey along the West Coast of South America, from Panama to Valparaiso.

Journal of the American Geographical Society of New York 10:ccxxvi–ccxxviii, 197–225.

Driesebach, James T., Harvey L. Jones, and Katherine Church Holland

1998 *Art of the Gold Rush*. University of California Press, Oakland Art Museum, and Crocker Art Gallery, Berkeley.

Drude de Lacerda, Luiz (editor)

2001 *Mangrove Ecosystems: Function and Management*. Springer, Dordrecht.

DuBard, Bryana

2013 The Key to All the Indies: Defense of the Isthmus of Panamá. Unpublished Master's thesis, Texas A&M University, College Station.

Dudenhoefer, David

2012 That Sinking Feeling. *Indian Country Today Media Network*, September 2. Available on *Before_It's_News.com*, http://beforeitsnews.com/native-american-news/2012/09/that-sinking-feeling-2443640.html.

Duncan, Brad

2011 "What Do You Want to Catch?" Exploring the Maritime Cultural Landscape of the Queenscliff Fishing Community. In *The Archaeology of Maritime Landscapes*, edited by Ben Ford, pp. 267–289. Springer, Dordrecht.

Duncan, Roland E.

1975 *Chile* and *Peru*: The First Successful Steamers in the Pacific. *American Neptune* 35(4):248–274.

Dwinelle, John W.

1931 The Diary of John W. Dwinelle, from New York to Panama in 1849. *Society of California Pioneers Quarterly* 8(2):105–129.

Earle, Peter

1981 *The Sack of Panama: Captain Morgan and the Battle for the Caribbean*. Thomas Dunne Books, New York.

Enscore, Susan I., Suzanne P. Johnson, Julie Webster, and Gordon Cohen

2000 *Guarding the Gates: The Story of Fort Clayton—Its Setting, Its Architecture, and Its Role in the History of the Panama Canal*. Construction Engineering Research Laboratory, U.S. Army Engineer Research and Development Center, Illinois.

Erlandson, Jon M., Michael H. Graham, Bruce J. Bourque, Debra Corbett, James A. Estes, and Robert S. Steneck

2007 The Kelp Highway Hypothesis: Marine Ecology, the Coastal Migration Theory, and the Peopling of the Americas. *Journal of Island and Coastal Archaeology* 2(2):161–174.

Espino, Ariel

2009 Integración Social y Desarrollo Económico: El caso del Casco Antiguo de Panamá. *Canto Rodado* 4:1–38.

Exquemelin, Alexander O.

1969 *The Buccaneers of America*. Translated by Alexis Brown. Penguin Books, Harmondsworth, UK. (Originally published in 1678 in Dutch as *De Americaensche Zee-Roovers*.)

Fernández de Oviedo y Valdés, Gonzalo
1851 *Historia Natural y General de Las Indias, Islas y Tierra Firme del Mar Océano,* edited by J. Amador de los Ríos. Real Academia de Historia, Madrid.
Ferris, A. C.
1891 Hardships on the Isthmus in '49. *Century Illustrated Magazine,* 2nd Series, 41(6):929–931.
Fike, Richard E.
1987 *The Bottle Book: A Comprehensive Guide to Historic, Embossed Medicine Bottles.* Gibbs M. Smith, Salt Lake City.
Flatman, Joe
2011 Places of Special Meaning: Westerdahl's Comet, "Agency," and the Concept of the "Maritime Cultural Landscape." In *The Archaeology of Maritime Landscapes,* edited by Ben Ford, pp. 311–329. Springer, New York.
Ford, Ben (editor)
2011 *The Archaeology of Maritime Landscapes.* Springer, New York.
Fortune, Armando
1958 Corsarios y Cimarrones en Panamá. *Revista Cultural Lotería* 33:77–97.
Frenkel, Stephen
2002 Geographical Representations of the "Other": The Landscape of the Panama Canal Zone. *Journal of Historical Geography* 28(1):85–99.
Gage, Thomas
1648 *The English-American his Travail by Sea and Land: or a New Survey of the West-India's. . . .* R. Cotes, London.
Gallardo Mejía, Francisco Roberto
2013 Registro y documentación histórica del pecio SS Colón en Acajutla, Departamento de Sonsonate, El Salvador. *Revista De Museología Kóot* 3(4):25–91.
Gallup Díaz, Ignacio
2004 *The Door of the Seas and the Key of the Universe: Indian Politics and Imperial Rivalry in the Darién, 1640–1750.* Columbia University Press, New York.
Galvin, Peter R.
1991 The Pirates' Wake: A Geography of Piracy and Pirates as Geographers in Colonial Spanish America, 1536–1718. Unpublished Ph.D. dissertation, Louisiana State University, Baton Rouge.
Garcés, Alejandra
2009 Loza panameña, mayólica Europea: Diferencias sociales en dos contextos arqueológicos de la primera ciudad de Panamá. Unpublished undergraduate thesis, Departamento de Antropología, Universidad del Cauca, Colombia.
Gardner, Hugh, and Norman Carpenter
1965 *World War I Fortifications of the Panama Canal.* Pamphlet 870-1, 193rd Infantry Brigade, Canal Zone, Panama.
Gibson, John M.
1950 *Physician to the World: The Life of General William C. Gorgas.* Duke University Press, Durham, North Carolina.

Gómez, Carlos

2007 Continuidad cultural en torno a las creencias religiosas coloniales. Unpublished undergraduate thesis, Universidad de Panamá.

Gorgas, Marie, and Burton J. Hendrick

1924 *William Crawford Gorgas: His Life and Work.* Doubleday, New York.

Goss, Helen Rocca

1953 An Ill-Starred Voyage: The S.S. *Golden Gate*, January 1854. *California Historical Society Quarterly* 32(4):349–361.

Greene, Julie

2009 *The Canal Builders: Making America's Empire at the Panama Canal.* Penguin, New York.

Gregory, Joseph W.

1850 *Gregory's Guide for California Travellers via the Isthmus of Panama.* Nafis and Cornish, New York.

Griggs, John C.

1995 Archaeological Survey and Testing in the Belén River Valley, Panamá. Unpublished Master's thesis, Texas Tech University, Lubbock.

2005 The Archaeology of Central Caribbean Panamá. Unpublished Ph.D. dissertation, Department of Anthropology, University of Texas, Austin.

Griswold, Chauncey D.

1852 *The Isthmus of Panamá, and What I Saw There.* DeWitt and Davenport, New York.

Gutierrez, Samuel A.

1993 *Taboga: Redescubrimiento de la isla y de su arquitectura.* Academia Panameña de la Historia, Panamá.

Hamilton, Earl J.

1929 Imports of American Gold and Silver into Spain, 1503–1660. *Quarterly Journal of Economics* 43(3):436–472.

1934 *American Treasure and the Price Revolution in Spain.* Cambridge University Press, Cambridge.

Hanselmann, Frederick H.

2010 *Preliminary Field Report: Río Chagres Cannon Recovery Project, Colón, Panamá.* Report submitted to the Institute of Nautical Archaeology, Texas A&M University, College Station, and Dirección Nacional de Patrimonio Histórico, Instituto Nacional de Cultura, Panamá.

Hanselmann, Frederick H., James P. Delgado, and Dominique Rissolo

2009 The Maritime Cultural Landscape of the Chagres River, Panama: A Preliminary Survey of More than 500 Years of Maritime Activity. In *ACUA Underwater Archaeology Proceedings 2009*, edited by Erika Laanela and Jonathan Moore, pp. 259-268. PAST Foundation, Columbus, Ohio.

Hanselmann, Frederick H., and James P. Delgado

2010 *El Paisaje Cultural Marítimo del Río Chagres: El Proyecto de las Naves Perdidas de Henry Morgan, Informe de Campo 2010.* Report submitted to the Meadows Center for Water and the Environment, Texas State University (San Marcos), and Dirección Nacional de Patrimonio Histórico, Instituto Nacional de Cultura, Panamá.

2010 *The Río Chagres Maritime Cultural Landscape Study: Lost Ships of Henry Morgan Project 2010 Field Report*. Report submitted to the Meadows Center for Water and the Environment, Texas State University (San Marcos), and Dirección Nacional de Patrimonio Histórico, Instituto Nacional de Cultura, Panamá.

Hanselmann, Frederick H., Bert Ho, and Andrés Diaz

2012 *El Paisaje Cultural Marítimo del Río Chagres: El Proyecto de las Naves Perdidas de Henry Morgan, Informe de 2011*. Report Submitted to the Meadows Center for Water and the Environment, Texas State University (San Marcos), and Dirección Nacional de Patrimonio Histórico, Instituto Nacional de Cultura, Panamá.

2012 *The Río Chagres Maritime Cultural Landscape Study: Lost Ships of Henry Morgan Project 2011 Report*. Report Submitted to the Meadows Center for Water and the Environment, Texas State University (San Marcos), and Dirección Nacional de Patrimonio Histórico, Instituto Nacional de Cultura, Panamá.

Hanselmann, Frederick H., Tomás Mendizábal, Bert Ho, Christopher Horrell, Melanie Damour, and José Espinoza

2014 *El Paisaje Cultural Marítimo del Río Chagres: El Proyecto de las Naves Perdidas de Henry Morgan, Informe de 2012*. Report Submitted to the Meadows Center for Water and the Environment, Texas State University (San Marcos), and Dirección Nacional de Patrimonio Histórico, Instituto Nacional de Cultura, Panamá.

2014 *The Río Chagres Maritime Cultural Landscape Study: Lost Ships of Henry Morgan Project 2012 Report*. Report submitted to the Meadows Center for Water and the Environment, Texas State University (San Marcos), and Dirección Nacional de Patrimonio Histórico, Instituto Nacional de Cultura, Panamá.

Hanselmann, Frederick H., Tomás Mendizábal, and Juan Guillermo Martín

2016 Plundering the Spanish Main: Henry Morgan's Raids in Panama. In *Pieces of Eight: More Archaeology of Piracy*, edited by Charles Ewen and Russell Skowronek, pp. 132–164. University Press of Florida, Gainesville.

Haring, Clarence H.

1918 *Trade and Navigation between Spain and the Indies in the Time of the Hapsburgs*. Cambridge University Press, Cambridge.

Harmon, Russell S. (editor)

2005 *The Rió Chagres, Panama: A Multidisciplinary Profile of a Tropical Watershed*. Springer, Dordrecht, Netherlands.

Harp, Susan

2001 *History of the Las Cruces Trail and Adjacent Canal Area*. Darién Information Systems, Albrook, Panama.

Harris, Lewis D.

1984a Rodrigo de Bastidas and the Discovery of Panama. *Geographical Review* 74(2):170–182.

1984b Columbus' Easternmost Discoveries in Panama: A Geographical Appraisal. *Terrae Incognitae* 16(1):25–36.

Herdendorf, Charles E.

1995 Science on a Deep-Ocean Shipwreck. *Ohio Journal of Science* 95(1), Special Issue:4–212.

Higgins, David A.

1986 *Archaeological Survey and Excavation of Indian and Early Colonial Sites in the San Blas Province of Panama*. Operation Raleigh, London.

Hinrichsen, Don

1998 *Coastal Waters of the World: Trends, Threats, and Strategies*. Island Press, Washington, D.C.

Hoffmann, Jon T., Michael J. Brodhead, Carol R. Byerly, and Glenn F. Williams

2009 *The Panamá Canal: An Army's Enterprise*. Center of Military History, United States Army, Washington, D.C.

Horton, Mark

1980 *Caledonia Bay, Panamá, 1979: A Preliminary Report on the Archaeological Project of Operation Drake*. Operation Drake, London.

2009 "To Transmit to Posterity the Virtue, Lustre and Glory of their Ancestors": Scottish Pioneers in Darien, Panama. In *Bridging the Early Modern Atlantic World: People, Products, and Practices on the Move*, edited by Caroline A. Williams, pp. 131–150. Ashgate, Farnham, Surrey, UK.

Hotchkiss, Charles F.

1878 *On the Ebb: A Few Log-Lines from an Old Salt*. Tuttle, Morehouse, and Taylor, New Haven, Connecticut.

Howe, James

1998 *A People Who Would Not Kneel: Panama, the United States, and the San Blas Kuna*. Smithsonian Institution Press, Washington, D.C.

2002 *The Kuna Gathering: Contemporary Village Politics in Panama*. Latin American Monographs No. 67. University of Texas Press, Austin.

Huck, Eugene R.

1970 Forty-Niners in Panama: Canal Prelude. In *Militarists, Merchants and Missionaries: United States Expansion in Middle America*, edited by Eugene R. Huck and Edward H. Moseley, pp. 55–62. University of Alabama Press, Mobile.

Hussey, Roland Dennis

1939 *Spanish Colonial Trails in Panama*. Pan American Institute of Geography and History, Mexico.

1960 Caminos Coloniales en Panamá. *Revista Lotería* 60:104–126.

Isthmian Canal Commission (ICC)

1909 *Canal Record*. Vol 2. Ancon, Canal Zone.

1911 *Canal Record*. Vol 4. Ancon, Canal Zone.

Jacob, Christian

2006 *The Sovereign Map: Theoretical Approaches in Cartography throughout History*. Translated by Tom Conley, edited by Edward H. Dahl. University of Chicago Press.

Jackson, Jeremy B.C., and Luis D'Croz

1997 The Ocean Divided. In *Central America: A Natural and Cultural History*, edited by Anthony G. Coates, pp. 38–71. Yale University Press, New Haven, Connecticut.

Jaén Suárez, Omar

1985 *Geografía de Panamá: Estudio Introductorio y Antología, Tomo 1.* Biblioteca de la Cultura Panameña, Universidad de Panamá, Panamá.

1998 *La Población del Istmo de Panamá: estudio de Geohistoria.* 3ra Edición. Agencia Española de Cooperación Internacional, Madrid.

2014 *Hacia una Historia Global: 500 años de la Cuenca del Pacífico.* Autoridad del Canal de Panamá, Panamá.

Jefferys, Thomas

1799 *The West Indian Atlas: Or A Compendious Description of the West Indies. . . .* Robert Laurie and James Whittle, London.

Johnson, Suzanne P. (researcher and compiler), and Richard M. Houle (editor)

1995a *An American Legacy in Panamá: A Brief History of the Department of Defense Installations and Properties, the Former Canal Zone, Republic of Panama.* Prepared for United States Army South (USARSO), Directorate of Engineering and Housing, Fort Clayton, Panama.

1995b *A History of Fort Amador and Fort Grant.* Graves and Klein, Panama.

Johnson, Theodore Taylor

1849 *Sights in the Gold Region, and Scenes by the Way.* Baker and Scribner, New York.

Jones, James P., and William Warren Rogers

1961 Across the Isthmus in 1850: The Journey of Daniel A. Horn. *Hispanic American Historical Review* 41(4):533–554.

Joseph, Joe W., Mark Swanson, and Mary B. Reed

1996 *Historic Properties Management Plan for the US Army South (USARSO), Republic of Panama, Central America.* Report drafted by IT Corporation and New South Associates, Inc., for the U.S. Army.

Juan, Jorge, and Antonio De Ulloa

1826 *Noticias Secretas de América (Siglo XVIII) Tomo 1.* R. Taylor, London.

Kapp, Kitt S.

1971 *The Early Maps of Panama up to 1865.* Map Collectors' Series No. 73. K. S. Kapp Publications, North Bend, Ohio.

Kaufman, Scott

2013 *Project Plowshare: The Peaceful Use of Nuclear Explosives in Cold War America.* Cornell University Press, Ithaca, New York.

Keith, Donald H., Toni L. Carrell, and Denise C. Lakey

1990 The Search for Columbus' Caravel *Gallega* and the Site of Santa María de Belén. *Journal of Field Archaeology* 17(2):123–140.

Keith, Donald H., and Toni L. Carrell

1991 The Hunt for the *Gallega. Archaeology* 44(1):55–59.

Kemble, John Haskell

1943 *The Panama Route, 1848–1869.* University of California Press, Berkeley.

1950 A Hundred Years of the Pacific Mail. *The American Neptune* 10:123–143.

Knapp, Herbert, and Mary L. Knapp

1984 *Red, White, and Blue Paradise: The American Canal Zone in Panama.* Harcourt Brace Jovanovich, New York.

Knight, Donald G., and Eugene D. Wheeler
1990 *Agony and Death on a Gold Rush Steamer: The Disastrous Sinking of the Side-Wheeler Yankee Blade*. Pathfinder, Ventura, California.

Kottmann, Aline
2006 *Implementación de un sistema de información geográfico (SIG) en las ruinas de Panamá Viejo*. DAAD research scholarship. Submitted to Patronato Panamá Viejo, Panamá.

LaFeber, Walter
1978 *The Panama Canal: The Crisis in Historical Perspective*. Cambridge University Press, New York.

Lange, Frederick W.
1992 Summary: Perspectives on Wealth and Hierarchy. In *Wealth and Hierarchy in the Intermediate Area: A Symposium at Dumbarton Oaks, 10th and 11th October 1987*, edited by Frederick W. Lange, pp. 423–443. Dumbarton Oaks Research Library and Collection, Washington, D.C.
1999 *Los recursos culturales, coloniales, historicos y contemporaneous en al area San Lorenzo/Ft. Sherman*. USAID, Ciudad de Panamá.

Lanzas, Gisela
2001 Clavos coloniales, Siglos XVI y XVII: Panamá La Vieja. Unpublished undergraduate thesis, Universidad de Panamá.

Larson, Curtis L., and Waldemar Albertin
1984 Controlling Erosion and Sedimentation in the Panama Canal Watershed. *Water International* 9(4):161–164.

Lasso, Marixa
2004 La Crisis Politica Post-Independentista: 1821–1841. In *Historia General de Panamá*, Vol. 2, edited by Alfredo Castillero, pp. 63–76. Comité Nacional del Centenario de la República de Panamá.

Lavery, Brian
1987 *The Arming and Fitting of English Ships of War, 1600–1850*. Naval Institute Press, Annapolis.

Letts, John M.
1852 *California Illustrated: Including a Description of the Panama and Nicaragua Routes*. William Holdredge, New York.

Linares, Olga F.
1977 *Ecology and the Arts of Ancient Panama: On the Development of Social Rank and Symbolism in the Central Provinces*. Studies in Precolumbian Art and Archaeology No.17. Dumbarton Oaks and the Trustees for Harvard University, Washington, D.C.

Linero, Mirta
2001 Cerámica criolla: muestra excavada en el pozo de las Casas de Terrin. In *Arqueología de Panamá La Vieja: Avances de investigación, época colonial*, Vol.1, edited by Beatriz Rovira and Juan Martín, pp. 149–163. Patronato Panamá Viejo, Panamá.

Linné, Sigvald
1929 *Darien in the Past: The Archaeology of Eastern Panama and North-Western Columbia*. Elanders Bocktryeri Aktiebolog, Goteborg, Sweden.

Liot, W. B.

1849 *Panamá, Nicaragua and Tehuantepec; Or, Considerations Upon the Question of Communication Between the Atlantic and Pacific Oceans.* Simpkin and Marshall, London.

Livingston, Noel B.

1909 *Sketch Pedigrees of some of the Early Settlers in Jamaica: Compiled from the Records of the Court of Chancery of the Island with a list of the Inhabitants in 1670 and Other Matter Relative to the Early History of the Same.* Educational Supply Company, Kingston, Jamaica.

Lloyd, J. A.

1831 Notes Respecting the Isthmus of Panams. *Journal of the Royal Geographical Society of London* 1:69–101.

Long, George

1967 Archaeological Investigations at Panamá Vieja. Unpublished Master's thesis, Department of Anthropology, University of Florida, Gainesville.

Long, George, George Richardson Porter, and George Tucker

1845 *America and the West Indies, Geographically Described.* Charles Knight, London.

Loosley, Allyn Campbell

1933 The Puerto Bello Fairs. *The Hispanic American Historical Review* 13(3):314–335.

Lusardi, Wayne R.

1998 Shipwrecked Swords: An Examination of Edged Weapons Recovered from Spanish Colonial Vessels and Archaeological Sites, 1492–1733. Unpublished Master's thesis, Program in Maritime History and Nautical Archaeology, East Carolina University, Greenville, North Carolina.

Mackenzie, Clyde L., Jr.

1999 A History of the Pearl Oyster Fishery in the Archipiélago de las Perlas, Panama. *Marine Fisheries Review* 51(2): 58–65.

McCain, William D.

1937 *The United States and the Republic of Panama.* Duke University Press, Durham, North Carolina.

McCollum, William S.

1960 *California As I Saw It: Pencillings by the Way of Its Gold and Gold Diggers! and Incidents of Travel by Land and Water.* Talisman, Los Gatos, California.

McCullough, David

1977 *The Path Between the Seas.* Simon and Schuster, New York.

McGovern, Terrance

1999 *The American Defences of the Panama Canal.* Edited by Athanassios Migos. Nearhos Publications, Wirral, UK.

McGuiness, Aims

2003 Defendiendo el Istmo: Las Luchas contra los Filibusteros en la Ciudad de Panamá en 1856. *Mesoamérica* 24(45):66–84.

2004 Aquellos Días de la California. *In Historia General de Panamá*, Vol. 2, edited by Alfredo Castillero, pp. 141–159. Comisión del Centenario de la República de Panamá.

2008 *Path of Empire: Panama and the California Gold Rush*. Cornell University Press, Ithaca, New York.

Mahan, Alfred Thayer

1911 Fortify the Panama Canal. *North American Review* 193(664):331–339.

Maigne, Charles M.

1914 The Guns of Panama: The Powerful Defenses at the Terminals of the Canal. *Scientific American* 110 (18):363, 385.

Major, John

1993 *Prize Possession: The United States and the Panama Canal, 1903–1979*. Cambridge University Press, New York.

Major, Richard Henry

1870 *Select Letters of Christopher Columbus with other original documents relating to the Four Voyages to the New World*. 2nd ed. Hakluyt Society, London.

Makarov, Nikolai A.

1994 Portages of the Russian North: Historical Geography and Archaeology. *Fennoscandia archaeological* 11:13–27.

Manning, W. R. (editor)

1935 *Diplomatic Correspondence of the United States, Inter-American Affairs, 1831–1860*. Volume 5: *Chile and Columbia*. Carnegie Endowment for International Peace, Washington, D.C.

Mantor, E. F.

1941 *A French Panama Canal, 1879–1903*. University of Wisconsin, Madison.

Manwayring, Henry

1644 *The Sea-mans Dictionary: or, an Exposition and Demonstration of all the Parts and Things Belonging to a Shippe. . . .* G. M. for John Bellamy, London.

Marken, Mitchell W.

1994 *Pottery from Spanish Shipwrecks, 1500–1800*.University Press of Florida, Gainesville.

Marley, David F.

2005 *Historic Cities of the Americas: An Illustrated Encyclopedia*. ABC Clio, Santa Barbara.

2010 *Pirates of the Americas*. ABC Clio, Santa Barbara.

Marryat, Frank

1948 *Mountains and Molehills; Or, Recollections of a Burnt Journal*. Edited by Marguerite Eyer Wilbur. Stanford University Press, Stanford.

Martin, Juan Guillermo

2001 Pisos coloniales en Panamá La Vieja: Una manera de afianzar el status. In *Arqueología de Panamá La Vieja: Avances de investigación, época colonial*, Vol. 1, edited by Beatriz Rovira and Juan Martín, pp. 25–238.

2002a Funerales en Panamá La Vieja: Existen patrones en la América Colonial? In *Arqueología de Panamá La Vieja: Avances de investigación*, Vol. 2, edited by Beatriz Rovira and Juan Martín, pp. 94–103.

2002b Excavaciones arqueológicas en el Parque Morelos (Panamá La Vieja). In *Arqueología de Panamá La Vieja: Avances de nvestigación*, Vol. 2, edited by Beatriz Rovira and Juan Martín, pp. 203–229.

2002c Panamá La Vieja y el Gran Darién. In *Arqueología de Panamá La Vieja: Avances de investigación*, Vol. 2, edited by Beatriz Rovira and Juan Martín, pp. 230–250.

2002d Estructuras arquitectónicas, bienes muebles y adornos personales: Alternativas de ostentación en la antigua ciudad de Panamá. *Revista de Antropología y Arqueología* 13:61–72.

2003 Panamá La Vieja: La recuperación de su traza urbana. *Revista de Arqueología Americana* 22:165–183.

2007 La cerámica prehispánica del parque Morelos: Un ejercicio de caracterización tecnológica. *Canto Rodado* 2:45–68.

2009 Arqueología de Panamá La Vieja: Del asentamiento prehispánico a la ciudad colonial. Unpublished Ph.D. dissertation, Universidad de Huelva, Huelva, España.

Martín, Juan Guillermo, and Julieta de Arango

2013 Panamá Viejo: Una experiencia exitosa de gestion patrimonial. *Revista de Estudios Sociales* 45:158–169.

Martín, Juan Guillermo, Alasdair Brooks, and Tania Andrade Lima

2012 Crossing Borders and Maintaining Identities: Perspectives on Current Research in South American Historical Archaeology. *Historical Archaeology* 46(3):1–15.

Martín, Juan Guillermo, Ana Caicedo, Bibiana Etayo, Alejandra Garcés, and Paola Sanabria

2007 Producción y comercialización de cerámicas coloniales en los Andes: El caso de las mayólicas de Popayán. *Boletín del Gabinete de Arqueología* 6:28–39.

Martín, Juan Guillermo, Richard G. Cooke, and Fernando Bustamante

2009 *Exploraciones arqueológicas en la Isla Pedro González, Archipiélago de las Perlas, Panamá*. Submitted to Dirección Nacional del Patrimonio Histórico, Panamá.

Martín, Juan Guillermo, and Claudia Díaz

2000 Enterramientos coloniales en la Catedral de Panamá La Vieja: Un ejercicio de reafirmación de las creencias religiosas. *Trace* 38:80–87.

Martín, Juan Guillermo, and Paula Figueroa

2001 Pasamanería colonial: El arte de trenzar y anudar hilos. *Arqueología de Panamá La Vieja: Avances de investigación*, Vol. 1, edited by Beatriz Rovira and Juan Martín, pp. 215–224.

Martín, Juan Guillermo, and Tomás Mendizábal

2009 Entre el Desarrollo Urbano y la Investigación Arqueológica: Nuevos Datos de la Panamá Amurallada. *Revista Cultural Vínculos*. 32:69–88. Museo Nacional de Costa Rica.

2010 Excavaciones Arqueológicas en la Catedral Metropolitana de Panamá. *Revista Memorias* 7(13):173–201.

Martín, Juan Guillermo, and Félix Rodríguez

2006 Los moluscos marinos de Panamá Viejo: Selectividad de recursos desde una perspectiva de larga duración. *Canto Rodado* 1:85–100.

Martín, Juan Guillermo, and Claudia Rojas

2008 *Arqueología funeraria de Panamá Viejo: Informe de Avance*. Submitted to Secretaria Nacional de Ciencia, Tecnología e Innovación, Panamá.

Martín, Juan Guillermo, and Beatriz Rovira

2012 The Panamá Viejo Archaeological Project: More Than a Decade of Research and Management of Heritage Resources. *Historical Archaeology* 46(3):16–26.

Martín, Juan Guillermo, and Luis A. Sánchez

2007 El istmo mediterráneo: intercambio, simbolismo y filiación social en la bahía de Panamá, durante el período 500–1000 D.C. *Arqueología del Área Intermedia* 7:113–122.

Martín, Juan Guillermo, and Toshiaki Yanaida

2007 La escala urbana como unidad de análisis: Métodos y estrategias de investigación para la recuperación de la traza urbana de la antigua ciudad de Panamá. In *Escalas menores-Escalas mayores: Una perspectiva arqueológica desde Colombia y Panamá*, edited by L. G. Jaramillo, pp. 95–108. Universidad de los Andes, Bogotá, Colombia.

Martín, Juan Guillermo, Annette Zeischka-Kenzler, Hans Mommsen, and Aline Kottmann

2008 Gres: La sutil presencia alemana en la Panamá colonial. *Canto Rodado* 3:65–94.

Marx, Deborah E.

2002 " . . . With the Speed of a Stag Hound," the Steamship Winfield Scott: A Case Study in Early United States Steam Navigation. Unpublished Master's thesis, Program in Maritime History and Nautical Archaeology, East Carolina University, Greenville, North Carolina.

Marx, Robert F.

1987 *Shipwrecks in the Americas*. Dover, New York.

Marx, Robert F., with Jenifer Marx

2004 *Treasure Lost at Sea: Diving to the World's Great Shipwrecks*. Firefly Books, Buffalo.

Masefield, John (editor)

1906 *Dampier's Voyages, Consisting of a New Voyage Round the World, a Supplement to the Voyage Round the World, Two Voyages to Campeachy, a Discourse of Winds, a Voyage to New Holland, and a Vindication*. . . . 2 vols. E. Grant Richards, London.

Mayo, Julia, and Richard G. Cooke

2005 La industria prehispánica de conchas marinas en Gran Coclé, Panamá: Análisis tecnológico de los artefactos de concha del basurero-taller del sitio Cerro Juan Díaz, Los Santos, Panamá. *Archaeofauna* 14:285–298.

Mellado, María E.

2010 Buscando Las Perlas: Aproximación al fenómeno del turismo como proceso social y cultural en el archipiélago de Las Perlas. *Canto Rodado* 5:145–184.

Mena García, María del C.

1984 La sociedad de Panamá en el siglo XVI. V Centenario del Descubrimiento de América No. 3. Publicaciones de la Excelentísima Diputación Provincial de Sevilla, Sevilla.

1992 *La ciudad en un cruce de caminos: Panamá y sus orígenes urbanos*. Publicaciones de la Escuela de Estudios Hispanoamericanos, Sevilla.

2011 *El oro del Darién: Entradas y Cabalgadas en la Conquista de Tierra Firme (1509–1526)*. Fundación Pública Andaluza Centro de Estudios Andaluces, Sevilla.

2012 A manera de introducción general: La Construcción del Mito del Héroe. In *Vasco Núñez de Balboa y los Cronistas de Indias*, edited by Luis Aritio, pp. 12–65.

Comisión Nacional para la Conmemoración del Quinto Centenario del Descubrimiento del Océano Pacífico, Panamá.

Mendez, Roberto (editor)

1992 *Panama Now: Portrait of the Nation*. Focus Publications, Panama.

Mendizábal, Tomás

1996 *Informe de Excavación: Casas de la Plaza, Temporada de Campo Abril-Septiembre*. Submitted to Patronato Panamá Viejo, Panamá.

1997 *Excavaciones en las Casas Terrín, Enero a Junio*. Submitted to Patronato Panamá, Viejo, Panamá.

1999 Current Archaeological Research in Panamá Viejo, Panamá. *Papers from the Institute of Archaeology* 10:25–36.

2003 Informe de Labores, Expedición BBC a Punta Escocés, Kuna Yala. Submitted to Dirección Nacional del Patrimonio Histórico, Instituto Nacional de Cultura, Panamá.

2004 Panamá Viejo: An Analysis of the Construction of Archaeological Time in Eastern Panamá. Unpublished Ph.D. dissertation, Institute of Archaeology, University College, London.

Mendizábal, Tomás, and Guillermina de Gracia

2014 *Prospección Arqueológica Nombre de Dios: Villa de Santiago del Príncipe*. Submitted to Dirección Nacional del Patrimonio Histórico, Instituto Nacional de Cultura, Panamá.

Mendizábal, Tomás, and Juan Guillermo Martín

2012 El Hornabeque de Manuel Hernández en la Explanada del Casco Antiguo de Panamá: Argumentos para una hipótesis. *Canto Rodado* 7:55–84.

2013 Arqueología del Convento de la Compañía de Jesús, San Felipe, Panamá. *Visiones Pretéritas. Encuentros Arqueológicos II*, edited by Iosvany Hernández Mora, pp. 87–104. Oficina del Historiador de Camagüey, Cuba.

Mendizábal, Tomás, and Dimitrios Theodossopoulos

2012 The Emberá, Tourism, and Indigenous Archaeology: "Rediscovering" the Past in Eastern Panamá. *Memorias: Revista digital de Historia y Arqueología desde el Caribe Colombiano* 9(18):88–114.

Meyer, Carl

1938 *Bound for Sacramento: Travel-Pictures of a Returned Wanderer*. Translated by Ruth Frey Axe. Saunders Studio, Claremont, California.

Miller, Hunter (editor)

1937 *Treaties and Other International Acts of the United States of America*. Volume 5, *1846–1852*. Government Printing Office, Washington, D.C.

Minter, John Easter

1948 *The Chagres: River of Westward Passage*. Rinehart, New York.

Missal, Alexander

2008 *Seaway to the Future: American Social Visions and the Construction of the Panama Canal*. University of Wisconsin Press, Madison.

Mojica, Alexis, Louis Pastor, Richard Vanhoeserlande, and María Salamanca-Heyman

2010 Using the Micro-resistivity Method to Detect Hispanic Ancient Floors at Nombre de Dios, Panamá. *Earth Sciences Research Journal* 14(2):127–134.

Moore, Sarah J.
2013 *Empire on Display: San Francisco's Panama-Pacific International Exposition of 1915*. University of Oklahoma Press, Norman.
Mora, Adrián
2011 *Prospección Arqueológica en la Isla de Taboga: Terrenos de la APAT, sector de Barlovento y la isleta del Morro*. Submitted to Dirección Nacional del Patrimonio Histórico, Panamá.
Morison, Samuel E.
1942 *Admiral of the Ocean Sea: A Life of Christopher Columbus*. Little, Brown, Boston.
Morrell, Capt. Benjamin
1832 *A Narrative of Four Voyages, to the South Sea, North and South Pacific Ocean, Chinese Sea, Ethiopic and Southern Atlantic Ocean, Indian and Antarctic Ocean, From the Year 1822 to 1831*. . . . J. and J. Harper, New York.
Muckelroy, Keith
1978 *Maritime Archaeology*. Cambridge University Press, Cambridge.
Murphy, Robert C.
1941 The Earliest Spanish Advances Southward from Panama along the West Coast of South America. *Hispanic American Historical Review* 21(1):3–28.
Myers, Mark D.
1988 An Archaeological Reconnaissance of Rio Belen, Panama. In *Underwater Archaeology Proceedings from the Society for Historical Archaeology Conference, Reno, Nevada, 1988*, edited by James P. Delgado, pp. 127-129. Society for Historical Archaeology, Ann Arbor, Michigan.
National Archives of the United Kingdom (TNA)
1669 Colonial Office Records, CO 1/33 no. 103a. Public Record Office, Kew, England.
1670 Colonial Office Records, CO 1/25 no. 51. Public Record Office, Kew, England.
1671 Colonial Office Records, CO 1/26 no. 51. Public Record Office, Kew, England.
Nelson, Wolfred
1889 *Five Years at Panama: The Trans-Isthmian Canal*. Belford Company, New York.
Niemeier, Jean G.
1968 *The Panama Story*. Metropolitan Press, Portland.
Nichols, Philip
1653 *Sir Francis Drake Revived*. Nicholas Bourne, London.
Nyrop, Richard F. (editor)
1981 *Panama: A Country Study*. Area Handbook Series, Department of the Army, Washington, D.C.
O'Sullivan, Aidan, and Colin Breen
2007 *Maritime Ireland: An Archaeology of Coast Communities*. Tempus, Gloucestershire, UK.
Orser, Charles E.
2009 World-Systems Theory, Networks, and Modern-World Archaeology. In *International Handbook of Historical Archaeology*, edited by T. Majewski and D. Gaimster, pp. 253–268. Springer, New York.
Osorio, Katti
2012 Los Atributos del Valor Universal Excepcional de una Propiedad Considerada

Patrimonio Mundial: El caso del sitio arqueológico de Panamá Viejo y distrito historico de Panamá. *Canto Rodado* 7:1–27.

Otis, Fessenden Nott

1867 *Isthmus of Panama: History of the Panama Railroad; and of the Pacific Mail Steamship Company.* . . . Harper and Brothers, New York.

Pacific Pearl Company

1865 *The Pacific Pearl Company, Incorporated Under the Laws of the State of New York.* E. S. Dodge, New York.

1866 *The Pacific Pearl Company: Incorporated Under the Laws of the State of New York.* John B. Lyon, New York.

Palka, Eugene J.

2005 Geographic Overview of Panama: Pathway to the Continents and Link between the Seas. In *The Rió Chagres, Panama: a Multidisciplinary Profile of a Tropical Watershed*, edited by Russell S. Harmon, pp. 3–18. Springer, Dordrecht, Netherlands.

Parker, Matthew

2008 *Panama Fever: The Epic Story of One of the Greatest Human Achievements of All Time—the Building of the Panama Canal.* Doubleday, London.

Parker, William H.

1871 *Remarks on the Navigation of the Coasts between San Francisco and Panama.* Slote and Janes, New York.

Parks, E. Taylor

1935 *Colombia and the United States, 1765–1934.* Duke University Press, Durham, North Carolina.

Parlane, James

1888 *Notes on the Scots' Darien Expedition, Taken from Books and Contemporary Pamphlets in My Possession.* Palmer and Howe, Manchester.

Pastor, Louis, Richard Vanhoeserlande, Nicolas Florsch, Isabelle Florsch, Jaime Toral, Joaquín González, María Lezcano, and Alexis Mojica

2001 Prospección Arqueogeofísica en Panamá La Vieja: Presentación de casos. *Arqueología de Panamá La Vieja: Avances de investigación, Época Colonial* 1:43–61.

Pastron, Allen G., and Eugene M. Hattori (editors)

1990 *The Hoff Store Site and Gold Rush Merchandise from San Francisco, California.* Society for Historical Archaeology, Pleasant Hill, California.

Patiño, Mariana, and Blaine Cliver

2003 Documenting the Panamá Canal: An International Achievement. In *19th CIPA Symposium, Antalya, Turkey, 30 September–4 October 2003 Proceedings*, edited by O. Altan. ICOMOS International Committee for Documentation of Cultural Heritage. http://cipa.icomos.org/fileadmin/template/doc/antalya/57.pdf, accessed July 2, 2014.

Patronato Panamá Viejo

2007 *Panamá Viejo: De la aldea a la urbe.* Editorial Patronato Panamá Viejo, Panamá.

Patzelt, Arno, Aline Kottmann, and Martin Waldhör

2007 Prospección geoeléctrica en la ciudad colonial de Panamá Viejo: Técnicas, mediciones y primeros resultados de las excavaciones. *Canto Rodado* 2:23–44.

Peacock, George

1879 *Notes on the Isthmus of Panama and Darien, Also on the River St. Juan, Lakes of Nicaragua &c. with Reference to a Railroad and Canal for Joining the Atlantic and Pacific Oceans. . . .* W. Pollard, Exeter, Devon, UK.

Pearson, Georges

2006 La industria lítica prehispánica de Panamá Viejo: Hacia una caracterización tipológica y tecnológica. *Canto Rodado* 1:133–156.

Pereira, Grégory

2002 Análisis de un entierro encontrado en la iglesia del Convento de las monjas de la Concepción de Panamá La Vieja. *Arqueología de Panamá La Vieja: Avances de investigación, Época Colonial* 2:104–112.

Pérez-Brignoli, Héctor

1989 *A Brief History of Central America.* Translated by Ricardo B. Sawrey A. and Susana Stettri de Sawrey. University of California Press, Berkeley.

Pérez-Venero, Alex

1978 *Before the Five Frontiers: Panama 1821–1903.* AMS Press, New York.

Peters, Tom F.

1996 *Building the Nineteenth Century.* MIT Press, Cambridge, Massachusetts.

Piperno, Dolores

2007 Prehistoric Human Occupation and Impacts on Neotropical Forest Landscapes during the Late Pleistocene and Early/Middle Holocene. In *Tropical Rainforest Responses to Climatic Change*, edited by Mark Bush, John Flenley, and William Gosling, pp. 193–218. Springer Berlin, Heidelberg, Germany.

Pizzurno, Patricia

2010 Hoteles emblemáticos de Panamá: Un siglo de renovación de la oferta hotelera (1850–1950). *Canto Rodado* 5:115–148.

Pratt, Julius H.

1891 To California by Panama in '49. *Century Illustrated Monthly Magazine* 41(6):901–916.

Prebble, John

1969 *The Darien Disaster: A Scots Colony in the New World, 1698–1700.* Holt, Rinehart, and Winston, New York.

Rains, Pat

2006 *Mexico Boating Guide.* Point Loma Publishers, San Diego.

Ranere, Anthony, and Richard G. Cooke

2003 Late Glacial and Early Holocene Occupation of Central American Tropical Forests. In *Under the Canopy: The Archaeology of Tropical Rain Forests*, edited by J. Mercader, pp. 219–248. Rutgers University Press, New Brunswick, New Jersey.

Ranft, Bryan McL. (editor)

1958 *The Vernon Papers.* Publications of the Naval Records Society, Vol. 99. Naval Records Society, London.

Reclus, Armand

1881 *Panama et Darien: Voyages d'exploration (1876–1878).* Hachette, Paris.

1997 *Exploraciones a los Istmos de Panamá y el Darién en 1876, 1877 y 1878.* Edited by V. Stamato. Biblioteca Cultural Shell, Panamá.

Reitz, Elizabeth J., C. Margaret Scarry, and Sylvia J. Scudder (editors)
2008 *Case Studies in Environmental Archaeology*. Springer, New York.
Richard, Alfred Charles
1990 *The Panamá Canal in American National Consciousness, 1870–1990*. Garland, New York.
Ripley, George, and Charles A. Dana (editors)
1858 *The New American Cyclopaedia: A Popular Dictionary of General Knowledge*. D. Appleton, New York.
Rivas, Raimundo
1915 *Relaciones Internacionales entre Colombia y los Estados Unidos, 1810–1850*. Imprenta Nacional, Bogotá, Colombia.
Robinson, Tracy
1907 *Panama: A Personal Record of Forty-six Years, 1861–1907*. Star and Herald, New York.
Rodríguez, Ana P.
2009 *Dividing the Isthmus: Central American Transnational Histories, Literatures and Cultures*. University of Texas Press, Austin.
Rojas y Arrieta, Guillermo
1929 *History of the Bishops of Panamá*. Imprenta de las Academica, Panamá.
Romoli, Kathleen
1953 *Balboa of Darién: Discoverer of the Pacific*. Doubleday, New York.
1987 *Los de la lengua de Cueva: Los grupos indígenas del Istmo Oriental en la época de la conquista española*. Ediciones Tercer Mundo, Bogotá, Colombia.
Roscoe, Theodore
1949 *United States Submarine Operations in World War II*. United States Naval Institute Press, Annapolis.
Rovira, Beatriz
1984 La cerámica histórica en la ciudad de Panamá: Tres contextos estratigráficos. In *Recent Developments in Isthmian Archaeology*, edited by F. Lange, pp. 288–315. British Archaeological Reports International Series, Archaeopress, Oxford.
1992 Excavaciones en la Aduana de Portobelo (Provincia de Colón, Panamá). Submitted to the Agencia de Cooperacion Española, Panamá.
1994 Vínculos Interdisciplinarios: Aspectos de la Relación entre Arquitectura y Arqueología en Restauración Monumental. In *Memoria del Ier Congreso Nacional del Patrimonio Cultural*, edited by Instituto Nacional de Cultura, pp. 117–131. Instituto Nacional de Cultura, Panamá.
1997 Hecho en Panamá: La manufactura colonial de mayólicas. *Revista Nacional de Cultura* 27:67–85.
2001a Presencia de mayólicas panameñas en el mundo colonial: Algunas consideraciones acerca de su distribución y cronología. *Latin American Antiquity* 12(3):291–303.
2001b Cerámicas ordinarias torneadas procedentes de un contexto de finales del siglo XVI y principios del SXVII. *Arqueología de Panamá La Vieja: Avances de investigación, Época Colonial* 1:117–148.

2002a Las cerámicas esmaltadas al estaño de origen europeo: una aproximación a la etiqueta doméstica en la Colonia. *Revista de Antropología y Arqueología* 13:6–25.

2002b Paredes no tan desnudas . . . La muestra de azulejos sevillanos del sitio de Panamá La Vieja. *Arqueología de Panamá La Vieja: Avances de investigación, Época Colonial* 2:167–183.

Rovira, Beatriz, James Blackman, Lambertus Van Zelst, Ronald Bishop, Carmen Rodríguez, and Daniel Sánchez

2006 Caracterización química de cerámicas coloniales del sitio de Panamá Viejo: Resultados preliminares de la aplicación de activación neutrónica experimental. *Canto Rodado* 1:101–131.

Rovira, Beatriz, and Juan Guillermo Martín

2008 Arqueología histórica de Panamá. La experiencia en las ruinas de Panamá Viejo. *Vestigios* 1(2):7–34.

Rovira, Beatriz, and Juan Guillermo Martín (editors)

2001 *Arqueología de Panamá La Vieja: Avances de investigación, época colonial.* Vol. 1. Patronato Panamá Viejo, Panamá.

2002 *Arqueología de Panamá La Vieja: Avances de investigación, época colonial.* Vol. 2. Patronato Panamá Viejo, Panamá.

Rovira, Beatriz, and Jazmín Mojica

2007 Encrucijada de estilos: la mayólica panameña: Gustos cotidianos en el Panamá colonial (Siglo XVII). *Canto Rodado* 2:69–100.

Rovira, Beatriz, and Felipe Gaitan-Ammann

2010 Los búcaros: De las indias para el mundo. *Canto Rodado* 5:39–78.

Russell Hart, Francis

1929 *The Disaster of Darien: The Story of the Scots Settlement and the Causes for its Failure, 1699–1701.* Houghton Mifflin, Boston.

Ryan, William Redmond

1850 *Personal Adventures in Upper and Lower California, In 1848–9; With the Author's Experience at the Mines.* William Shoberl, London.

Salamanca-Heyman, María F.

2007 *Arqueología Histórica en el Puerto Colonial Español de Nombre de Dios, Panamá.* Technical report submitted to Department of Anthropology, Center for Archaeological Research, College of William and Mary, Williamsburg, Virginia.

2009 The Urban Archaeology of Early Spanish American Ports of Call: The Unfortunate Story of Nombre de Dios. Unpublished Ph.D. dissertation, College of William and Mary, Williamsburg, Virginia.

Sanabria, Paola

2007 Transformaciones en cultura-ambiente generadas por la introducción de los animals domésticos a Panamá durante la Colonia. Unpublished undergraduate thesis. Universidad del Cauca, Colombia.

Sánchez Laws, Ana Luisa

2011 *Panamanian Museums and Historical Memory.* Berghahn Books, New York.

Sauer, Charles O.

1966 *The Early Spanish Main.* University of California Press, Berkeley.

Scarlett, Peter Campbell

1838 *South America and the Pacific; Comprising a Journey Across the Pampas and the Andes, From Buenos Ayres to Valparaiso, Lima and Panamá, With Remarks upon the Isthmus.* Henry Colburn, London.

Schreg, Rainer

2010 Panamanian Coarse Handmade Earthenware as Melting Pots of African, American and European Traditions? *Postmedieval Archaeology* 44(1):135–164.

Scott, Riley E.

1914 Can the Panama Canal Be Destroyed from the Air? *Sunset: The Pacific Monthly* 32(4):775–784.

Seed, Patricia

1995 *Ceremonies of Possession in Europe's Conquest of the New World, 1492–1640.* Cambridge University Press, Cambridge.

Semmes, Raphael

1869 *Memoirs of Service Afloat during the War between the States.* Kelly, Piet, Baltimore.

Severino de Santa Teresa, Padre

1956 *Historia Documentada de al Iglesia en Urabá y Darién desde el Descubrimiento hasta Nuestros Días.* Editorial Kelly, Bogotá.

Schott, Joseph L.

1967 *Rails across Panama: The Story of the Building of the Panama Railroad, 1849–1855.* Bobbs-Merrill, Indianapolis.

Selfridge, Thomas O.

1874 *Reports of Explorations and Surveys to Ascertain the Practicability of a Ship-Canal Between the Atlantic and Pacific Oceans By Way of the Isthmus of Darién.* Government Printing Office, Washington, D.C.

Shulsky, Linda

2001 Porcelana china de sitios coloniales españoles del sur de Norteamérica y el Caribe. *Arqueología de Panamá La Vieja: Avances de investigación, Época Colonial* 1:203–214. Patronato Panamá Viejo, Panamá.

Skinner, James M.

1988 *France and Panamá: The Unknown Years, 1894–1908.* Peter Lang, New York.

Small, Charles S.

1981 *Rails to the Diggings: Construction Railroads of the Panama Canal.* Railroad Monographs, Greenwich, Connecticut.

1983 *Military Railroads on the Panama Canal Zone.* Second printing. Railroad Monographs, Greenwich, Connecticut.

Smith, Bolling W.

1993 [1912] Type or "Panama" Fourteen-Inch Disappearing Gun Batteries. *Coast Defense Study Group Journal* 7(2):33–48.

Snapp, Jeremy S.

2000 *Destiny by Design: The Construction of the Panama Canal.* Pacific Heritage House, Lopez Island, Washington.

Sorsby, Victoria G.

1975 British Trade with Spanish America under the Asiento. Unpublished Ph.D. dissertation, University College, London.

Stark, Barbara L., and Barbara Voorhies

1978 *Prehistoric Coastal Adaptations: The Economy and Ecology of Maritime Middle America*. Academic Press, New York.

Sternbeck, Alfred

1930 *Filibusters and Buccaneers*. Robert M. McBride, New York.

Stier, Frances Rhoda

1979 The Effect of Demographic Change on Agriculture in San Blas, Panama. Unpublished Ph.D. dissertation, University of Arizona.

Storrs, Christopher

1999 Disaster at Darien (1698–1700): The Persistence of Spanish Imperial Power on the Eve of the Demise of the Spanish Habsburgs. *Economic History Quarterly* 29(1):5–38.

Strassnig, Christian

2010 Rediscovering the Camino Real of Panama: Archaeology and Heritage Tourism Potentials. *Journal of Latin American Geography* 9(2):159–168.

Suarez, Loreto

1994 Excavaciones Arqueológicas en Portobelo. In *Memoria del Ier Congreso Nacional del Patrimonio Cultural*, edited by Instituto Nacional de Cultura, pp. 84–101. Instituto Nacional de Cultura, Panamá.

Talty, Stephen

2005 *Empire of Blue Water: Captain Morgan's Great Pirate Army, the Epic Battle for the Americas, and the Catastrophe that Ended the Outlaw's Bloody Reign*. Crown Publishers, New York.

Tardieu, Jean P.

2009 *Cimarrones de Panamá: La forja de una identidad Afroamericana en el siglo XVI*. Iberoamericana Editorial Vervuert, Madrid.

Taylor, B.

1949 *Eldorado; Or, Adventures in the Path of Empire. . . .* Alfred A. Knopf, New York.

Tate, E. Mowbray

1986 *Transpacific Steam: The Story of Steam Navigation from the Pacific Coast of North America to the Far East and the Antipodes, 1867–1941*. Cornwall Books, New York.

Tejeira Davis, Eduardo

2001 La Ciudad, sus Habitantes y su Arquitectura. In *El Casco Antiguo de la Ciudad de Panamá*, edited by Eduardo Tejeira and Vanessa Spadafora, pp. xx. Oficina del Casco Antiguo, Panamá.

2011 Los orígenes de la ciudad de Colón: Fundamentos para el estudio de un patrimonio arquitectónico y urbanístico excepcional. *Canto Rodado* 6:33–73.

2013 *Panamá: El Casco Antiguo y la dinámica de sus transformaciones*. Oficina del Casco Antiguo, Panamá.

Ten Broeck, Dr. P.G.S.

1854 Diary, Manuscript HM 16999. Henry E. Huntington Library, Pasadena.

Thrower, John
2001 Colonial Nombre de Dios: The "Treasure Mouth of the World." *Terrae Incognitae* 33(1):1–12.
Thornton, Jessy Quinn
1864 *Oregon and California in 1848, With an Appendix, Including Recent and Authentic Information on the Subject of the Gold Mines of California. . . .* Vol.2. Harper and Brothers, New York.
Thrower, Jon
2001 Colonial Nombre de Dios: The "Treasure Mouth of the World." *Terrae Incognitae* 33(1):1-12.
Tice, Karin E.
1995 *Kuna Crafts, Gender and the Global Economy.* University of Texas Press, Austin.
TNA. *See* National Archives of the United Kingdom.
Tomes, Robert
1855a *Panamá in 1855. An Account of the Panamá Rail-Road, Cities of Panamá and Aspinwall, With Sketches of Life And Character On The Isthmus.* Harper and Brothers, New York.
1855b A Trip on the Panamá Railroad. *Harper's New Monthly Magazine October 1855,* 616–622.
Torres, Roman Rivera
2003 *The Legend of the Golden Gate.* Grupo Editorial Regiomontano, Cancun.
Torres de Araúz, Reina
1992 *Natá Prehispánico. En Conmemoración del Vto Centenario del Descubrimiento de América: Encuentro de Dos Mundos.* Instituto Nacional de Cultura, Panamá.
Tucker, Spencer
1989 *Arming the Fleet: U.S. Navy Ordnance in the Muzzle Loading Era.* Naval Institute Press, Annapolis.
United States Board of Consulting Engineers
1906 *Message of the President of the United States, Transmitting the Report of the Board of Consulting Engineers and of the Isthmian Canal Commission on the Panama Canal, Together With a Letter Written by Chief Engineer Stevens.* Senate Document No. 231, 59th Congress, 1st session. Government Printing Office, Washington, D.C.
United States House of Representatives
1978 *Disposition of Cemeteries in the Panama Canal Zone Where American Veterans Are Buried: Effect of Proposed Panama Canal Treaty on Americans Buried in the Panama Canal Zone.* Hearings before the Subcommittee on Cemeteries and Burial Benefits of the Committee on Veterans' Affairs, House of Representatives, 95th Congress, 2nd session. Government Printing Office, Washington, D.C.
United States Hydrographic Office
1893 *The West Coasts of Mexico and Central America from the United States to Panama including the Gulfs of California and Panama.* Government Printing Office, Washington, D.C.
1904 *The West Coasts of Mexico and Central America from the United States to Panama including the Gulfs of California and Panama, Chiefly from Surveys by the United*

States Steamers Narragansett, Tuscarora, Ranger, and Thetis, between 1873 and 1901. Government Printing Office, Washington, D.C.

Varela, Consuelo, and Juan Gil
1997 *Cristobal Colón: Textos y Documentos Completos.* Alianza Editorial, Madrid.

Verlinden, Charles, Jozef R. Mertens, and Gerardo Reichel-Dolmatoff
1958 Santa Maria la Antigua del Darien première "Ville" coloniale de la Terre Ferme américaine Expédition du Roi Léopold de Belgique (Janvier-février 1956). *Revista de Historia de América* 45 (June):1–15, 17–48.

Wafer, Lionel
1903 [1699] *A New Voyage and Description of the Isthmus of America.* Edited by G. P. Winship. Burrows Brothers, Cleveland.

Wake, Thomas A.
2006 Prehistoric Exploitation of the Swamp Palm (*Raphia taedigera*: Arecacae) at Sitio Drago, Isla Colón, Bocas del Toro, Panama. *Caribbean Journal of Science* 42:11–19.

Wake, Thomas A., Douglas R. Doughty, and Michael Kay
2013 Archaeological Investigations Provide Late Holocene Baseline Ecological Data for Bocas del Toro, Panama. *Bulletin of Marine Science* 89(4):1015–1035.

Wake Thomas A., Jason de Leon, and Carlos Fitzgerald
2004 Prehistoric Sitio Drago, Bocas del Toro, Panama. *Antiquity.* 78(300). http://antiquity.ac.uk/ProjGall/wake/, accessed January 24, 2015.

Wake, Thomas A., and Tomás Mendizábal
2010 Sitio Drago (Isla Colón, Bocas del Toro, Panama): Una aldea y centro de intercambio en el Caribe panameño. In *Mucho mas que un puente terrestre: Avances de la arqueología panameña y sus implicaciones en el contexto regional*, edited by Juan Guillermo Martin and Richard Cooke. Manuscript on file, Patronato Panamá Viejo, Panamá.

Wake, Thomas A., Alexis O. Mojica, Michael H. Davis, Christina J. Campbell, and Tomás Mendizábal
2012 Electrical Resistivity Surveying and Pseudo Three-Dimensional Tomographic Imaging at Sitio Drago, Bocas del Toro, Panama. *Archaeological Prospection* 19(1):49–58.

Ward, Christopher
1993 *Imperial Panamá: Commerce and Conflict in Isthmian America, 1550–1800.* University of New Mexico Press, Albuquerque.

Ward, Eliot D. C.
1985 The Castles of Portobelo: Spanish Strategy and Tactics in the Defence of Empire, 1597–1760. Unpublished Ph.D. dissertation, University of Florida, Gainesville.

Watt, Douglas
2007 *The Price of Scotland: Darien, Union and the Wealth of Nations.* Luath Press, Edinburgh.

Wagner, Moritz
1861 *Beiträge zu einer physisch-geographischen Skizze des Isthmus von Panamá.* Justus Perthes, Gotha, Germany.

Weaver, Peter L., and Gerald P. Bauer

2004 *The San Lorenzo Protected Area: A Summary of Cultural and Natural Resources.* General Technical Report No. IITF-GTR-25. Submitted to the International Institute of Tropical Forestry, USDA Forest Service.

Weber, David J.

2005 *Bárbaros: Spaniards and Their Savages in the Age of Enlightenment.* Yale University Press, New Haven, Connecticut.

Webster, Edwin.

1973 El Sitio de Venta de Chagres. In *Actas del IV Simposium Nacional de Antropología, Arqueología y Etnohistoria de Panamá, 1973.* Universidad de Panamá, Ciudad de Panamá. http://www.indrakeswake.co.uk/Society/Research/ventadechagre.htm (English version), accessed on October 7, 2013.

Weddle, Robert S.

1992 Spanish Exploration of the Texas Coast, 1519–1800. *Bulletin of the Texas Archeological Society* 63: 99–122.

Westerdahl, Christer

1992 The Maritime Cultural Landscape. *International Journal of Nautical Archaeology,* 21(1):5–14.

1998 The Maritime Cultural Landscape: On the Concept of Transport Zones of Geography. Institute of Archaeology and Ethnology, University of Copenhagen. https://www.abc.se/~pa/publ/cult-land.htm, accessed October 4, 2013.

Wheelwright, William

1844 *Observations on the Isthmus of Panama.* William Weale, London.

Williams, Mary Wilhelmine

1916 *Anglo-American Isthmian Diplomacy, 1815–1915.* American Historical Association, Washington, D.C.

Winthrop, Theodore

1866 *The Canoe and the Saddle, Adventures Among the Northwestern Rivers and Forests; and Isthmiana.* Ticknor and Fields, Boston.

Wiskowski, Lance

1988 History under the Canal. Manuscript Proposal on file, Panama Canal Commission.

Zapatero, Juan M.

1985 *Historia del Castillo San Lorenzo el Real de Chagre.* Servicio Historico Militar, Biblioteca CEHOPU, Madrid.

Zárate, Diana

2004 La cerámica con engobe rojo en Panamá Viejo (1519–1671): Caracterización y análisis. Unpublished undergraduate thesis. Universidad de los Andes-Bogotá, Colombia.

INDEX

Page numbers in *italics* indicate illustrations.

James P. Delgado is a maritime archaeologist specializing in the maritime frontiers of the last 500 years. He has led field projects around the world in a four-decades-long career, including a decade of work in Panáma. His published works include *To California By Sea: A Maritime History of the Gold Rush*, *Gold Rush Port: The Maritime Archaeology of San Francisco's Waterfront*, and *Misadventures of a Civil War Submarine: Iron, Guns and Pearls*, which documents his several years of work in Panamá on the wreck of *Sub Marine Explorer*.

Frederick H. Hanselmann ("Fritz") directs programs in underwater archaeology and underwater exploration in the Department of Marine Ecosystems and Society in the Rosenstiel School of Marine and Atmospheric Sciences at the University of Miami. He is also a fellow of the Meadows Center for Water and the Environment at Texas State University. His research ranges from submerged prehistoric deposits in springs and caves to historic shipwrecks in Latin America and the Caribbean, including the wreck of the *Quedagh Merchant*, abandoned by Captain Kidd in 1699 off the coast of Hispaniola. Fritz led the first-ever archaeological survey off the mouth of the Chagres River in Panamá and codirects the Río Chagres Maritime Cultural Landscape Study as well as the Lost Ships of Henry Morgan Project. He is a principal investigator with the Monterrey Shipwreck Project in the Gulf of Mexico, codirector of the Sunken Ships of Colombia project, and principal investigator with the Spring Lake Underwater Archaeology Project. He is widely featured in global print and electronic media, including documentaries, films, and programs with the National Geographic Channel, the Sundance Film Festival, and the Travel Channel, among others.

Tomás Mendizábal is an archaeologist specializing in the colonial and nineteenth-century occupations of Panamá City, Panamá, and the former Canal Zone. He has been director of Museo Antropológico Reina Torres de Araúz, the national museum of Panamá. As an independent consultant he has excavated extensively in the Pearl Islands, Panamá City's Casco Antiguo, and the ruins of Panamá la Vieja. Currently he is the contract archaeologist for the Panama Canal Expansion Program.

Dominique Rissolo is an archaeologist at the University of California, San Diego. His interdisciplinary research focuses on paleocoastal human ecology and the development of ancient maritime trade networks along the Yucatan coast. His work on the Yucatan Peninsula has also focused on ancient Maya and Paleoamerican cave and cenote use as well as coastal and near-coastal settlement patterns and the rise of social complexity in the region. In addition to codirecting the Proyecto Costa Escondida in Quintana Roo, Mexico, since 2006, Dominique has conducted archaeological research in Belize, El Salvador, and Panamá. Dominique coordinated and participated in the 2008 and 2010 Río Chagres field seasons and shares a lasting interest in region.